The Self-Directed Search®
and Related Holland
Career Materials:
A Practitioner's Guide

Related Publications
from
Psychological Assessment Resources, Inc.

Dictionary of Holland Occupational Codes

by

Gary D. Gottfredson, PhD, and John L. Holland, PhD

This 768-page book is an essential reference for those who use the Holland occupational codes in career counseling.

Making Vocational Choices: A Theory of Vocational Personality and Work Environments

by

John L. Holland

This 312-page book presents the most recent formulation of John L. Holland's RIASEC theory of careers and its successful application to vocational life.

The Self-Directed Search (SDS) in Business and Industry: A Resource Guide

Edited by

Michael Shahnasarian, PhD

This 170-page book helps Human Resource professionals develop a consistent and systematic approach to employee selection, training, and career development.

The Self-Directed Search® and Related Holland Career Materials: A Practitioner's Guide

ROBERT C. REARDON, PhD
JANET G. LENZ, PhD

PAR Psychological Assessment Resources, Inc.

Dedication

We dedicate this work to our parents,
Etta Marie and Tommy Reardon and Emily and Stanley Lenz,
whose lives shaped and supported our career journeys.

Library of Congress Cataloging-in-Publication Data

Reardon, Robert C.
    The self-directed search and related Holland career materials :
a practitioner's guide / Robert C. Reardon, Janet G. Lenz.
        p.   cm.
        Includes bibliographical references.
        ISBN 0-911907-28-9
        1. Occupational aptitude tests.   2. Vocational guidance.
        3. Holland, John L.   I. Lenz, Janet G., 1957-   II. Title.
        HF5381.7.R4   1998
        158.6—dc21   97–45675
                                                                                            CIP

PAR **Psychological Assessment Resources, Inc.**•16204 N. Florida Ave., Lutz, FL 33549
Toll-Free 1.800.331.TEST• www.parinc.com

9 8 7 6 5 4 3 2   Reorder #RO–3895   Printed in the U.S.A.

Preface

In writing this book on John Holland's Self-Directed Search (SDS) and related Holland-based career interventions, we undertook a task that was sometimes daunting and almost overwhelming, but one that became captivating and thoroughly engaging. The amount of information available on Holland's RIASEC theory and the practical tools and scholarly research flowing from that work is enormous. It is an incredibly rich body of work that we fear is not always fully appreciated by some career researchers and practitioners. This authorship experience has provided us a glimmer of what John Holland learned long ago in his 40-year fascination with RIASEC theory and the SDS.

In conducting SDS workshops and training hundreds of practitioners to use these materials with increased skill and confidence, we have been stimulated to learn more about the application of RIASEC theory and research to practice. We have been humbled and heartened by the committed and creative efforts of the many practitioners in the field who are using Holland's interventions (most of these unreported in the literature). In some instances, professional scholars and reviewers minimize Holland's contributions, but this is not the case with the practitioners in the field.

As we wrote this book, we imagined we were speaking directly to the practitioners in our SDS workshops or to graduate students learning to be career counselors or advisors. These practitioners include professional career counselors and career guidance technicians, as well as librarians, social workers, teachers, and other persons in helping professions. We thought about those persons who had been handed a pack of SDS materials and didn't know what to do with them; or those sole practitioners working in high school guidance offices, one-stop career centers, Human Resource Development and outplacement programs, rehabilitation centers, and community colleges; and even those practitioners from other countries seeking to help their fellow citizens explore new career options as they make the transition to a market-based economy. We also thought of those persons teaching careers courses for graduate or undergraduate students, or those supervising paraprofessional or preprofessional counselors interested in learning more about the SDS. These are the groups for whom this book was written, and for simplicity we refer to them generically as "counselors."

Because these counselors are often SAE types, our goal was to deliver the information with them in mind. We realize, of course, that many Social types would rather get their information about the SDS and Holland's theory in a workshop or a class (where there are many opportunities for discussion and practice), so we are writing this book with limited referencing, statistics, and academic detail. Much of the literature about RIASEC theory has been written by Investigative types for other researchers and scholars, so we moved in a different direction in this book.

We each wrote six chapters: Reardon was the principal author of chapters 1, 2, 3, 4, 11, and 12; and Lenz drafted chapters 5, 6, 7, 8, 9, and 10. Then we critiqued and rewrote parts of every chapter, making this a truly collaborative effort. Not everyone will read this book chronologically, and to some extent that realization affected both our writing strategies and the inclusion of topics in various chapters. We deliberately chose to be repetitive across chapters with regard to some topics. Lest you think we were being lazy or uncoordinated in our efforts, as often happens with jointly authored books, let us share our thinking on this matter. Beginning practitioners, who have very little experience with Holland's work, may choose to read each chapter in sequence. We hope that any repetition they notice will simply serve to reinforce their learning (i.e., make the point stick.) Other, more experienced SDS users may choose to read only selected chapters. These readers are likely to encounter the content on a particular subject only one time. If they desire more, we have made every effort to provide cross-references to similar topics found in other chapters. The following paragraphs provide brief synopses of each chapter.

Chapter 1, "John L. Holland: A RIASEC Perspective," includes material from the Holland biography in the 1995 APA award citation printed in the *American Psychologist*. Major points include a review of Holland's philosophy and purpose in creating the Vocational Preference Inventory (VPI) and the SDS, Holland's own SDS code, and recognition of Holland's unique role in developing the RIASEC theory and its practical applications. The purpose of this chapter is to help the reader identify in a personal way with John Holland as the creator and developer of the SDS.

Chapter 2, "RIASEC Theory: Past and Present," provides a chronology of the major developments leading to the RIASEC theory and describes the most recent evolution of the theory. Major points include an analysis of where Holland's work fits in relation to other theories, a review and discussion of the eight assumptions undergirding the theory, and an explanation of how understanding the theory is essential for effectively using the SDS and other materials.

Chapter 3, "Types and Environments More Fully Examined," describes, compares, and contrasts the RIASEC personality types and the RIASEC environmental models, thus providing the necessary background and concepts for practitioners to use the SDS and related instruments more effectively. Major points include an explanation of how the types have been researched in various studies, the Rule of Asymmetrical Distribution of Types and Subtypes, personality characteristics of types, an analysis of what characteristics are typically included in an environment, the Rule of Intraoccupational Variability, labor market and census data related to RIASEC types, and methods for determining codes for environments.

Chapter 4, "Review of the SDS Form R and My Vocational Situation," reviews the SDS as a paper-and-pencil simulated career counseling activity and discusses how the MVS can help determine how the SDS might be used. Major points include a review of the SDS as it imitates an interest inventory, a review of the SDS Daydreams Section as a measure of expressed vocational interests and procedures for scoring this section, a review of the scope and content of each of the five SDS content sections and how they produce a measure of assessed vocational interests, a review of what published reviews have said about the SDS, and an overview of the The Occupations Finder and You and Your Career booklets as components of a basic SDS career guidance intervention.

Chapter 5, "Comparing and Contrasting SDS Forms and Formats," reviews the alternative forms of the SDS and the paper and computer formats. Major points include an analysis of the various features and administration costs of SDS Forms R, E, CP, and Career Explorer; an analysis of the various SDS administration options, a summary of published reviews on the alternate forms of the SDS; and a review of the features and costs of computer-based SDS systems.

Chapter 6, "Non-SDS Holland-Based Program Materials," reviews Holland-based career guidance materials other than the SDS that can help persons learn about their career options and make appropriate career plans. Major points will include using the *Dictionary of Holland Occupational Codes* (DHOC), Educational Opportunities Finder (EOF), and Leisure Activities Finder (LAF) to learn about options in occupations, education, and leisure; using the Position Classification Inventory (PCI) in career management, supervision, and organizational development; using the VPI in interest assessment; local adaptations of RIASEC theory reported in the literature; a summary of published reviews of SDS products; and using the Career Attitudes and Strategies Inventory (CASI) in career counseling.

Chapter 7, "Interpreting the SDS," reviews the basic and secondary interpretive ideas regarding the SDS. Major points include an explanation of congruence and high-point code as basic interpretive ideas; and coherence of aspirations, vocational identity, consistency, differentiation, commonness, and professional judgment as secondary interpretive ideas. The chapter includes a table showing decision rules for identifying and interpreting diagnostic signs on the SDS; it also discusses using the Career Information Exercise for working through options generated by the SDS and using the RIASEC Game in working with the SDS.

Chapter 8, "Linking RIASEC and Cognitive Information Processing," examines Cognitive Information Processing as a way of linking RIASEC theory and career service delivery. Major points include a review of the pyramid of information processing domains and the CASVE cycle, introduction and use of the Career Thoughts Inventory (CTI) as an assessment of negative career thoughts that interfere with successful career decision making and problem solving, and suggestions for reframing negative statements for more effective career work.

Chapter 9, "Using Diagnostic Signs in Career Assistance," examines how negative signs drawn from the SDS, MVS, and CTI with regard to a client's Personal Career Theory can assist practitioners in developing a career intervention plan. Major points include a review of how to use the RIASEC hexagon and pyramid of information processing domains to understand the client's situation, how to read the Professional Summary from the computer versions of the SDS, a review and analysis of a case study using diagnostic signs from the SDS and related tools, how to intervene with high and low undifferentiated profiles, and a review of guidelines for using the SDS and other Holland-based interventions.

Chapter 10, "Six Case Studies," examines additional cases that systematically vary from the one examined in chapter 9. We focus on two older workers, a college junior, an adult returning to college, a high school senior, and a prison inmate seeking career assistance.

Chapter 11, "Program Development Strategies," examines an application of a systems approach to SDS program development and staff training that makes extensive use of Holland-based materials. The CASVE problem-solving model is used to guide the development of a program proposal, and a brief middle school career guidance application is described. The chapter also shows how the National Career Development Guidelines can be used in program development and staff training.

Chapter 12, "Evaluation and Future Trends," provides information about the overall scope and impact of RIASEC theory and the SDS. Comments by reviewers of Holland's contributions are cited, along with Holland's own self-evaluation of the theory and the SDS.

Finally, we want to thank many persons who have helped us in producing this work: John Holland for 25 years of insights into career research and practice and for inspiring us to become better in integrating both scholarship and service into our own careers; our boss, Jeff Garis, who has given us space and considerable support in pursuing our interests and work; and the staff at PAR, Bob Smith, Serje Seminoff, and Sandra Schneider, who patiently pursued and fully supported us in this project. We also acknowledge the special contributions (both ideas and legwork) of Jim Sampson, Gary Peterson, Jeff O'Dell, Mike Railey, Steve Leierer, and Gary Gottfredson. We are grateful to those individuals and organizations who volunteered to provide case material. Finally, we especially acknowledge the questions and ideas about the SDS from hundreds of career advisors working in the Florida State University Career Center and workshop participants from across the nation—their stimulation has energized us in this endeavor.

Robert C. Reardon, PhD
Janet G. Lenz, PhD
Tallahassee, Florida
October, 1997

Table of Contents

List of Tables

List of Figures

1

John L. Holland:
A RIASEC Perspective

Some might think it is unusual to begin a book about the Self-Directed Search with a chapter about John Lewis Holland. One might have thought it would begin with the SDS itself, or perhaps with RIASEC theory. But the more I thought about it, the more I wanted to begin this book with a personal "sketch" of John Holland. In many ways, Dr. Holland is the original source of everything associated with the SDS and RIASEC theory, so it makes sense to me to begin this book with him. Many things should be examined: What is his background? What were and are his motives? What is he like? What was he trying to do in his life and career? Why did he create the SDS? What is he doing now? How have others reacted to his work? This chapter will explore these questions and other topics.

As counselors, we sometimes select tests and materials although we know very little about the author or authors. In fact, some guidance and counseling products don't even list an author. With the SDS, there is no doubt: The author is John L. Holland. The SDS was not produced by a committee, a task force, or a corporation. There were no government grants, no foundation awards, and no agency initiatives in 1960 when Holland began to create the SDS and other works. The SDS and its related products have come from the imagination, intelligence, creativity, concern, drive, determination, persistence, and persuasiveness of John Holland. Given that he is the principal figure behind this enterprise—and it is a big business that he has created—we'll begin with him.

As counselors, we can make better use of professional products and materials when we know something about the philosophy, goals, values, and aims of their authors. With this personal insight, we can further identify with the authors' missions and, in my judgment, make more effective use of their materials. Tests and other practical tools, even theories, are developed by authors with specific purposes in mind. They aren't intended to be everything a professional might need or use, only something that might be helpful or thought-provoking for a counselor or client. My purpose, then, is to demonstrate how my own knowledge of John Holland has enabled me to be a better user of the

SDS and other materials that he has created. I hope my sharing of these personal perspectives will help other interested persons identify with the spirit and essence of Holland's work.

A Personal History

My contacts with John Holland began in 1970 when I read about the creation of a new interest inventory that could be self-scored and used in a self-guided way. It was just what I had been looking for. It was the missing piece for our self-help-oriented career services program. Here's what happened.

In our university counseling center at that time, most of the counselors, including clinical psychologists and social workers, were not very interested in doing educational or vocational counseling—even though this was what 75% of the clients reported that they wanted. Given the staff reluctance to provide career counseling, we proposed a program that would provide an alternative to the counselor-based "intake—testing—follow-up appointment" service system that sometimes produced a client waiting list and other delays. This new program put more responsibility for educational and career services directly into the hands of the clients.

So, we set out to create a self-directed career decision-making program that would involve establishing a series of self-help stations in an empty office in our counseling center. Each station had a module: The first five consisted of (a) an introduction to the program, (b) some instruction on decision making, (c) a self-assessment of interests, (d) indexes to files of information and the *Occupational Outlook Handbook* (OOH; Bureau of Labor Statistics, 1996), and (e) the names of faculty contacts and other referral sources for additional information. We had already created all of the stations except the third one on self-assessment. (Interested persons can read more about the development and evaluation of this program, the Curricular-Career Information Service [CCIS], in Peterson, Sampson, & Reardon [1991] and Reardon [1996]).

Our Module 3 options were the Strong Vocational Interest Blank (SVIB; Campbell, 1971), the Kuder Interest Inventory (Form DD; Kuder & Diamond, 1979), the Jackson Vocational Interest Survey (Jackson, 1985), and some others, all of which required machine scoring or the use of scoring stencils. None provided the kind of stand-alone assessment we needed. When we reviewed our prepublication copy of the Self-Directed Search (SDS), we knew our self-directed career program idea would work. From the very beginning, the SDS has been the mainstay of career services at our university. We've been using between 600 and 1,000 copies a year since 1972, when our CCIS program was started.

Early on, Holland wrote about a self-directed career planning program (Holland, Hollifield, Nafziger, & Helms, 1972), and we have also written about the use of self-directed approaches in career services. It is no small irony that the "self-directed" feature of the SDS remains one of the least fully understood and least exploited aspects of this career service delivery innovation. After conducting more than 35 workshops on the SDS around the nation since 1974, we still have the feeling that many counselors use the SDS just as they would any other interest test. For example, the counselor assigns the SDS, and then the client makes a second appointment with the testing office to complete the instrument. The testing office sends the results and perhaps a report back to the counselor for interpretation.

In situations like this, the SDS remains an underused tool for helping clients quickly and efficiently obtain information that will help them solve educational and occupational decision-making problems. The opportunity to provide an immediate, full response to the client at the time of his or her initial contact for service is wasted. The problem may be that counseling services have not been able to revise their service delivery scheme to efficiently serve drop-in clients at the time of initial contact. Too many offices require that the use of assessments be tied to service delivery schemes that involve counselor-based appointments. The SDS makes it possible to deliver services in a quicker, more efficient way.

Viewing Holland From the RIASEC Perspective

What Is Holland's RIASEC Code?

In December 1990, Stephen Weinrach convinced John Holland and Donald Super to complete a series of inventories and psychological tests that included the SDS. Holland's scores were R (Realistic) = 26, I (Investigative) = 27, A (Artistic) = 29, S (Social) = 26, E (Enterprising) = 29, and C (Conventional) = 8. His code was A/EI. The first two letters were tied, and the first five letters were separated by only 3 points. Experienced users of the SDS will recognize this as a case of an undifferentiated profile that is on the high side. The C code was clearly different from the other five. It is also useful to note that because the A and E were tied, a slight edge went to the A because it had more points on the Occupations Scale of the SDS, 8 versus 5. The Occupations Scale is actually a shortened form of the Vocational Preference Inventory (VPI; Holland, 1985b), which is an established, reliable measure of RIASEC codes.

Holland's own calculation of his code was AEI/R/S (Weinrach, 1996). How did he arrive at this? He probably remembered the "Rule of 8," which is based on the standard error of measurement of the SDS, whereby score differences of fewer than 8 points on the SDS may be considered as trivial. In addition, Holland also probably noted that his Occupational Daydreams scores on the SDS were S=15, A=13, E=11, R=6, I=5, and C=0, creating a code of SAE. We'll talk more about "scoring daydreams" in later chapters. Holland listed eight occupations in the Daydreams section: psychologist/researcher (social psychologist = ASE), writer (AES), research administrator (research worker = IER), vocational counselor (counselor = SAE), college teacher (SEI), counseling center director (counselor = SAE), musician = (ASI), and engineer (RES). In chapters 4, 5, 9, and 10, we will discuss more fully the importance and significance of these ideas in interpreting SDS results. Readers might note that the third edition of the *Dictionary of Holland Occupational Codes* (Gottfredson & Holland, 1996a) lists a new code (IAE) for Holland's first aspiration, social psychologist, but this does not change his Aspirations summary code from SAE.

What Do These SDS Results Tell Us About Holland?

In reviewing these results, Holland observed to Weinrach (1996) that both he and Super were social types "who might have benefited from some career counseling or who might have pursued any one of several related occupations" (p. 12). I think it is important to keep an eye on the Artistic aspect of Holland's personality. "A" was the first letter of the codes for his first two Daydream occupations, and it was tied for the highest code in his SDS summary score. As we will learn in chapter 2, A types are very independent, creative, innovative, and imaginative. They also tend not to conform to some social conventions or to some common rules for doing things. Indeed, the Self-Directed Search and many of the resources that grew out of John Holland's work are most understandable when viewed from an Artistic perspective.

As noted earlier, Holland's Daydreams Summary Code, the combined code of all eight occupations he listed, is SAE. This is also the code for Vocational Counselor. In this sense, Holland is "one of us." He has many of the personality traits and interests of practicing counselors. I think this can help us as practitioners relate to what Holland and his work are all about.

Introducing "A Man of All Types"

As we noted earlier, Holland has an undifferentiated or "flat" RIASEC profile; he has many interests and competencies. Sometimes this makes it difficult to get a quick picture of what he is like as a person. In 1987, I was asked to introduce John Holland at a workshop on the SDS, and I was having trouble figuring out what to say about him. So I consulted someone who had done some writing with Holland and who had been associated with him for several years, Adam Lackey. Before writing this chapter, I contacted him again for an update.

Lackey (1975) noted that the SDS is the most frequently reported and used vocational assessment device in counseling history, as reported by Watkins, Bradford, Lew, and Himmell (1986), and has been translated into more than 20 languages. It is used throughout the world. During the past 25 years, more than 14 million persons have used the SDS; Psychological Assessment Resources reports that over 21 million persons worldwide have used the various Holland-based guidance materials.

Holland has a knack for getting his friends and associates to do work with and for him. He must have written more than 200 articles, many of which have been coauthored. This is especially important because he never had a group of graduate students around to do his work or a federal sponsor to support them.

According to Lackey, Holland really did read all 12,099 occupations in the *Dictionary of Occupational Titles* (DOT; U.S. Department of Labor, 1977) to determine whether his first letter codes matched those generated empirically by a formula devised by Gary Gottfredson (1984). He found 35 that did not.

Lackey also noted that when Holland retired from Johns Hopkins University in 1980, he was in the top .1% of publishing psychologists in America. He had averaged six publications per year since 1953.

There is additional evidence about the diversity of Holland's interests. In the late 1970s, we developed a tactile board version of the SDS for use by persons with visual disabilities (Barker, White, Reardon, & Johnson, 1980; Reardon & Kahnweiler, 1980). When John Holland met the woodworker who had crafted the boards, they got into an intense discussion about the biological origins of the woods used in the boards. In listening to that exchange, I learned that Holland was a woodworker who had collected woods from around the world. Holland told Weinrach (1980) about his interests in furniture-making and wood crafts.

One last thing regarding Holland's varied types: Holland reports that

> he took piano lessons from age 12 to 22 and toyed with becoming a musician until he noticed in the typical stair-step recitals that there was always some little kid who made everyone else look bad. He took a year of harmony in college and also discovered he wasn't a potential composer. (American Psychological Association, 1995, p. 236)

Later, Holland noted that in retirement he "still pursues his aborted musical career by taking piano lessons and added voice lessons in 1993" (APA, p. 238). Holland told Weinrach (1980) about purchasing a grand piano with some early royalties from the SDS and about his interest in collecting art.

After reading about John Holland and thinking about RIASEC codes, it is probably easier to understand why Holland's code is undifferentiated. But we're not quite finished yet. Think about the name Adam Lackey. Can you think of a time you might have referred to someone as a "lackey"? We can't finish a profile of John L. Holland without noting his sense of humor. Adam Lackey, dear reader, does not in fact exist as a colleague of Holland's; he is a pseudonym, a name that Holland and his colleagues created to acknowledge authorship of a work for which no one wanted to take primary credit.

Holland's Background

Interesting insights into Holland's personality can be found in much of his writing, such as the "Some Common Questions" section in the back of the *Self-Directed Search Professional User's Guide* (Holland, Powell, & Fritzsche, 1994), and several other good sources. Among those offering an inside look into Holland's personality are a videotape of Holland commenting on RIASEC theory and the SDS (Career Design Associates, 1988), a published interview conducted by Steve Weinrach (1980), a videotape of a presentation he made at a 1992 career theory conference at Michigan State University (Savickas & Lent, 1993), an article reporting the test results of inventories completed by Super and Holland (Weinrach, 1996), and the citation written about Holland on the occasion of his receiving the American Psychological Association Award for Distinguished Professional Contributions (APA, 1995). The following paragraphs, using a question-and-answer format, will draw upon these materials.

What is Holland's Family Background?

Holland "was born in Omaha, Nebraska, on October 21, 1919, into a lower-class family of English-Irish ancestry. His father had immigrated from London at age 20, worked as laborer, took night courses at the YMCA, and eventually became a successful advertising executive (AES). His mother had been an elementary school teacher (SEC) before her marriage. Both parents had marked intellectual interests and put all four children (John was the second of three boys, and a girl) through college" (APA, 1995, p. 236).

As an adult, Holland and his wife Elsie, to whom *Making Vocational Choices* (MVC; Holland, 1997) is dedicated, had three children, two girls (ISA, ASE) and one boy (RSA) (Weinrach, 1980). Elsie, a secretary (CSE) working at a YWCA, died after Holland retired from Johns Hopkins in 1980. The case studies shown in the *SDS Professional User's Guide* include the SDS profiles of his children, as well as friends and other family members.

What Kind of Student Was Holland?

Holland started off in music at the Municipal University of Omaha, tried the physical sciences, but switched to psychology and liked it. He graduated in 1942 and then spent $3\frac{1}{2}$ years in the army working in psychological and social services. Upon leaving the army, Holland had decided to become a psychologist and entered the University of Minnesota in counseling psychology. Self-described as an "average student," Holland was probably not highly congruent with the strong empirical, data-driven characteristics of the Minnesota environment. "In the 1940s, psychology at Minnesota was pro 'show me the evidence' and anti-Freud, Rogers, typologies, and most of all, anti-speculation" (APA, 1995, p. 237). Holland's dissertation focused on a validation of some speculations about art and personality, a topic that he noted did not sit well with fellow students or faculty (1995). (Readers will recall my earlier suggestion to keep an eye on Holland's A.)

Spokane and Shultheis (1996) also noted that "Holland was not entirely in the 'Minnesota Mold' when he graduated in 1952" (p. 27). "A rebel by nature, Holland was as interested in the intervention side of measurement as he was in the scaling side" (p. 28). However, Spokane and Shultheis noted that Holland was more steeped in the Minnesota tradition than is often acknowledged. "His research style was and still is characterized by relentless empirical trials and examinations, followed by theoretical reformulations. This combination of theory and data is largely responsible for the success of the theory and its numerous inventories and interventions" (p. 28).

Did Holland Really Get Fired at ACT?

In the interview with Weinrach (1980), Holland talked about the experience of involuntary job loss at the American College Testing Program in 1969 as one of the most painful in his life. Holland had come to ACT as a vice president after working for several years at the National Merit Scholarship Corporation. He reports developing a serious administrative disagreement about an ACT product and walking out of a meeting to protest a management decision. Upon his dismissal, he sued ACT for improper termination, and after 5 years a settlement was reached. Getting on the phone the day he was fired, he obtained several offers and about a month later accepted a position at Johns Hopkins University. In characteristic tone, Holland told Weinrach, "My interpretation of what happened eventually was that I was the wrong type for that environment. The ACT people were more business-minded than I was. I was more interested in developing knowledge about college students and their institutions" (Weinrach, p. 412).

Holland's Creation of the SDS

How Did the Army and Minnesota Experiences Affect Holland's Thinking?

Holland's work in the army involved a brief 15-minute interview with recruits gathering personal information, and he soon learned that, despite the infinite complexity of the human personality, he could correctly anticipate responses because of the stable, common core of personality characteristics. In these brief interviews, Holland began to observe the personal typology in operation. Holland reported that his 4-year practicum experience in counseling centers, devoted largely to career counseling, plus an early job as a career counselor at Western Reserve University, were sufficiently frustrating and depressing that he began to look for alternatives. "...scoring delays and incomplete information about a person's interests and occupational aspirations were hard to cope with. In 1953, Holland began the development of the Vocational Preference Inventory (VPI) as a lark. Why not use only occupational titles as items and create scales for the main kinds of occupations rather than for single occupations?" (American Psychological Association, 1995, p. 237). (Remember the A.)

The VPI has been revised eight times; it became the research tool that inductively verified the existence of the RIASEC typology and later led to the development of the SDS itself.

Why Did Holland Develop the SDS?

On September 20, 1973, Holland was invited back to the University of Minnesota to give a speech at the annual conference of the Minnesota Statewide Testing Programs. The speech, entitled "Some Practical Remedies for Providing Vocational Guidance for Everyone," was published in the *Educational Researcher* (Holland, 1974). In his remarks, Holland identified and responded to some popular "myths" that he judged had restrained progress in career theory and practice. The following paragraph shows his response to one of these myths:

> "Counseling Must Be Personal." The counseling and teaching professions attract a large proportion of friendly people who must love and be loved in order to get through the day. Consequently, they believe that other people also must have the same needs with the same intensity. As a natural corollary, many also believe that any form of vocational intervention must provide for a person-to-person situation. These beliefs have prevented any major revision of the delivery system for vocational services. Some experience and recent experiments strongly imply that most people want help,

not love. In no case has an impersonal information or guidance system received a lower average rating than local counselors. To the contrary, most tests reveal that impersonal schemes are more highly rated as well as infinitely cheaper, have better attendance records, and are generally more dependable. In short, there is ample empirical evidence to support more impersonal approaches for the solution of vocational problems. (Holland, 1974, p. 10)

This quote provides a partial insight into Holland's development and use of the Self-Directed Search and related tools. In another quote taken from the *SDS Professional Users Guide* (Holland, Powell, & Fritzsche, 1994), Holland responded to the question, "Why did you develop the SDS?" with the following comment:

My recollections of the origins of the SDS and of my motivation at that time (1970) now vary from year to year. The more stable memories are that I wanted to see if I could create an inventory that would be self-scored and would avoid the problems involved in separate answer sheets, mailing, scoring, and so on. I did not anticipate the positive reactions that the SDS stimulated in users and professionals. (p. 51)

How Did Holland Go about Creating the SDS?

In an interview with Stephen Weinrach (1980), Holland described the people, events, and ideas that led to the development of the Self-Directed Search. I will briefly summarize them, but readers are encouraged to read the original materials cited in this chapter to get the full story.

Holland credits many others for little things involving the creation of the SDS. For example, he credits Tom Magoon, the former director of the Counseling Center at the University of Maryland, who provided the words "self-directed," and Chuck Elton, who gave him the idea of self-scoring.

In the Weinrach (1980) interview, Holland noted that the SDS evolved over a period of years, roughly 1953-1970, in rhythm with the development of the RIASEC theory and the VPI. For example, the VPI came first and demonstrated that short scales of equal length scored "yes" and arranged in RIASEC order could provide a basis for effective measurement.

Early products that had some features of what later became the SDS were developed at the National Merit Scholarship Corporation and at ACT. In particular, the College Guidance Profile, developed at ACT in 1967, had things in common with the SDS Assessment Booklet, but it turned out to be a financial and artistic failure, according to Holland (Weinrach, 1980). One of the things that Holland gained from these experiences was the realization that a self-scored instrument would be useful only if there was a corresponding list of occupational possibilities.

After arriving at Johns Hopkins from ACT, Holland acquired several sets of data about occupations, including SVIB archives data donated by Dave Campbell (Weinrach, 1980). These events enabled Holland to begin developing a comprehensive occupational classification and to begin to develop a prototype SDS booklet in 1970.

> I asked Joan, my daughter, to take it. Joan could follow the directions, but I had forgotten to work out the self-scoring procedure. Nor did I have any good ideas of how to do it. As it turned out, the scoring was the final and most difficult task. With the aid of neighborhood kids, my family, and Tom Magoon and his University of Maryland students, we tried multiple techniques to develop a simple scoring procedure. We obtained a useful method in 1970, but some remaining difficulties were not effectively dealt with until the revision of the scoring procedure in 1977. (Weinrach, 1980, p. 409)

The *SDS Professional User's Guide* (Holland, Powell, & Fritzsche, 1994) provides a brief review of the changes made in the succeeding editions of the SDS in 1977, 1985, and 1994. Readers are cautioned to be suspicious of earlier criticisms of the SDS because many of these have been corrected in subsequent editions of the instrument.

Recognition of Holland's Unique Contribution

In 1995, John Holland received an award from the American Psychological Association for "Distinguished Professional Contributions to Applied Psychology as a Professional Practice." No other counseling psychologists and no other career psychologists have been so recognized. The first recipient of this award was Carl R. Rogers in 1972. This award puts Holland in a highly esteemed class of research and professional psychologists and helps practitioners verify that the body of work that Holland has created is well respected and important within psychology. The scope and quality of Holland's contributions can be a source of inspiration and confidence for us as practitioners working with clients.

At the time of Holland's retirement from Johns Hopkins University in 1980, Gary Gottfredson and others prepared a written celebration of his work. Gottfredson (1980) identified four important contributions that Holland had made to the field:

Intellectual contributions. Holland's studies of college environments and students' personalities in relation to college adjustment; the Environmental Assessment Technique, with its focus on the environment when other career theorists were looking exclusively at personality; the RIASEC theory of careers; Holland's responses to critical reviews, with additional empirical research studies or modification of earlier views; and studies of nonacademic predictors as useful measures of student academic performance.

Practical devices. Holland's Vocational Preference Inventory (VPI; Holland, 1985b); the Self-Directed Search (SDS Forms R, E, CP, and Career Explorer); the Vocational Exploration Insight Kit (VEIK; Holland, 1992); My Vocational Situation (MVS; Holland, Daiger, & Power, 1980); the *Dictionary of Holland Occupational Codes* (DHOC); the Career Attitudes and Strategies Inventory (CASI; Holland & Gottfredson, 1994); and the Position Classification Inventory (PCI; Gottfredson & Holland, 1991) are all practical career resources. RIASEC theory has been incorporated into many other career interventions, including the Strong Interest Inventory (Harmon, Hansen, Borgen, & Hammer, 1994); most computer-based guidance systems (i.e., Discover, Choices); many career information reference materials; and Bolles' (1996) best-selling *What Color Is Your Parachute?*

"Unfrocking" contributions. Holland has poked at some "sacred cows" in the career guidance field. Gottfredson noted that Holland repeatedly challenged popular, prevailing views among psychologists and that he used empirical evidence to present sharply divergent, usually practical points of view. During a conversation years ago, Holland told me about an SDS presentation he made at a conference: An esteemed measurement psychologist stood up in a crowded room and, with a very red face and wagging his finger, said, "You can't do that." There are many aspects of the SDS, as we shall learn later, that could have triggered that response.

Influence on others. Holland has influenced the thinking and work of others; he is in the top .1% of publishing psychologists, and his work is widely cited (Watkins et al., 1986). Perhaps as you read this book and other materials that Holland has written, you, too, may come to count yourself among those he has influenced.

Conclusion

John Holland's own SDS summary code (AEI/R/S) and his Aspirations summary code (SAE) reveal much about his personality and interests and the beliefs and values that led him to create the SDS and other practical guidance tools. Understanding Holland's personality can be useful in understanding the design and development of the SDS. It can also enable users to extend the use of RIASEC theory and instruments in new, creative ways that are consistent with the original purposes of the author, John L. Holland.

2

RIASEC Theory: Past and Present

In teaching a career theories course for the past 20 years and in leading more than 35 SDS workshops, I have come to recognize how difficult it is to sell THEORY to busy practitioners. The popular view seems to be that theory is unrelated to practice or practical things. Theory is for academics in an ivory tower, who have little experience with the real world. Indeed, theory gets in the way of practice, and should be avoided at all costs. Counselors should ignore, or even better, avoid theory because it doesn't help much. That might be true for *some* career theory, which was designed more as a tool to understand career development as a component of human development, rather than as a guide for delivering career interventions.

But Holland's RIASEC theory is different. It is a user-friendly theory, especially for busy counselors and their clients. Indeed, when the results of the early evaluations of the SDS were completed, high school students noted that it was the "theory" about the types in the SDS that was especially helpful (Zener & Schnuelle, 1976). In chapter 1, we learned that the development of the SDS and RIASEC theory occurred in an interactive, reciprocal process, each influencing the other. Holland's theory is useful and practical in almost every way, and understanding the theory is important and worthwhile for effective, professional career counseling.

In this chapter, we examine some of the major developments in RIASEC theory over the years, especially as they affect the design and use of the SDS. We will explore the eight assumptions presently undergirding RIASEC theory and briefly examine Holland's theory in relation to other career theories.

Holland's RIASEC Theory

Several good, current, brief statements of RIASEC theory are available in the literature and are described later in this section. However, it is important for persons using the SDS and other Holland-based tools to read the theory as written by John Holland himself, because he says it better than anybody else. The best single source of information about RIASEC theory is Holland's (1997) *Making Vocational Choices: A Theory of Vocational Personalities and Work Environments.* This is the third, complete formal statement of the theory by Holland (the second edition of the book was published in 1985). The first complete statement was the original edition of *Making Vocational Choices: A Theory of Careers* (Holland, 1973).

Readers sometimes debate how much the theory changed between the 1973 and 1997 books. On the one hand, it is important that the theory show stability and continuity over time. If the theory changed dramatically each time it was revised, we might wonder if it were any good. On the other hand, the theory should be modified as new research further clarifies and extends it. My own view is that the theory changed about 20% from 1973 to 1985 and another 15% in 1997; Holland would probably view the change as less. Perhaps the most important thing to note is that it is essential to read the most recent statements of the theory because some ideas have evolved and have been refined over time. Additional perspectives on the quality and evolution of the theory are presented in chapter 12. In general, what you learned about RIASEC theory years ago in a class or a workshop may no longer be accurate.

Information about RIASEC theory is also included in the *SDS Professional User's Guide* (Holland, Powell, & Fritzsche, 1994) and the *SDS Technical Manual* (Holland, Fritzsche, & Powell, 1994). A brief review of some of the highpoints in the life of the theory is included in Holland's address on receiving the 1995 award from the American Psychological Association (Holland, 1996a).

Two other important and useful statements about RIASEC theory appear in recent literature. These include a chapter by Arnie Spokane and Susan Shultheis (1996), "There Is Nothing so Practical as a Good Theory," in *The Self-Directed Search (SDS) in Business and Industry*, edited by Mike Shahnasarian, and a chapter by Spokane (1996), "Holland's Theory," in a career theory textbook, *Career Choice and Development*, edited by Duane Brown and Linda Brooks (1996).

Authors and researchers develop theories for various purposes. Each theory seeks to explain something, to increase our understanding of some event or happening. Holland has been very clear about the purposes of his theory, and it is very important to keep these in mind when working with RIASEC theory. In *Making Vocational Choices* (Holland, 1985, p. 1), he lists three questions his theory seeks to address:

1. What personal and environmental characteristics lead to satisfying career decisions, involvement, and achievement, and what characteristics lead to indecision, dissatisfying decisions, or lack of accomplishment?

2. What personal and environmental characteristics lead to stability or change in the kind of level and work a person performs over a lifetime?

3. What are the most effective methods for providing assistance to people with career problems?

These three questions provide the rationale or basis for the work that has led to the development of Holland's RIASEC theory. As we note later, some persons criticize Holland's theory because of what it does *not* do, but it is more fair to be critical only if a theory fails to accomplish its purpose. If these three questions are important to you as a practicing career services provider or to those you seek to help, then Holland's typological theory may be very useful to you.

Below is the brief account of the theory that Holland provided recently in the *American Psychologist* (Holland, 1996a):

> The typology assumes it is useful to characterize people according to their resemblance to six personality types and to characterize environments according to six ideal environments. Each type is assumed to flourish in an environment having the same label. For example, Realistic types flourish or do well in a Realistic environment, because it provides opportunities, activities, tasks, and roles that are congruent with the Realistic type's competencies, interests, and self-beliefs. More explicitly, it is assumed—other things being equal—that congruence of person and job environment leads to job satisfaction, stability of career path, and achievement. Conversely, incongruence (i.e., person and job are mismatched) leads to dissatisfaction, instability of career path, and low performance. (p. 397)

If the old adage that "a picture is worth 1,000 words" has any merit, it is especially true in understanding RIASEC theory. Indeed, it is just not possible to really understand this theory apart from the hexagon model in Figure 1. In an interview with Weinrach (1980), Holland recalls that he and a research colleague, Doug Whitney, were "searching for a way to order the typology by recording the correlations between the different scales of the VPI. If Anne Roe had not preceded me, we would have called it a circle. I remember telling Doug Whitney that Roe had a circle, so we called the resulting configuration a hexagon. Actually, it's a misshapen polygon. But I did see that it might be a way to organize the relations among all the constructs in the theory and to define degrees of consistency and congruency" (Weinrach, 1980, p. 408).

This comment about the hexagon and the circle by Holland is especially noteworthy because there is considerable "energy" being expended in the research literature regarding the true shape of the hexagon. Some suggest that the RIASEC hexagon is better described as a circular arrangement, circumplex structure, or a concentric circle model of interests (Tracey & Rounds, 1995). We will leave the debate and further investigation of these issues to other

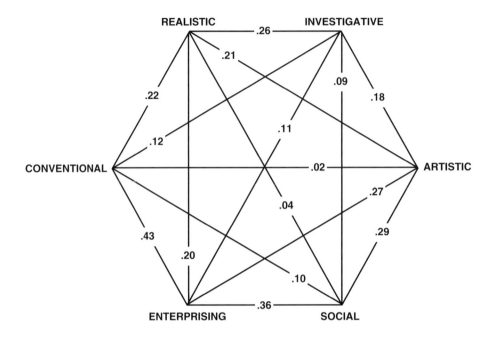

Figure 1. A hexagonal model for interpreting inter- and intra-class relationships among personality types and environments. From the *Self-Directed Search Technical Manual* (p. 4), by J. L. Holland, B. A. Fritzsche, and A. B. Powell, 1994, Odessa, FL: Psychological Assessment Resources, Inc. Copyright © 1985, 1987, 1994 by Psychological Assessment Resources, Inc., Odessa, FL. Reproduced by permission.

researchers, and stay the course with our focus on the hexagon as Holland originally described it.

Before the creation of a RIASEC hexagon (Cole, Whitney, & Holland, 1971), Holland's theory was much less orderly. It is almost as if the types were free-floating in space, but by attaching each of the types to one of the six points in the hexagon figure and in the prescribed order, Holland was able to introduce more order and predictability into the theory. As shown in Figure 1, the correlation numbers indicate the approximate strength of the relationships among the types. The numbers are generally higher between the types that are closest on the hexagon, and lower for those types farthest apart. In the early days, Holland called this "calculus," because it showed the predictable relationships among the six types.

The invention of the hexagon was an important, pivotal event in the historical development of career theory and practice. Indeed, many of our most popular career tools use this powerful idea. Ironically, the article reporting the creation of the RIASEC hexagon was in the first issue of the *Journal of Vocational Behavior* (Cole et al., 1971). Borgen (1991) has referred to the

RIASEC hexagon as "vocational psychology's icon" (p. 273) and Holland's logo. "Few ideas in the social science, and none in vocational psychology, have had such heuristic impact on subsequent research and application" (Borgen, p. 272).

Assumptions of the Theory

Figure 1 provides much of the fundamental information about RIASEC theory and a framework for discussing seven of the eight basic assumptions presently included in the theory (Holland, 1997; Holland, Powell, & Fritzsche, 1994). In this section, we will examine these assumptions in some detail because they are key components in understanding and using the SDS and other Holland-based interventions. Brief definitions of many of the terms used in the theory are provided in the Glossary (Appendix A).

1. *Most People Can Be Categorized As One of Six Personality Types.*

Persons can be categorized as one of six personality types: Realistic, Investigative, Artistic, Social, Enterprising, or Conventional. These six types are briefly defined below. It may be noted that these definitions were taken from the interpretive report for the SDS Form R, which provides a tangible link between RIASEC theory and practice because this report is intended to be read by clients.

Realistic (R) people like realistic careers, such as auto mechanic, aircraft controller, surveyor, electrician, and farmer. The *R* type usually has mechanical and athletic abilities and likes to work outdoors and with tools and machines.

The *R* type generally likes to work with things more than with people. The *R* type is described as conforming, frank, genuine, hardheaded, honest, humble, materialistic, modest, natural, normal, persistent, practical, shy, and thrifty.

Investigative (I) people like investigative careers, such as biologist, chemist, physicist, geologist, anthropologist, laboratory assistant, and medical technician. The *I* type usually has math and science abilities and likes to work alone and to solve problems.

The *I* type generally likes to explore and understand things or events, rather than persuade others or sell them things. The *I* type is described as analytical, cautious, complex, critical, curious, independent, intellectual, introverted, methodical, modest, pessimistic, precise, rational, and reserved.

Artistic (A) people like artistic careers, such as composer, musician, stage director, dancer, interior decorator, actor, and writer. The *A* type usually has artistic skills, enjoys creating original work, and has a good imagination.

The *A* type generally likes to work with creative ideas and self-expression more than routines and rules. The *A* type is described as complicated, disorderly, emotional, expressive, idealistic, imaginative, impractical, impulsive, independent, introspective, intuitive, nonconforming, open, and original.

Social (S) people like social careers, such as teacher, speech therapist, religious worker, counselor, clinical psychologist, and nurse. The *S* type usually likes to be around other people, is interested in how people get along, and likes to help other people with their problems.

The *S* type generally likes to help, teach, and counsel people more than engage in mechanical or technical activity. The *S* type is described as convincing, cooperative, friendly, generous, helpful, idealistic, kind, patient, responsible, social, sympathetic, tactful, understanding, and warm.

Enterprising (E) people like enterprising careers, such as buyer, sports promoter, television producer, business executive, salesperson, travel agent, supervisor, and manager. The *E* type usually has leadership and public speaking abilities, is interested in money and politics, and likes to influence people.

The *E* type generally likes to persuade or direct others more than work on scientific or complicated topics. The *E* type is described as acquisitive, adventurous, agreeable, ambitious, attention-getting, domineering, energetic, extroverted, impulsive, optimistic, pleasure-seeking, popular, self-confident, and sociable.

Conventional (C) people like conventional careers, such as bookkeeper, financial analyst, banker, tax expert, secretary, and radio dispatcher. The *C* type has clerical and math abilities and likes to work indoors and to organize things.

The *C* type generally likes to follow orderly routines and meet clear standards, avoiding work that does not have clear directions. The *C* type is described as conforming, conscientious, careful, efficient, inhibited, obedient, orderly, persistent, practical, thrifty, and unimaginative.

Each of these six types is a theoretical model against which we can measure real persons. Holland was aware that no person would completely resemble all of the characteristics of any one of the six basic types, but would more properly have some combination of several types in his or her personality. By using three types to characterize a person's personality, it is possible to identify 720 combinations of types, representing a rather complex array of personality options. In this way, the RIASEC typology reflects some of the complexity in human personality.

It is important to note that Holland picked six types—others urged him to pick another number, (i.e., 5 or 8 or 12), but he picked six. He picked six for reasons, including simplicity and usefulness. This matter continues to receive attention by researchers who support the use of eight scales (Tracey & Rounds, 1995), or seven scales (Campbell, 1995), or the overlay of dimensions (i.e., people-things and data-ideas) to the six RIASEC scales (Prediger & Vansickle, 1992). Other typological theories, such as the one represented in the Myers-Briggs Type Indicator (MBTI; Myers & McCaulley, 1992), have more categories of types (i.e., 16). Murray's needs-press theory (1938) has eight. There have been numerous typological theories in psychology over the years, including the work of Carl Jung (1933), on which the MBTI is loosely based. Additional information about the six Holland types will be presented in chapter 3.

2. There Are Six Model Environments: Realistic, Investigative, Artistic, Social, Enterprising, and Conventional.

The second assumption of the RIASEC theory is that there are six corresponding environments, dominated by a given type of personality and related physical characteristics. For example, an artistic environment is dominated by artistic types of personalities, and the environment is characterized by such things as musical instruments, dramatic and studio work settings, and persons working alone. Environments reflect the interests, talents, skills, and attitudes of the people who populate the setting. Environments can be measured or assessed by counting the numbers of types in the environment and establishing a percentage of the six types. For example, a given environment might be considered a pie graph, with each of the six slices representing the percentage of the environment composed of each of the six types. The Artistic environment would have proportionally more Artistic types present.

Holland's early efforts with the National Merit Scholarship Corporation and the American College Testing Program enabled him to look at colleges as environments. Later he focused on occupations as environments. Almost any social setting can be considered an environment in terms of RIASEC theory. For example, a family-owned business might be characterized in terms of RIASEC environments, or a classroom, or a marriage, or a work group. Every aspect of the theory can be applied to all of these different kinds of environments.

3. *People Search for Environments That Will Let Them Exercise Their Skills and Abilities, Express Their Attitudes and Values, and Take on Agreeable Problems and Roles.*

This third assumption is sometimes called the "birds of a feather" assumption, because it builds on the idea that "likes" will attract "likes." Holland's work has been criticized by some because it does not explain how types are developed, or because it is a simple, outdated "matching" theory. We find this third assumption to be developmental in nature because it suggests that over time persons will increasingly find environments that enable their type to flourish and grow. Further, we have often seen patterns in families where children grow up in a particular environment and develop personality types similar to those of their parents. For example, we often see children of A type parents becoming A types as well. And finally, environments often work to attract compatible types through job recruiting and referral, advertising, and other social mechanisms. In this sense, the theory is quite interactive and dynamic, rather than static or stolid.

Holland (1996a) has labeled this assumption the "congruency hypothesis" and has offered the following observation:

> This incomplete review of hard and soft research implies that congruency of interests is conducive to stability and satisfaction in both interpersonal and person-job relations. A few studies also imply that the explanations of interactions given by research participants parallel the explanations from the theory. These findings suggest that...people are active participants in their interactions with environments. (p. 401)

Later, Holland noted that despite the usefulness of the congruency hypothesis, some inefficiencies should be corrected by revising the typology, especially as it might pertain to environments. In general, however, this third assumption is a good one, and practitioners can take heart in the research that is available to support it.

4. *A Person's Behavior Is Determined by an Interaction Between His or Her Personality and the Characteristics of the Environment.*

This assumption is directly related to the preceding one, and it suggests that we can use information about types and environments to predict a person's behavior in a given environment. Such behavioral outcomes might include job changes, meritorious performance, high salary, stomach ulcers, anxiety, or persistence in a job. Recalling the three basic questions identified earlier in this chapter that Holland sought to answer with the theory, this assumption is very important. The typology helps us explain why some persons absolutely "love" their jobs and why other persons "hate" theirs.

For example, an RIA person in an RIA job would likely be characterized by shared interests with coworkers and supervisors, support and rewards for values and behavior typical of RIA types, low job stress, high job satisfaction, high job ratings with annual salary rewards, and desire to persist in the job. Conversely, an RIA person in an SEC job would probably have little in common with coworkers or supervisors, have many interests and activities outside of the job, not get high job ratings or rewards for work performance, report low job satisfaction, experience job stress and have little sick leave remaining, and spend considerable time thinking about some other kind of job.

The four preceding assumptions have been identified as the basic or primary assumptions of the theory. Holland has offered four other "secondary" assumptions to help "prop up" or explain the first four more fully. These secondary assumptions help explain why and how the first four assumptions might not be fully met, and they add some complexity to the RIASEC typology itself. We tend to think of them as additional theoretical ideas that enable us to stay within the theory itself when seeking explanations about how the typology really works.

5. *The Degree of Congruence (or Agreement) Between a Person and an Occupation (Environment) Can Be Estimated by a Hexagonal Model.*

As shown in Figure 1, there are levels or degrees of congruence between a person and an environment, or between any two sets of codes for that matter, and the hexagon helps us measure this. For example, the highest level of congruence occurs with an R person in an R job, and the lowest is with an R person in an S job because the S is opposite the R on the hexagon. The next highest level occurs with the two letters adjacent to the R on the hexagon, I and C, followed by the A and E. Thus, the hexagon enables us to estimate or measure four levels of congruence on the hexagon. We can obtain even more precise levels of congruence if we use three-letter codes rather than one-letter codes. Later, we will learn how the Iachan Index, used in the SDS computer version, provides a way to measure 28 different levels of congruence between three-letter codes. But for now, it is important to remember that levels of congruence involve matching one code with another code according to the array of RIASEC codes on the hexagon.

This is important because the typology may influence a person's behavior, depending on the level of congruence present. If the degree of congruence is only of average level, the typology may not work very well in explaining some aspects of vocational behavior. It is interesting to note that if congruence is either high or low, the typology may work quite well in explaining a person's job or educational situation.

6. *The Degree of Consistency Within a Person or an Environment Is Also Defined by Using the Hexagonal Model.*

Consistency is easy to confuse with congruence. One way to keep them separate is by remembering that *consistency* has to do with the relationship between **the first two letters** within one code; *congruence* has to do with the relationship between **two separate codes**. As with congruence, we use the hexagon to measure or estimate the level of consistency within a code. Levels of consistency are defined as follows:

- *high* level of consistency: the first two letters are adjacent (e.g., RC or RI) on the hexagon

- *moderate or medium* level of consistency: the first two letters are alternate on the hexagon (e.g., RA or RE)

- *low* level of consistency: the first two letters are opposite on the hexagon (e.g., RS)

Why is this important? Codes are generally considered more stable and predictable when consistency is higher. In other words, the typology works better when consistency is present. Consistency predicts both the kind of study or work likely in the future and the stability of the person's current job or aspiration. This can have very practical significance. For example, persons with RS codes might have considerable difficulty in balancing their interests in "things" and "people" and find relatively few fields of study or jobs that have both R and S characteristics. The same can be said for AC and IE codes. Inconsistent codes may be more likely to change over time. In this way, a low level of consistency in a code helps explain why the RIASEC typology might not work very well in a particular situation.

Recently, Holland (1997) has introduced the concept of *coherence of aspirations* as a special form of consistency (i.e., the consistency of vocational aspirations). Coherence of aspirations has not yet become one of the basic assumptions of RIASEC theory, but it is an important theoretical concept and one that has practical implications for effective use of the SDS. Counselors with experience in looking at the way clients complete the Daydreams section of the SDS are aware that the codes of the daydream occupations are sometimes very different with respect to the RIASEC typology. For example, the first letters of the occupations listed under daydreams may all begin with a different letter (i.e., they lack coherence). Conversely, all of the occupations listed may begin with the same RIASEC letter. This notion of the coherence of aspirations is a powerful one. The level of coherence of aspirations may indicate a need for the user to learn more about his or her interests and about how occupations relate to one another. Holland, Gottfredson, and Baker (1990) have indicated that coherence may become increasingly important in the research and practical implications associated with RIASEC theory. The idea of coherence of aspirations will be discussed further in chapters 4, 7, 8, and 12.

7. The Degree of Differentiation of a Person or an Environment Modifies Predictions Made From a Person's RIASEC Profile, From an Occupational Code, or From the Interaction of the Two.

In developing the RIASEC theory, Holland was looking for a way to measure or describe the strength of the type. For example, was a person a "big" E type or a "little" E type; was the E really different from the other RIASC letters? Did the person endorse or agree with most of the likes, preferences, and characteristics of the E type, or were only a few of the preferences endorsed? Endorsing many E preferences on the SDS or VPI would mean that fewer of the other RIASC preferences would be selected, and we could say the person's E code was differentiated from the other five codes. If the person was a big E, then the characteristics of the type would be more manifest and prominent; the person would think and act more like the model Enterprising type.

The original method for determining differentiation of a person's code was simple and direct: Subtract the lowest SDS RIASEC summary score from the highest score to obtain a difference or d-score. For example, if a college male's highest score was 45 on the Enterprising scale and his lowest score was 10 on the Investigative scale, the difference or d-score would be 35, and inspection of Table B.1 (Holland, Powell, & Fritzsche, 1994) would reveal this score to be at the 89th percentile. In other words, this d-score was higher than that of 89 out of 100 college males in the sample and indicative of a highly differentiated profile.

At this point it might be useful to review the first assumption of the RIASEC theory and to carefully study the adjectives used to describe the six types. Because each of the six types is quite different, the strength of the type present in any given situation modifies the predictions of the theory. What does this mean? A big E type in a big E environment will most likely be characterized by all aspects of the theory, whereas a little E type in a big E environment might not function as well, even though high congruence was present. Similarly, a big E type in a weak E environment would not experience all of the expected influences of the E environment. Holland noted that well-defined or differentiated people or environments are most likely to show all of the expected aspects of their code.

If the codes are not highly differentiated from one another, however, we would say the person or environment is undifferentiated. In other words, the six RIASEC types are each present in about the same amount, but persons might be either undifferentiated high (i.e., they like many aspects of all six RIASEC areas a great deal) or undifferentiated low (i.e., they like few aspects of any of the six RIASEC areas). This idea is discussed more fully in chapters 7 and 9.

Although Holland, Powell, and Fritzsche (1994) listed only seven assumptions in the *SDS Professional User's Guide*, another assumption might be included here. In *Making Vocational Choices*, Holland (1985a, 1997) discussed the concept of vocational identity, and he elaborated on this idea in a recent article in the *American Psychologist* (Holland, 1996a). The eighth assumption might read something like the following:

8. *The Identity Level of a Person or an Environment Modifies Predictions Made From a Person's RIASEC Profile, From an Occupational Code, or From the Interaction of the Two.*

Vocational identity provides an estimate of the clarity and stability of a person's identity or the identity of an environment. "Personal identity is defined as the possession of a clear and stable picture of one's goals, interests, and talents" (Holland, 1985a, p. 5). "High scorers are vocationally mature people who possess many constructive beliefs about career decision-making; are interpersonally competent; are relatively free of disabling psychological problems; are conscientious, hopeful, and responsible; have a clear sense of vocational identity; and are not easily put off by barriers or environmental difficulties" (Holland, 1997, p. 149). If a person's vocational identity is high, he or she will more likely find a congruent environment or persist in searching for one. Vocational identity is measured directly by the 18 items on the Identity scale of My Vocational Situation (Holland, Daiger, & Power, 1990).

Holland also observed that "environmental identity is present when an environment or organization has clear, integrated goals, tasks, and rewards that are stable over long time intervals" (Holland, 1985a, p. 5). More recently, Holland (1997) has reported on the development of an experimental scale, the Environmental Identity scale (Gottfredson & Holland, 1996b). This scale taps a worker's beliefs about the explicitness and consistency of an organization's goals, work rules, and rewards for performance. A high score indicates that an environment provides clear and consistent direction and reward. The construct of environmental identity is patterned after vocational identity, and future research will provide information about the usefulness of the scale in explaining congruence in the RIASEC typology.

Holland has noted that consistency, differentiation, and identity are all concerned with the clarity, definition, or focus of the first four assumptions dealing with the RIASEC models of persons and environments. They help verify that the RIASEC type or environment is stable, that "matching" will occur, and that the predicted outcomes will happen. Differentiation and identity estimate the level of stability of a current aspiration or job, and consistency also estimates the kind of aspiration or job. Although consistency and differentiation are weaker secondary constructs, vocational identity "has proved to be a robust variable with substantial validity and practical value" (Holland, 1997, p. 169). In summary, persons and environments with a clear sense of identity have a greater likelihood of finding "partners" with congruent codes.

The Importance of Aspirations

From the very beginning, Holland has urged counselors to pay close attention to what clients say about the occupations they are considering. It is ironic that many counselors will systematically ignore clients' expressed aspirations. I recall leading a workshop several years ago where the counselors spoke about the need to find out how many students entering this very large community college needed career assistance. In the process of discussing the situation, I remember one counselor saying that they never paid any attention to what the new students said about their vocational interests because that information was biased and unreliable. Others emphatically agreed. How did we get into this situation where we ignore clients' expressions of their occupational interests, and what happens when we do?

In one of his most recent statements about the theory, Holland (1996a) has continued to argue for the practical and theoretical importance of occupational aspirations as a measure of *expressed* interests. Vocational inventory results, (i.e., Strong, Kuder), are considered measures of *assessed* interests. Psychologists have known for more than 40 years that occupational aspirations are powerful predictors of future occupational activity (Dolliver, 1969; Holland, 1996a; Holland, Fritzsche, & Powell, 1994). Dolliver reported almost 30 years ago that occupations identified by clients as their primary interest were just as predictive of future occupational activity as those reported on a test. In other words, a client's expressed interest was just as predictive of future occupational activity as his or her assessed interest. The supportive research on this topic provides a sound basis for giving serious consideration to expressed interests.

Holland extended this basic idea by applying the typology to occupational aspirations. In other words, the occupation listed by the client was important in and of itself, but it was also important because of the RIASEC type it represented. Holland included a measure of expressed interests in the Self-Directed Search (Form R) as the Daydreams section. We will discuss the importance and use of this measure of interests in chapter 4.

RIASEC Theory in Relation to Other Career Theories

As noted earlier, career theories differ in numerous ways. Some theories were developed for practitioners, and some for research psychologists. Some career theories were explicitly connected to learning or developmental theories in psychology, whereas others were not. Over the past 50 years, some career theories have faded, and others seem to be increasing in impact and importance. Because career theories are not all the same, I have found it useful to develop a model for comparing and contrasting them. My analysis is not perfect by any means, and it is quite subjective.

Career theories are most often characterized as either structured or developmental. Indeed, Brown and Brooks (1996) reflected this in their book on career theory by using the words "choice" and "development" in the title. Figure 2 shows a horizontal line with this continuum. Structured theories are also sometimes characterized as matching, person-environment, instrumental, choice, and trait-factor. Theories at the structured end of the continuum are among the oldest theories and have generally produced the most tools and practical devices used in the career guidance and counseling field. For example, most of our tests and informational materials are connected to structured theories. I sometimes think of these theories as more "conservative," in that they deal with the more concrete matters of jobs, economics, personality traits, and work adjustment or satisfaction.

At the opposite end from structured theories are the developmental or process-oriented theories developed later in this century (e.g., Ginzberg, Super). In general, these theories focus on the process of career development as it occurs over a person's lifetime and include the multiple life roles that characterize adult life (i.e., parent, spouse, citizen, student, worker, annuitant) and the way they are blended into life/career. I sometimes think of these theories as more liberal, in that they deal with more humanistic, philosophical, and esoteric issues associated with life satisfaction and development.

Figure 2 shows a vertical axis, which I characterize in terms of impact. At the top are career theories that are having the greatest impact on practice and research; the bottom of the axis marks those theories with less current importance. Some of these theories were more important at an earlier time but

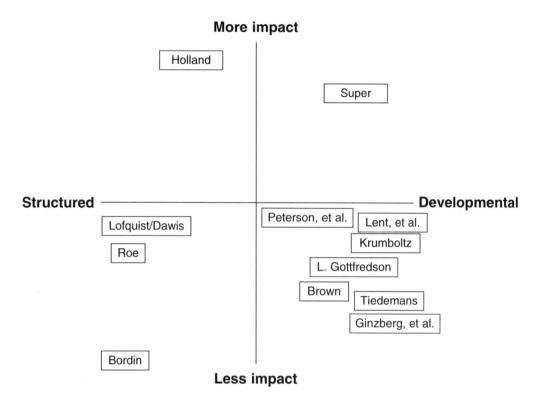

Figure 2. Career theories viewed from dimensions of structure vs. process orientation and impact on research and practice.

have faded, whereas others may be relatively more important in research or practice, but not both.

Given this orientation to the model undergirding Figure 2, I would place Holland's RIASEC theory in the most powerful position. There is little disagreement that RIASEC theory is currently stimulating more research than any other theory and impacts practice in many ways. Hyland and Muchinsky (1991) reported several years ago that about 700 studies had been conducted on Holland' theory, and many more are published each year. Holland's critics would probably place his work farther to the left in Figure 2 because they focus on the structured matching model inherent in the typology. I place Holland's work more toward the middle because I think that human learning and other developmental processes are associated with several of the theory assumptions discussed earlier in this chapter (i.e., Assumptions 4, 5, 7, and 8). I believe persons learn more about their own types as they grow older, and they learn more about how to analyze environments that will be congruent or how to make compromises when appropriate. I view Holland's theory as dynamic-interactive, not static-matching.

The position where I locate RIASEC theory on Figure 2 is a powerful one. Besides being the most active, impactful theory, it occupies the center, moderate position. Just like Republicans and Democrats, theorists prefer to work from the middle position, whereas their critics prefer to paint them as extremists. A theory in the middle has broader appeal and relevance to various career problems that counselors encounter in varied settings. Given these observations and comments about Holland's RIASEC theory, readers can infer the basis for my placements of other career theories in Figure 2. Interested readers might wish to read Brown and Brooks (1996) and other career theory texts reviewed in chapter 12 to develop their own schemes for locating Holland and the other theorists on the model. In chapter 12, we will return to RIASEC theory and Holland's impact to discuss more fully the future developments of the theory as well as the evaluations of the theory offered by several critics and observers.

Conclusion

Holland's RIASEC theory is based on an easily understood typology of persons and environments. The theory is based on four primary assumptions and four secondary assumptions that help to explain the circumstances under which the typology operates most efficiently. Holland's theory dominates the field because of its impact on research and practice and because it blends both structured-choice and developmental-process elements of career theory.

3

Types and Environments
More Fully Examined

In this chapter, we will explore in more detail both the RIASEC personality types and the way the typology applies to environments. With the personality types, we want to examine the psychological bases of RIASEC theory, and with the environments we will be drawing upon the disciplines of sociology and economics to increase our understanding of the theory. The field of counseling has sometimes been described as applied behavioral science. This chapter will draw upon these rich, interdisciplinary perspectives to help us learn more about the implications of RIASEC theory for career services. It is important for us to plunge a bit more deeply into the RIASEC typology because it is a rich source of information that can help our clients become more skillful career problem solvers and decision makers. The contents of this chapter can be used by career guidance practitioners in many aspects of their practice, from individual counseling to teaching credit courses.

Several years ago during my lecture on Holland's theory in a undergraduate career planning class, one of the students asked a question that troubled me: "Is that all there is to it?" In other words, this fellow Holland comes up with the idea of six kinds of people, and then says there are six kinds of jobs, and then says it will be OK when the same kinds of persons and jobs get together. Is that it? As I have thought about that question over the years and heard similar expressions by leading career theorists and practitioners at professional meetings, I am convinced that it is important for everyone to take a closer, more thoughtful look at this theory. Is it really so simple? In some ways it is, but in other ways it is not.

This chapter begins by comparing and contrasting the six RIASEC types and continues with a brief examination of what we know about the personality traits and characteristics of each, including multicultural and international perspectives. Then the chapter analyzes the six environmental models and some of the characteristics associated with these environments when applied to jobs, occupations, and training programs. In reviewing both aspects of the typology, the implications of this information for career counseling and guidance will be explored and explained. This richer, more complex understanding of RIASEC theory then sets the stage for a review of the design and use of the SDS and related Holland-based interventions.

RIASEC Types More Fully Examined

In this section, we examine several major points regarding the six RIASEC personality types, with implications for career counseling interventions. Four topics are covered: (a) comparing and contrasting the types, (b) analyzing the distributions of types, (c) the stability of interests and work histories, and (d) the multicultural and international aspects of types.

Distinguishing Among the Types

Although it seems to be an obvious point, it is nevertheless important to realize that the six RIASEC types represent real, qualitative differences in basic personality characteristics. As models of personality, the types represent genuine differences among persons with respect to interests, values, skills, outlooks, interpersonal styles, achievement orientations, and work styles. It is especially noteworthy that a type is more than just interests. Many research studies have shown that the personal adjectives used to describe the six types are empirically derived; they are not just made up by some researcher or simple constructions out of thin air. For example, the adjectives used to describe the six types under Assumption 1 of the theory (see chapter 2) are based on research data from numerous personality inventories used in studying the six RIASEC types.

When writing the adjective descriptions of the six types for the computer-based SDS interpretive reports, some thought that the term "hardheaded" should not be used to describe Realistic types because of its negative connotation. However, John Holland pointed out that R types typically describe themselves this way. Of course, many of us Social types found it difficult to appreciate how this could be true. In reading the descriptions of each of the types, you might also notice that some of the personality traits are not flattering or positive, at least to another type.

Gottfredson and Holland (1996a) developed a table summarizing characteristics among the types. Table 1 includes summary information about the six RIASEC personality types across five attributes:

1. A person's preferences for activities and occupations.

2. A person's values.

3. How a person sees himself or herself.

4. How others see the person.

5. What a person avoids.

Table 1
A Brief Description of the Holland Personality Typology

Attribute	Personality Type					
	Realistic	Investigative	Artistic	Social	Enterprising	Conventional
Preferences for activities and occupations	Manipulation of machines, tools and things	Exploration, understanding and prediction or control of natural and social phenomena	Literary, musical, or artistic activities	Helping, teaching, treating, counseling, or serving others through personal interaction	Persuading, manipulating, or directing others	Establishing or maintaining orderly routines, application of standards
Values	Material rewards for tangible accomplishments	Development or acquisition of knowledge	Creative expression of ideas, emotions or sentiments	Fostering the welfare of others, social service	Material accomplishment and social status	Material or financial accomplishment and power in social, business, or political arenas
Sees self as	Practical, conservative, and having manual and mechanical skills—lacking social skills	Analytical, intelligent, skeptical and having academic talent—lacking interpersonal skills	Open to experience, innovative, intellectual—lacking clerical or office skills	Empathic, patient, and having interpersonal skills —lacking mechanical ability	Having sales and persuasive ability —lacking scientific ability	Having technical skills in business or production—lacking artistic competencies
Others see as	Normal, frank	Asocial, intellectual	Unconventional, disorderly, creative	Nurturing, agreeable, extroverted	Energetic, gregarious	Careful, conforming
Avoids	Interaction with people	Persuasion or sales activities	Routines and conformity to established rules	Mechanical and technical activity	Scientific, intellectual, or abstruse topics	Ambiguous or unstructured undertakings

Note. From *Dictionary of Holland Occupational Codes* (3rd ed., p. 3). by G. D. Gottfredson and J. L. Holland, 1982, 1989, 1996, Odessa, FL: Psychological Assessment Resources. Copyright © 1996 by Psychological Assessment Resources, Inc. Reproduced with permission of the publisher.

Table 1 reveals a wide range of differences across these five dimensions. (Interested persons may want to examine a more detailed table showing characteristics of the types in the *SDS Professional User's Guide* (Holland, Powell, & Fritzsche, 1994, p. 25).

Holland (1997) recently noted that RIASEC interests may have a larger inherited component than earlier thought. He cites studies suggesting that 36-50% of the variance in interests may be inherited and 50-64% may be the result of environmental influences. In light of this, Holland (1997) suggests that

> counselors and clinicians should be both more sensitive to a person's aspirations, vocational interests, and family history, and more skeptical about attempts to change a person's aspirations and interests in substantial ways unless there is persuasive evidence that those interests have been distorted by lack of experience, discrimination, or some other negative influence. (p. 152)

A very active area of research involves examining Holland's RIASEC vocational typology and the five-factor personality theory (Costa & McCrae, 1992). The latter is a taxonomy of major personality dimensions which have been shown to underlie most personality constructs and is measured by the Revised NEO Personality Inventory (NEO PI-R). The so-called "Big-Five Factors" include Extraversion (reclusive–sociable, cautious–adventurous), Neuroticism (calm–anxious, secure–insecure), Agreeableness (irritable–good-natured, uncooperative–helpful), Conscientiousness (undependable-responsible, disorganized–well-organized), and Openness to Experience (conventional–original, unreflective–intellectual). Tokar and Swanson (1995) found substantial relationships between Holland's (1997) typology and the five-factor model. For example, Extroversion for men correlated .56 and .45 with the E and S scales, respectively, and Openness correlated .57 and .53 with the Artistic scale for men and women. Tokar and Swanson suggested that career interest assessment and personality assessment become less mutually exclusive. Holland has gone so far as to recommend that practitioners read "anything that Costa and McCrae have written about personality, its stability, structure, and the implications for therapy" (Holland, Powell, & Fritzsche, 1994, p. 61).

Holland (1997) reports the study by DeFruyt and Mervielde (1997) as the most comprehensive study to date of NEO and SDS relationships. Using the 30 facets or subscales of the NEO, the researchers were able to clarify differences among SDS types. For example, the facet scales for Extroversion imply that S and E types share some characteristics to about the same degree (e.g., Gregariousness and Positive Emotions), but E types probably have more Assertiveness, Active or Energetic, and Excitement-Seeking characteristics. S types may exhibit more warmth. Holland notes that the facet correlations from the NEO appear to mirror the hexagonal model.

Understanding and appreciating the differences among these six RIASEC personality types is the first step in using Holland's theory in interpreting the results of the SDS. It is the beginning point from which all other measures and interpretations are based. This cannot be overemphasized, because I sometimes encounter situations where counselors are using the SDS and have failed to account fully for the client's type in using or interpreting the test results or in planning a career intervention. For example, a counselor plans to have a client with an R or I type engage in informational interviews, without considering the fact that this may be very difficult for this client to do easily or well. Clients with S or E types might do this more easily. The counselor might have been more effective in helping the client if information about the Realistic type had been used (i.e., interpersonal style, preferred methods of getting information, typical life skills). These ideas are discussed more fully in chapters 5 and 9.

This information about personality types is perhaps the most important single source of data for using SDS results to help persons learn more about career problem solving and decision making. In many ways, the SDS is based on a powerful theory of personality that provides new knowledge for use in career guidance. No other theory of career choice or development has such a model available to guide career interventions. Once a person's RIASEC type is known that knowledge can be used by the counselor to select career interventions, develop a plan for providing career assistance, identify alternative career goals, and estimate the likelihood of particular career outcomes. (In the following chapter, we will examine two ways—expressed and assessed measurement—to ascertain a person's RIASEC type.)

One of the most provocative, yet humorous, essays on the characteristics of types can be found in an early, satirical article by John Hollifield (1971) in the *Personnel and Guidance Journal*. The article, "An Extension of Holland's Theory to Its Unnatural Conclusion," describes a RIASEC scenario of the end of the world. Holland's War in the 1990s, according to Hollifield, grew out of deep conflict among the RIASEC types and their inability to coexist in the United States. A national advertising board composed of proper proportions of the types was also part of Hollifield's scenario. In reading the article, one can grasp an offbeat understanding of how the types interact and the roles they play in society. You can speculate on how the scenario plays itself out. Which type do you think remained at the end? Was it the resourceful Realistics? The creative Artistics? The helpful Socials? The dutiful Conventionals? The idealistic Investigatives? Or would it have been the competitive Enterprisings? How well do you know the types? In Hollifield's version, the E types survived the longest, but they eventually did one another in because each wanted to be the final leader. Interestingly, Holland (1997) cites research suggesting that, other things being equal, achievement will be associated with the interest profile ESAICR.

Rule of Asymmetrical Distribution of Types and Subtypes

In developing guidelines for effectively using the Self-Directed Search, Holland offered several "rules" for interpreting the results. One is the "Rule of Asymmetrical Distribution of Types and Subtypes." What does this mean?

Normative data included in the Self-Directed Search manuals (Holland, Fritzsche, & Powell, 1994; Holland, Powell, & Fritzsche, 1994) reveal that RIASEC codes vary across persons of various ages and gender. Table 2, reported by Holland, Powell, and Fritzsche (1994), shows the distribution of two-letter codes for high school students in the normative sample. The most common code for high school boys was RE, followed by RI and ES. No boys had an AC or CA code. In comparison, high school girls most frequently had SE, SA, AS, or SI codes. The girls were least likely to have codes of CR, RC, RS, or RI.

There are several practical implications of this fact for career guidance practice:

1. Persons with rare or uncommon codes may have more difficulty in finding compatible, congruent environments. The *SDS Professional User's Guide* (Holland, Powell, & Fritzsche, 1994) and *Technical Manual* (Holland, Fritzsche, & Powell, 1994) both include tables showing the norms for one-, two-, and three-letter RIASEC codes.

2. Persons with rare and uncommon codes may display combinations of traits and personality characteristics that are not typically associated with one another. Such combinations of interests and traits may require compromises in interests, activities, and goals as a part of educational and career planning. Rare or uncommon codes are also characterized by fewer occupational listings; indeed, the SDS Form R Occupations Finder specifies no occupations for several codes (i.e., ACR, ACE, SAR, CAI). In chapter 4, we will review the "Rule of Full Exploration," which provides strategies for working around problems associated with rare codes. The RIASEC theory helps us specify which codes are less common among persons and occupations, and it also gives us tools to overcome these problems. We will explore this idea more fully in chapter 7.

3. Third, Holland (1997) argues that interest inventories that use normative data adjust interest scores based on sex, which distorts scores for women because large proportions of most female samples prefer Social occupations. With normed results, higher scores are more easily obtained on scales that are less popular among women; this can lead to confusion. For example, a high

Table 2
Distribution of Two-Letter SDS Codes for High School Students
in the 1985 and 1994 Samples

Males						Females					
1994 (n=344)			1985 (n=2,169)			1994 (n=475)			1985 (n=2,447)		
Code	f	%	Code	f	%	Code	f	%	Code	f	%
RI	46	13.4	RS	301	13.9	SE	77	16.2	SA	595	24.3
RE	36	10.5	RI	290	13.4	SA	60	12.6	SC	433	17.7
RA	29	8.4	IR	202	9.3	AS	50	10.5	SI	307	12.5
ES	21	6.1	IS	171	7.9	IS	45	9.5	SE	274	11.2
ER	19	5.5	SE	138	6.4	SI	44	9.3	AS	251	10.3
IR	19	5.5	RE	128	5.9	ES	36	7.6	CS	231	9.4
IA	17	4.9	RA	111	5.1	SC	26	5.5	IS	138	5.6
RS	16	4.7	SR	102	4.7	CS	16	3.4	IA	37	1.5
SE	14	4.1	SI	96	4.4	AI	14	3.0	AI	31	1.3
AR	12	3.5	AS	89	4.1	AE	13	2.7	SR	23	0.9
EI	12	3.5	ES	68	3.1	CE	11	2.3	CA	19	0.8
EC	11	3.2	SA	67	3.1	EC	10	2.1	ES	18	0.7
EA	10	2.9	IA	61	2.8	SR	10	2.1	AC	13	0.5
IS	10	2.9	IE	46	2.1	IA	8	1.7	CE	13	0.5
AS	9	2.6	RC	39	1.8	EA	6	1.3	IR	11	0.5
SR	9	2.6	AI	38	1.8	IC	6	1.3	AE	9	0.4
AE	8	2.3	SC	32	1.5	IE	6	1.3	RS	8	0.3
AI	7	2.0	AR	31	1.4	RE	6	1.3	IC	7	0.3
IE	7	2.0	ER	24	1.1	CA	4	0.8	RI	5	0.2
RC	7	2.0	CS	21	1.0	CI	4	0.8	CI	5	0.2
SA	6	1.7	AE	20	0.9	IR	4	0.8	AR	4	0.2
SI	5	1.5	CE	17	0.8	RA	4	0.8	EC	4	0.2
CE	4	1.2	EI	16	0.7	AC	3	0.6	EI	3	0.1
CR	4	1.2	EC	15	0.7	AR	3	0.6	CR	3	0.1
IC	2	0.6	IC	13	0.6	EI	3	0.6	IE	2	0.1
SC	2	0.6	CR	13	0.6	ER	3	0.6	RE	1	0.1
CI	1	0.3	EA	10	0.5	RC	1	0.2	ER	1	0.1
CS	1	0.3	CI	9	0.4	RI	1	0.2	EA	1	0.1
AC	0	0.0	CA	1	0.1	RS	1	0.2	RA	0	0.0
CA	0	0.0	AC	0	0.0	CR	0	0.0	RC	0	0.0

Note. Sample size varies slightly because not all respondents completed all items. *f* = frequency. From *The Self-Directed Search Professional User's Guide* (p. 80), by J. L. Holland, A. B. Powell, and B. A. Fritzsche, 1994, Odessa, FL: Psychological Assessment Resources. Copyright © 1985, 1987, 1994 by Psychological Assessment Resources, Inc. Adapted with permission of the publisher.

school female with little interest or skill in the Realistic area may obtain a high score on this scale and wonder where it came from, given her lack of strong interest in that area.

Stability of Interests and Work Histories

In reviewing 40 years of work with the theory, Holland (1996a) noted that the application of the RIASEC typology to aspirations and work histories was one of the most successful outcomes. Despite the impressions often given in the popular media that people are constantly changing jobs, there is substantial continuity over time in the kinds of work that people do and the kinds of vocational aspirations they identify related to the typology. Holland cited studies by Gottfredson (1977, 1982) and others of adult work histories to support this conclusion. McLaughlin & Tiedeman (1974) found that the RIASEC category of vocational aspiration or intention of high school students predicted the category of actual employment 11 years later. Similar findings have been reported in studies where standardized interest inventories were used (Holland, 1996a; Holland, Powell, & Fritzsche, 1994). Crenshaw (1995) reported that workers today are spending as many years at the same job as they always did. He suggested that the average worker today has been at the same job longer than someone of comparable age 20 or 30 years ago, despite a common perception to the contrary.

Career interests are most likely to be changeable through about age 25, but they may not change a great deal thereafter in terms of RIASEC codes. Codes or interests become more stable with increasing age. For example, a person might change from an interest in Criminal Lawyer (code ESA) to Columnist (code AES), but would be less likely to change to an occupation completely outside the E code. In summary, Holland has concluded that a person's expressed aspirations and inventoried interests can be considered reliable and valid assessments of RIASEC types.

RIASEC Types: A Multicultural and International View

Counselors in our workshops often ask about the validity of the RIASEC typology in a multicultural society such as that of the U.S. or the usefulness of the typology in other countries. How does the typology apply to Hispanic youth, Asian college students, or African-American adults? What about gay/lesbian/bisexual persons? Does the typology apply to people in other countries? This section focuses on these topics.

Researchers have studied the application of the RIASEC typology across cultures for more than 20 years. In 1992, several articles on Holland's theory in a special issue of the *Journal of Vocational Behavior* (Tinsley, 1992) were devoted to this topic. More recently, James Rounds and Terence Tracey (1996) of the

University of Illinois, together with other researchers, have reported numerous studies of research in this area. The basic issue seems to boil down to whether the RIASEC hexagon, as a model for the structure of interests, exists in non-Western cultures (e.g., Asian, African). The results are conflicting. Spokane (1996) noted that although sampling, translation, and cross-cultural measurement problems abound, the possibility that the hexagon or some similar structural representation of RIASEC interests does not exist across various cultures could be an important concern for the profession. This issue quickly becomes both a technical discussion about statistical factor structures of vocational interests and the search for the perfect hexagon. Holland and Gottfredson (1992) have suggested that scholars may be seeking to apply too much precision to the study of the hexagon and that more efforts should be devoted to studying the practical effects of using interest inventories with varied kinds of persons.

Cultural subgroups in the U.S. have a sufficiently common social and educational experience that we may confidently apply RIASEC theory and the SDS to almost everyone (Day, Rounds, Tracey, & Swaney, 1996). After examining data from more than 49,000 results of the Unisex Edition of the ACT interest inventory, they concluded, "The structure of minority vocational interests seems to be well represented by Holland's RIASEC model, and instruments based on such theories have validity for diverse groups in the United States" (p. 6). Of course, persons who differ greatly from average in any characteristic (i.e., very poor or very rich, very slow or very smart, very special talent or genetic characteristic) may be outside the range of what the typology seeks to help us understand or explain.

Not everyone agrees that ethnic subgroups in the U.S. appear to be no different than the White, majority culture with respect to the RIASEC typology (Fouad & Dancer, 1992; Swanson, 1992). These authors argued that the application of the typology to U.S. cultural minority groups is only suggestive and requires more research. Related to this point of view, a study of the career interests and aspirations of gay men who used the SDS (Chung & Harmon, 1994) suggested that gays, compared to heterosexuals, were less Realistic- and Investigative-oriented and more Artistic- and Social-oriented. Gay men's aspirations were also less traditional for males. Chung and Harmon urged counselors to be alert to the social barriers for gay men in pursuing nontraditional occupations.

Nevertheless, Holland and Gottfredson (1992) concluded that we have a rather comprehensive account of how the typology and the SDS apply successfully to Whites, Blacks, men, and women in this country. Indeed, Holland (1997) recently noted that in the 1994 revision of the SDS, the largest mean differences are for gender, not ethnicity. "In short, women are more similar in interest to women in other cultures or races than they are to men of the same culture or race" (Holland, 1997, p. 157). In general, practitioners can have confidence in using the SDS and related Holland-based materials with varied cultural minorities in the U.S. As with any assessment device, however, the development of local norms may enhance the use of the instrument (Gade, Fuqua, & Hurlburt, 1984).

The VPI and the SDS have been translated into more than 20 languages, sometimes only for research purposes. Commercial editions of the SDS are available for Australian, Canadian, Danish, Dutch, French, German, Hebrew, Icelandic, Japanese, New Zealand, Norwegian, Slovenian, South African, Spanish, and Vietnamese clients. Lokan and Taylor (1986) provided one of the most detailed discussions of the application of Holland's work in other countries in their book, *Holland in Australia: A Vocational Choice Theory in Research and Practice*. Although comparative studies have not been conducted with many of these translations, most studied comparisons have indicated that principles of both the RIASEC typology and the instruments may be generalized across nations. In addition, there are few reports of complaints about the accuracy or validity of the theory or the instruments by users in these other countries (Holland & Gottfredson, 1992). The work of Jin (1986) is cited as an example of the robustness of RIASEC theory with another group. In a study of 800 Chinese high school students who completed an SDS translation, Jin found strong support for the hexagon model and the use of the SDS. More recently, Yu and Alvi (1996) administered the Chinese version of the SDS to 409 high school students in China. They found that the six types distributed across fields of study consistent with the theory and that the relationships among types hypothesized by the hexagonal model were fully supported.

Although Holland's work is known and recognized throughout the world, it might be noted that he has not traveled to other countries to present papers about his research or the theory. Although Holland made a trip to Australia in the early 1980s, he has not appeared outside the U.S. except for meetings of the American Psychological Association held in Canada.

A Word of Caution

Some observers have noted that Holland's typology is really a personality theory and that he should just come clean and promote and use it as such. However, counselors must be cautious and not use the typology to stereotype or label clients. The RIASEC types are, after all, theoretical models against which we compare real people to learn more about their characteristics and behavior. The personality types should be used by counselors to explore hypotheses with clients about career interests and aspirations, not to pigeonhole people. Moreover, as we shall see in the following section, there is more to RIASEC theory than personality types; indeed, the application of the typology to environments may be one of the most powerful features of Holland's theory.

RIASEC Environments More Fully Examined

Many counselors know relatively more about and have an understanding of the personality typology, but not about the environmental models. There may be several reasons for this. As a psychologist, Holland has spent more time concentrating on that part of the theory. Sociologists, economists, and organizational/industrial psychologists have not conducted as much research on RIASEC theory. The connections between Holland's theory and these fields have not been fully explored and, in some cases, may be relatively unknown. Counselors are more oriented to psychology, and many of the tools and interventions used in career guidance have psychological bases. Much of Holland's work has not been incorporated into the Department of Labor occupational information resources. For example, RIASEC codes are not used in the *Occupational Outlook Handbook* (Bureau of Labor Statistics, 1996), the *Dictionary of Occupational Titles*, or the *Guide for Occupational Exploration* (U.S. Department of Labor, 1979). These are major tools for informing career counselors and others about occupations and the world of work. For these and other reasons, the application of the environmental models in the RIASEC typology has received less attention.

In this section, we will examine aspects of environments in terms of RIASEC theory in an effort to increase our understanding of and skill in using this part of the typology. After all, our clients live their lives and do their jobs in environments. Applying RIASEC ideas to these social, economic, and organizational situations can provide new and helpful ideas for career exploration and adjustment.

Distinguishing Among Environments

As with personality types, Gottfredson and Holland (1996a) developed a table (Table 3) summarizing the six RIASEC environmental models across five attributes: (a) what the environment requires, (b) what it demands and rewards the display of, (c) what it values or the personal styles that are allowed expression, (d) what occupations or other environments involve, and (e) sample occupations. As with the personality typology (Table 1), the environmental typology reveals a wide range of differences. These model environments operate quite differently from one another, and understanding how these environments pull and push people is a key factor in understanding how Holland's RIASEC theory operates. Rather than being a simple matching model, the personality types and environments might be likened to electrically charged particles, each carrying a blend of forces that pull, push, and neutralize one another. The types and environments interact, and the results of these interactions affect how persons and organizations (or even interpersonal relationships) function.

Table 3
A Brief Description of the Holland Environmental Typology

Attribute	Environmental Type					
	Realistic	Investigative	Artistic	Social	Enterprising	Conventional
Requires	Manual and mechanical competencies, interaction with machines, tools, and objects	Analytical, technical, scientific, and verbal competencies	Innovation or creative ability, emotionally expressive interaction with others	Interpersonal competencies, skill in mentoring, treating, healing, or teaching others	Skills in persuasion and manipulation of others	Clerical skills, skills in meeting precise standards for performance
Demands and rewards the display of	Conforming behavior, practical accomplishment	Skepticism and persistence in problem solving, documentation of new knowledge, understanding or solution of problems	Imagination in literary, artistic or musical accomplishment	Empathy, humanitarianism sociability, friendliness	Initiative in the pursuit of financial or material accomplishment; dominance; self-confidence	Organizational ability, conformity, dependability
Values or personal styles allowed expression	Practical, productive and concrete values; robust, risky, adventurous styles	Acquisition of knowledge through scholarship or investigation	Unconventional ideas or manners, aesthetic values	Concern for the welfare of others	Acquisitive or power-oriented styles, responsibility	Conventional outlook and concern for orderliness and routines
Occupations or other environments involve	Concrete, practical activity; use of machines, tools, materials	Analytical or intellectual activity aimed at trouble-shooting or creation and use of knowledge	Creative work in music, writing, performance, sculpture, or unstructured intellectual endeavors	Working with others in a helpful or facilitating way	Selling, leading, manipulating others to attain personal or organizational goals	Working with things, numbers, or machines to meet predictable organizational demands or specified standards
Sample occupations	Carpenter, truck operator	Psychologist, microbiologist	Musician, interior designer	Counselor, clergy member	Lawyer, retail store manager	Production editor, bookkeeper

Note. From *Dictionary of Holland Occupational Codes* (3rd ed., p. 4), by G. D. Gottfredson and J. L. Holland, 1982, 1989, 1996, Odessa, FL: Psychological Assessment Resources. Copyright © 1996 by Psychological Assessment Resources, Inc. Reproduced with permission of the publisher.

Because the theory enables us to categorize and understand environments, we can use this information to find more compatible jobs, colleges, training programs, or leisure activities for persons to explore. We can also use this information to understand why a person might be unhappy in his or her job or how we can change a job to make it more satisfying to a person. In addition, managers can use this information to redesign jobs (e.g., make a job more Realistic) or to examine why some work teams don't function well together (e.g., the team is composed of five Es, two Ss, and one A). RIASEC theory has much to offer regarding our increased understanding of environments, especially as it applies to career counseling

RIASEC Codes Applied to the DOT

As we have noted earlier, Holland did not receive federal funding for his work; indeed, government-supported efforts to develop and disseminate labor market information have until recently ignored RIASEC theory. At the same time, Holland wanted to improve a counselor's ability to use labor market information such as the *Dictionary of Occupational Titles* (DOT).

In 1982, Gottfredson, Holland, and Ogawa produced the first *Dictionary of Holland Occupational Codes* (DHOC), which formally connected the DOT with RIASEC theory. Second and third editions of this book were published in 1989 and 1996. The DHOC, which will be discussed more fully in other chapters of this book, is a treasure of information. One nugget is shown in Table 4, summarizing data from the DHOC in relation to the DOT (Gottfredson & Holland, 1989).

This table shows the extent to which our knowledge of occupations, as revealed in the DOT, is biased in the direction of Realistic and Enterprising occupations. Relatively speaking, Artistic and Investigative occupations are not

Table 4
Number of 1982 DOT Occupations With Each Code Letter
Appearing Somewhere in the First Three Letters

Code	Number of occupations
Realistic	10,708
Investigative	2,551
Artistic	570
Social	66,064
Enterprising	10,405
Conventional	5,999

Note. From *Dictionary of Holland Occupational Codes* (3rd ed., p. 710), by G. D. Gottfredson and J. L. Holland, 1996, Odessa, FL: Psychological Assessment Resources. Copyright © 1982, 1989, 1996 by Psychological Assessment Resources, Inc. Reproduced with permission of the publisher.

well represented in the DOT. In other words, when our clients go to the DOT to learn about occupations, they are finding about 21 times as many occupations with Realistic codes as occupations with Artistic codes. Fewer than 5% of DOT occupations have an Artistic code letter. Our knowledge about Realistic and Enterprising jobs is much greater than our knowledge about Artistic jobs. What does this mean? On the one hand, it may be a factual truth. Some RIASEC types of occupations may actually occur more frequently, or be more common, than other types. This was the shape of the industrial economy in the U.S. On the other hand, this finding may reflect the fact that Artistic work is often part-time or temporary. It is harder to document and report because it doesn't typically occur in large organizations with good personnel records. Artistic types often free-lance or work at home.

At any rate, the data in Table 4 reveal that when we examine the world of work through a RIASEC looking glass, we can obtain a new perspective on work environments. The world of work looks a little different through a RIASEC lens. This information can be used to inform clients about work and to increase their understanding of occupations and employment.

Rule of Intraoccupational Variability

In developing guidelines for effective use of the Self-Directed Search, Holland offered several "rules" for interpreting the results. Earlier we mentioned "The Rule of Asymmetrical Distribution of Types and Subtypes," and now we move to another rule, "The Rule of Intraoccupational Variability." This rule refers to research findings which indicate that occupations and fields of study include a variety of types and subtypes. Many occupations tolerate a variety of types. Individuals employed in the same occupation often have a variety of Holland codes. Different positions within the same occupation also often have a variety of codes. Put another way, codes describe people in an occupation on average, but it is a mistake to assume that all persons or positions in an occupation have the same SDS or Position Classification Inventory (PCI; Gottfredson & Holland, 1991) profiles. Below is an illustration of this rule.

Of the 24 counselors who completed the PCI, a measure of codes for specific job positions (see Table 5), 23 had a high-point code of Social, 7 had a code of SAE (the RIASEC code for counselor), and 6 had other code combinations with Social.

A study by John Holland and his daughter Joan (Holland & Holland, 1977a) reported differences across many occupations and fields of study. Of particular interest is their finding regarding the intraoccupational variability of career counselors (Holland, Powell, & Fritzsche, 1994). Figure 3 shows the percentages of 113 counselors with various codes. The code letters near the circles show the

Table 5
PCI Codes for 24 Counselors' Job Descriptions

PCI Code	N
S Profiles	**23 (96%)**
SAE	7
SAI	4
SIA	4
SEA	3
SEC	2
SCI	2
SAC	1
A Profiles	**1 (4%)**
ASI	1

Note. Data from *Position Classification Inventory Professional Manual* (p. 13), by G. D. Gottfredson and J. L. Holland, 1991, Odessa, FL: Psychological Assessment Resources. Copyright © 1991 by Psychological Assessment Resources, Inc. Adapted and reproduced with special permission of the publisher.

most common codes reported and the size of the circle approximates the number of counselors with the high point code. This figure graphically shows that every code except Conventional is represented in this sample of career counselors, but that 67% of them are either Social or Artistic.

These data, and other studies reported in the *SDS Professional User's Guide* (Holland, Powell, & Fritzsche, 1994), *SDS Technical Manual* (Holland, Fritzsche, & Powell, 1994), and *Making Vocational Choices* (Holland, 1985a), reveal that occupations vary in the range of types present. All we have to do is count the numbers of different types in an environment to verify this fact. Some environments tolerate a wide diversity of types, whereas others are more homogeneous or restricted. The "Rule of Intraoccupational Variability" reminds us that the RIASEC theory is not a perfect correlation of types and environments. A person does not absolutely have to be a certain type to function successfully in a particular environment or occupation. But the typology does provide counselors and clients with a set of models for thinking about the possible relationships between persons and their career options.

An example comes to mind. Several years ago a colleague was helping elementary school teachers incorporate more career education activities into their classroom instruction. The setting was a rural, northwest Florida town on the Gulf coast, surrounded by a national forest. As part of their training, the teachers took the SDS. The consultant was surprised when many of the teachers, almost all of whom were women, had codes with first or second letters that were Realistic, given that the code for elementary teacher is SEC. As they discussed

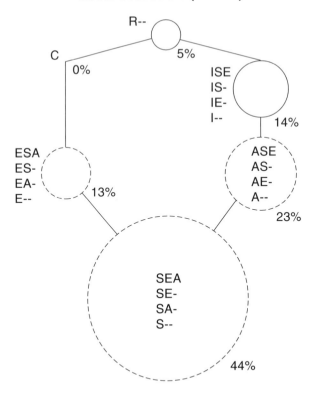

Career Counselors (*N* = 113)

Figure 3. Distributions of types and subtypes employed in career counseling (SEA). Sizes of circles are proportional to the percentage of people with that high-point code. Dotted circles represent expected codes. Three-letter codes within or adjacent to circles indicate the most common codes. Reprinted from "Distributions of Personalities Within Occupations and Fields of Study" by J. L. Holland and J. E. Holland, *Vocational Guidance Quarterly, 25,* 1977, pp. 226-231. Copyright © American Counseling Association. Reprinted with permission. No further reproduction authorized without written permission of the American Counseling Association.

this situation, they realized that many of the teachers were avid hunters, boaters, and outdoor types. Indeed, their spouses and students shared those Realistic traits. The larger environment, including the geography and history of the region, provided an explanation for the "intraoccupational variability" of the codes for this group of teachers.

RIASEC Codes of Workers

How does the work force look in RIASEC terms? What is the distribution of workers according to Holland codes? We can examine census data for the

U.S. population and the numbers of persons engaged in various occupations to determine the distribution of RIASEC types in the nation. These census data reveal that the distribution of various RIASEC types is not equal or proportional. Similarly, the distribution also varies by ethnic group. Table 6 shows that 57% of the men worked in Realistic occupations and only 2% were engaged in Artistic work, whereas 24% of the women worked in Realistic occupations and only 1% were engaged in Artistic endeavors. These findings are based on 1980 census data (Gottfredson & Decision Research Associates, 1984).

Given that RIASEC types are not spread equally across the population and combinations of types are also unequally distributed, some types are found less often in the population. As members of a "minority group," they may experience some of the feelings and perceptions associated with minority group status (i.e., not understood, seen as different or unusual, sense of isolation). Relatively speaking, there are fewer people with Artistic and Investigative code letters than other types.

Table 6 also shows differences in educational (GED) levels across the RIASEC types. For example, Investigative work does not even appear in the table until GED levels 5 and 6, indicating college and postgraduate education.

In addition to gender, GED levels, and number employed, RIASEC codes may be used to examine Specialized Vocational Preparation (SVP) levels and earnings. SVP ratings for occupations range from 1 to 10, with the higher number indicating the longest periods of inservice, on-the-job training required for the occupation. Table 7 was developed from information reported in the 1989 edition of the DHOC (Gottfredson & Holland, 1989) and shows the relationships among selected two-letter codes, GED levels, SVP levels, earnings, number of persons employed, and percentage of female workers. The estimated earnings are based on census data of actual workers, and includes those working part-time or unemployed during the year.

Several things from Table 7 can be incorporated into career guidance presentations. First, the codes with I and E are characterized by higher earnings, as well as higher GED and SVP ratings. High school students wanting to make more money can see where they are, at least in RIASEC terms. Second, the lowest earnings are associated with occupations having Conventional codes and codes having the highest percentage of women workers. This may reflect the nature of what was traditionally women's work (i.e., periodic, part-time), as well as the persistently lower salaries provided for female employees. And although one might speculate that things may have changed dramatically for women workers since this 1980 census, a review of Table 8 reveals that women workers still tend to be clustered in "traditionally" female occupations, occupations that have a predominance of S, E, and C codes.

Table 6
Kind and Level of Work Done by Men and Women
Ages 16 and Above in 1980 (Thousands)

Kind of work	General Educational Development level						Total	
	1	2	3	4	5	6		
Men								
Realistic	369	8,214	11,767	13,154	1,039	73	34,616	(57%)
Investigative	–	–	–	–	1,273	1,501	2,774	(5%)
Artistic	–	–	6	106	528	292	932	(2%)
Social	–	22	611	607	2,351	342	3,933	(7%)
Enterprising	–	321	1,815	3,524	8,421	505	14,586	(24%)
Conventional	–	259	1,201	684	636	–	2,748	(5%)
						Total	59,621	(57%)
Women								
Realistic	553	4,082	4,536	982	350	77	10,580	(24%)
Investigative	–	–	–	–	412	467	879	(2%)
Artistic	–	–	1	43	431	37	512	(1%)
Social	–	16	2,068	2,018	5,103	243	9,448	(21%)
Enterprising	–	384	2,113	3,634	3,115	100	9,346	(21%)
Conventional	–	103	5,792	7,190	411	–	13,496	(31%)
						Total	44,261	(43%)

Note. Based on a reclassification of detailed occupational data from the 1980 census of population. From the *Dictionary of Holland Occupational Codes* by G. D. Gottfredson, J. L. Holland, and D. Ogawa, 1982, Palo Alto, CA: Consulting Psychologists Press. Copyright © 1982 by Psychological Assessment Resources, Inc. Reprinted with permission.

It is important to review one additional study related to this topic. In examining 1980 census data, Arbona (1989) found differences within ethnic groups in the percentage of men and women employed in each Holland type of work.

Table 9 shows a higher percentage of Black and Hispanic Americans engaged in Realistic work than Whites. A converse difference appears in the Investigative and Enterprising areas.

Altogether, Tables 3 through 9 give us some insight into how jobs and the work force are distributed according to the typology. These tables help us understand how the types really do differ when viewed from sociological and economic perspectives.

In a more recent study, Downes and Kroeck (1996) observed discrepancies between existing jobs and a person's vocational interests. Using normative data from the 1994 edition of the SDS for both high school students and adults,

Table 7
Training, Earnings, and Employment (Thousands)
for Occupations Grouped by Holland Category

Code	GED	SVP	Earnings	Number employed	% Women
RS	3.10	5.60	$12,782	219	39
RI	3.98	6.34	16,161	149	10
RC	2.82	3.02	10,428	160	32
IE	5.83	5.67	20,391	80	14
IS	5.85	8.00	19,740	27	35
IR	5.47	7.53	22,271	71	22
AS/E	4.75	7.33	12,188	117	45
SR	4.11	6.00	10,737	28	57
SE	4.82	6.89	13,876	259	49
SI	5.55	7.46	13,783	144	65
EI	5.00	7.50	24,092	119	30
EC	3.20	3.80	10,156	173	63
ES	4.09	5.87	15,194	154	35
CS	3.56	4.52	9,546	539	78
CR	2.62	3.30	9,489	62	53
CE	3.44	4.11	11,970	224	65

Note. Based on analysis of detailed data from 503 selected occupations in the 1980 population census. From "An Empirical Classification of Occupations Based on Job Analysis Data: Development and Applications" by G. D. Gottfredson, 1980. Paper presented at the annual meeting of the American Psychological Association, Toronto, Canada. Reprinted with permission.

together with employment figures for the 292 occupations listed in the June 1993 issue of the *Monthly Labor Review*, the authors reported a lack of person-environment fit with respect to some individual interests and employment. For example, they reported low interests in the Enterprising and Conventional areas relative to the large number of jobs for both high school and adult groups. The two normative groups, however, differed in their interests across the six RIASEC areas. For example, unlike adults, high school students showed little interest in the Realistic area. The changes in vocational interests over the lifespan in relation to employment realities are examined more fully later in this chapter.

How can these data about the work force from a RIASEC perspective help us become better counselors? First, they help us understand that work reflects different interests and skills for most men and women. Occupational activity differs according to gender. Second, these data help us understand that even

Table 8
20 Leading Occupations of Employed Women
With Holland Codes (1996 Annual Averages)

Occupations	Employed women (numbers in thousands)	Women as % of total employed (both sexes)	Holland code
Secretaries	3,119	98.6	CSE
Cashiers	2,230	78.1	CSE
Managers and Administrators, n.e.c.	2,074	29.2	ES[a]
Registered nurses	1,853	93.3	SIE
Sales supervisors and proprietors	1,689	37.5	ESA
Nursing aides, orderlies, and attendants	1,636	88.4	SER/SRE
Bookkeepers, accounting, and auditing clerks	1,631	91.9	CSI/CSR
Elementary school teachers	1,538	83.3	SAE
Waiters and waitresses	1,071	77.9	ESC/A
Sales workers, food, drugs, commodities	1,026	68.4	ESA
Handlers, equipment cleaners, helpers, and laborers	971	19.3	REI
Receptionists	930	96.9	CSE
Machine operators, assorted materials	915	32.1	RCE
Cooks	869	42.2	RES
Accountants and auditors	862	56.0	CSI/ESI
Textile, apparel and furnishing machine operators	793	74.1	RCE
Janitors and cleaners	769	34.9	RES
Administrative support occupations, n.e.c.	697	76.9	ESC
Investigators and adjusters, excluding insurance	692	76.3	SIE/ESR
Secondary school teachers	686	55.9	SAE

Note. Employment data from the U.S. Department of Labor Women's Bureau, 1997. Holland codes from the *Dictionary of Holland Occupational Codes* (3rd ed.), 1982, 1989, 1996, by G. D. Gottfredson and J. L. Holland, Odessa, FL: Psychological Assessment Resources. Copyright © 1996 by Psychological Assessment Resources, Inc. Adapted with permission of the publisher.
[a]Third letter varies by specific type of manager.

though work may be declining in some areas, the Realistic environment still provides work for a large percentage of the population, particularly men. Third, these data show how education is related to the typology. Investigative work is closely connected to education and training. An understanding of these basic ideas can help counselors and clients become more informed about labor markets and employment.

Table 9
Percentage of Men and Women Employed in
Each Holland Type of Work Within Ethnic Groups (1980)

| | Ethnic group | | | | | | | | |
| | White | | | Black | | | Hispanic | | |
Type of work	M	F	Total	M	F	Total	M	F	Total
Realistic	54	24	41	68	37	53	71	41	59
Investigative	5	2	4	2	1	2	2	1	2
Artistic	2	2	2	1	1	1	1	1	1
Social	8	22	14	10	26	18	6	16	10
Enterprising	23	15	20	9	7	8	12	10	11
Conventional	8	35	19	10	28	19	8	31	17

Note. From "Hispanic Employment and the Holland Typology of Work," by C. Arbona, *The Career Development Quarterly*, *37*, p. 263. Copyright © 1989 by American Counseling Association. Reprinted with permission. No further reproduction authorized without written permission of the American Counseling Association.

The Isomorphism Assumption

What happens to types who can't find a compatible environment? After all, RIASEC theory assumes that every type will find a matching environment, doesn't it? In countries where there is little economic freedom or freedom of vocational choice, persons can only aspire to occupations that the state has determined are needed in the work force. In market-driven economies, some might argue that it is the unrealistic or naive clients who aspire to types of occupations that are not available in the economy. Whyte and Rayman (1985) wondered about this and speculated about this so-called "isomorphism assumption." Isomorphism has to do with the study of sameness or commonness across things. Under this assumption, in an ideal world, you would have a correspondence in the relative frequency of RIASEC types and occupations in the economy. How good is this assumption?

Citing a 1975 study by G. Gottfredson, Holland, and L. Gottfredson, Whyte and Rayman (1985) examined unevenness or lack of isomorphism with respect to certain RIASEC codes. Using census data for jobs and an SDS male sample of high school age and older, it was revealed that the IAS code accounted for 18% of jobs and 51% of the sample. Likewise, the RCE code accounted for 52% of jobs and 49% of the sample. What causes this lack of balance between persons and jobs? What does it mean and what should counselors do about it? Does this mean the theory doesn't work? Whyte and Rayman (1985) offered several observations about this phenomenon. First, they noted that isomorphism is a macro level issue related to the economy and work force as a whole; specific individuals might not be affected at all. Second, they noted two methods by which society may deal with a lack of isomorphism. On the one hand, *circumstantial incongruence* is more temporary and may occur when unemployed persons take temporary jobs to make ends meet while looking for more congruent, permanent positions. On the other hand, *structural incongruence* is more permanent because it is related to low isomorphism and the lack of congruence in society between persons and jobs according to the typology. For example, we know that the U.S. economy is slowly moving from one of goods-producing (Realistic) to services (Social, Enterprising) and information (Investigative, Artistic).

What does this mean for career guidance practitioners? Whyte and Rayman (1985) identified possible redistribution mechanisms operating at the societal level to increase isomorphism. These included the idea that incongruent persons are less likely to replicate themselves over time (i.e., incongruent parents will push their children into more congruent options). An example might be parents in mining, farming, or fishing who find their industries declining and thus encourage their children to learn other skills and get into some other line of work. Related to this, persons who must change their jobs because of structural incongruence (e.g., factories are closing and Realistic jobs are lost) may find it easier to make a transition to other more readily available jobs, such as selling building supplies (ESR work), than to continue to pursue potentially declining Realistic employment. Also, persons whose personality type is incompatible with the jobs available in their area may find leisure activities and/or entrepreneurship a useful mechanism to increase congruence in their lives. For example, Realistic persons experiencing low isomorphism because of factory closings might explore R-type hobbies or start a lawn maintenance business. We will explore these issues in later chapters.

Vocational Aspirations and Labor Market Realities

As we explained in earlier chapters, occupational aspirations are an essential element of Holland's theory and interventions. The relationship between occupational aspirations and isomorphism is of interest and practical relevance. Table 10 shows the results of a study conducted by Linda Gottfredson (1979) with a sample of employed men and the aspirations of men aged 16 and 28 with respect to RIASEC codes. The older men had occupational aspirations that were more closely related to the actual distribution of workers. As they grew older, the men had changed their occupational aspirations to accommodate some of the realities of available jobs in the work force. More specifically, they aspired to more R and E types of jobs. A very large shift occurred in the Investigative area. Perhaps this is a normal part of the socialization process and is evidence of the power of environments to shape a person's vocational interests and goals. These findings provide some assurance to counselors and clients regarding the mechanisms at work in RIASEC theory that lead to increased isomorphism and congruence in the workplace. Exactly how these mechanisms are carried out in the lives of workers are not fully understood.

Table 10
Percentage of Employed Men and the Aspirations of 16- and 28-Year-Olds

Code	Employed men	Aspirations of 16-year-olds	Aspirations of 28-year-olds
R	47	36	43
I	9	27	10
A	2	7	2
S	10	14	11
E	26	12	30
C	6	3	4

Note. Data from "Aspiration–Job Match: Age Trends in a Large, Nationally Representative Sample of Young White Men," by L. Gottfredson, 1979, *Journal of Counseling Psychology, 26,* pp. 319-328. Copyright © 1979 by the American Psychological Association. Adapted with permission.

Economic and Labor Market Changes from a RIASEC Perspective

Technological changes in the economy and the resulting impact on workers and jobs are widely acknowledged among career counselors. Some have argued that these changes make Holland's theory irrelevant because the economy is now very different than it was in the 1950s when the theory was developed. Is RIASEC outdated in the new economy?

In his research, Richard Sharf (1997a), a career counselor and author, has concluded that it is possible to view technological change as described by sociologists and economists from a Holland perspective. Sharf (1997b) developed a table that summarizes technological trends in relation to RIASEC codes (Table 11). Sharf suggested that technological changes have come from the Investigative environment and have had the most impact on Realistic and Conventional environments. This has contributed to a decline of opportunities in those environments. The impact of the Investigative environment on the Social, Artistic, and Enterprising environments has been less direct. Counselors and clients may find this table helpful in understanding how technological changes are affecting occupations and how RIASEC theory remains relevant in light of these changes.

Robert Reich (1992), the former Secretary of Labor, identified three broad categories of emerging work in his book, *The Work of Nations.* Reich argues that

Table 11
Technological Trends for Holland Environments

Holland environment	Technological trends
Realistic	Changes in technology tend to automate some tasks. New equipment and processes can contribute to job elimination. More growth exists in installation and repair or Realistic work *relatively* unaffected by technology, such as construction and transportation.
Investigative	Investigative environments are the source for the design, development, and implementation of technological change and offer relatively good job prospects.
Artistic	Technology has affected visual arts and broadcasting through new computer design software and communications technology.
Social	The more an environment is purely Social, the less likely it is to be affected by technology. However, most social and educational institutions use software for budgeting, planning, scheduling, and/or record keeping.
Enterprising	Enterprising environments are made more productive and easy to use through the use of computer software and related technology.
Conventional	The use of new billing, dictating, filing, and record keeping technology has adversely affected employment growth for many Conventional environments.

Note. From "Using Career Development Theory to Understand Technological Change," by Richard S. Sharf, January 1997. Paper presented at the annual meeting of the National Career Development Association, Daytona Beach, FL. Adapted with permission.

three areas of work (i.e., routine production services, in-person services, and symbolic-analytic services) are emerging in all nations and include 75% of American jobs, that Americans are becoming part of an international labor market, and that the only sure career path in the future lies in solving, identifying, and brokering new problems. We have studied Reich's three areas of emerging work in light of RIASEC theory (Table 12). Holland's typology is very useful in helping counselors and their clients understand what is happening in the economy and what it might mean in individual career planning.

Reich (1992) noted that persons working in the *routine production services* area, Conventional-Realistic in terms of the typology, must be able to read and perform simple computations, but their cardinal virtues are reliability, loyalty, and the capacity to take direction. Their work products will compete in international markets. This is similar to the characteristics of CR-type work in the past. *In-person services* workers, Social-Enterprising types, will provide their work in local markets on a person-to-person basis; they will be in direct contact with the beneficiaries of their work, their customers. This is quite consistent with

Table 12
Emerging Categories of Work in Relation to
RIASEC Codes and Employment Growth

Service category	Occupational example and code	Forecast
Routine production	Assembler and tester, electronics (RIC)	25% of jobs and declining
	Assembly-line inspector (CRS)	
	Auto mechanic (RSE)	
	Data entry clerk (CSR)	
	Payroll clerk (CRS)	
	Medical records clerk (CSI)	
	Court clerk (CSE)	
	Library clerk (SCR)	
	Production coordinator (ESR)	
	Office manager (ESR)	
In-person	Janitor (RES)	30% and growing rapidly
	Salesperson, general (ESA)	
	Waiter/waitress (CES)	
	Hotel clerk (ECS)	
	Cashier-checker (CES)	
	Day-care worker (SER)	
	Housekeeper (ESR)	
	Hospital attendant/orderly (SRE)	
	Nursing aide (SER)	
	Taxi driver (IRE)	
	Real estate clerk (CSR)	
	Secretary (CSE)	
	Hair stylist (SER)	
	Auto mechanic (RSE)	
	Security guard (SEC)	
	Physical therapist (SIE)	
Symbolic-analytic	Research associate (IRC)	20% and stable
	Engineer, chemical (IRE)	
	Public relations (EAS)	
	Manager, financial institution (ESR)	
	Lawyer (ESA)	
	Real estate agent (ESR)	
	Accountant (CRS)	
	Consultant (IER)	
	Information resources director (ISR)	
	Psychologist, industrial/organizational (SEI)	
	Planner, program services (EIS)	
	Systems analyst (IER)	
	Professor, faculty member (SEI)	
	Writer/editor (AES)	
	Advertising account executive (AES)	
	Musicians (ASI)	

the emerging services-oriented economy in the U.S. and clearly understood in terms of the typology. Finally, the products of *symbolic-analytic services* workers, Investigative-Artistic types, are also provided and traded worldwide; these workers may not come in direct contact with their customers, but may have careers that are not linear or hierarchical, may work alone or in small groups, and may have advanced degrees. These work situations and characteristics might be expected of IA types according to Holland's typology.

Environmental Forces

How do RIASEC environments affect persons? How do the environments pull and attract more congruent types or push and repel the less congruent types? What is the nature of the social power of an environment? Holland (1985a) offered speculations about this process. Staying within the typological theory, Holland suggested that environments that were more *consistent* (i.e., first two letters adjacent) or more *differentiated* (i.e., proportionally higher numbers of persons with the same high-point code) would have a more powerful impact on persons than environmental codes marked by low consistency and differentiation. The consistency and differentiation of an environment could be readily determined by using the Environmental Assessment Technique (Holland, 1985a) to assess the distribution of types (census) in the environment. For example, in a moderately large bank employing 200 persons, how many employees were Conventionals, Socials, Enterprisings, etc.?

Holland also suggested that environments characterized by high identity would have more power and influence on people. This means that a high identity organization would be more likely to influence persons toward the dominant RIASEC type in the environment. Holland defined the level of identity of an environment as the *inverse* of the number of behavior settings, where behavior setting was defined as different kinds of positions. For example, the more positions or occupations present in an organization, the lower the identity of the organization. In a small accounting firm, the identity score might be very high because only a small number of occupations are represented (e.g., secretary, accountant, lawyer). We could guess that everyone in that firm would probably have some C in their code. On the other hand, Florida State University has a very low environmental identity score because more than 5,000 persons are employed in more than 300 different occupations, including glass blower (work in the chemistry lab), football coach, circus manager, and nuclear physicist. A large, complex environment with a very low identity such as this university has a very different impact on persons with regard to the RIASEC typology than a small firm with a very high identity.

As we noted in chapter 2, Holland (1997) has recently reported on the development of an experimental scale, the Environmental Identity scale (EIS)

(Gottfredson & Holland, 1996b). This scale taps a worker's beliefs about the explicitness and consistency of an organization's goals, work rules, and rewards for performance. A high score means that an environment provides clear and consistent direction and reward. Persons interested in learning more about how an environment affects a person (i.e., a worker or student) will be following the development of the new EIS very closely. If this instrument becomes as powerful and useful as the Identity scale in My Vocational Situation, counselors will have a valuable new instrument to assess the impact of work environments on their clients.

Gottfredson (1985) has suggested another factor that might help us understand how environments influence persons' behavior. He defines *proximity* of an environment as the probability that it will reward or punish behavior. Within the typology, a *high*-proximity environment would punish behavior or traits incongruent with the environment and praise or reward congruent behavior. A *low*-proximity environment may be thought of as weak, in that it does not clearly specify the most desirable behaviors for members, the behaviors are difficult to observe and monitor, and rewards or punishments are not available or used in the environment. As we noted earlier, some environments (e.g., a large company or university) may exercise weak social power or proximity over persons, whereas others (e.g., a small, family-owned business or an individual's spouse) would provide much more social power for shaping behavior.

The implications of these ideas about environments for career services providers can be summarized as follows. First, the social power available in an environment might be related to its history, size, and complexity. Clients can research organizations to learn more about these variables. Weak environments with low proximity or low identity might be more likely to tolerate varied types. On the other hand, a high level of congruence between worker and job might be much more important to consider in organizations having high proximity and identity. Such organizations might be more likely to punish employees who did not have a code congruent with the position. The typology can be used by clients in these ways to examine work options. Second, it is important to remember the nature of the RIASEC types themselves in considering environments. For example, we might expect that large Social organizations would be more tolerant of diversity than small Conventional environments. Organizations or work environments with low consistency and differentiation, low identity, and low proximity are less likely to punish incongruence or to reward congruence. Finally, in work environments with high levels of proximity associated with higher education levels and on-the-job training, there may be more of a tendency to "punish" (i.e., not hire, not promote, not reward) those who do not have the necessary degrees and inservice training experiences to work in such an organization.

Methods for Assessing Environments

Since the late 1960s and early 1970s when RIASEC theory first appeared, many advances have been made in the way environments are measured and assessed. In the beginning, Holland (1985a) used the Environmental Assessment Technique, a method of measuring an environment by conducting a census of the types found in the environment. A company, school, occupation, or profession was measured by the numbers of RIASEC types present. Later, job analysis data obtained from such instruments as the Position Analysis Questionnaire (PAQ; McCormick, 1979) were used to measure the characteristics of an environment in accordance with what was predicted by the theoretical model. For example, was an Enterprising job actually comprised of the features that the theory predicted should be there?

The publication of the first edition of the *Dictionary of Holland Occupational Codes* (DHOC) in 1982 (Gottfredson, Holland, & Ogawa, 1982) signaled a new, breakthrough procedure for measuring occupational environments. Using data compiled by the Bureau of Labor Statistics, Gottfredson developed a statistical model that used 47 data elements compiled by labor researchers in predicting three-letter RIASEC codes for every occupation in the *Dictionary of Occupational Titles* (DOT; U.S. Department of Labor, 1977). To check the accuracy of the predictive model, John Holland independently read the definitions of the DOT occupations and assigned a first letter code to each one. When the expert judgment and formula were compared, the comparative hit rate was very high. Only 35 of the 12,099 occupations examined were not assigned the same first letter. Second and third editions of the DHOC were published in 1989 and 1996; the second edition (Gottfredson & Holland, 1989) includes tables showing changes in labor market information in the intervening years.

In 1991, another breakthrough occurred in measuring environments when Gottfredson and Holland developed the Position Classification Inventory (PCI). The PCI enables researchers and practitioners to assess a specific job with respect to RIASEC characteristics in a matter of moments. It is now possible for the first time to assess work environments at the individual level in terms of RIASEC theory.

The uses of the DHOC and the PCI in career counseling and guidance will be examined more fully in chapter 6. These recent developments in the study of environments have significantly increased our understanding of this aspect of the RIASEC typology.

Conclusion

In this chapter we have examined several aspects of Holland's RIASEC theory more closely, in terms of the models associated with both the personality typology and the environmental typology. We have sought to delve more deeply into the theory, in a way that informs our professional practice in career services. In discussing each topic in this chapter, we have offered our thinking on the practical implications of the theory or research presented and noted where it will be even more fully examined in later chapters of this book.

4

Review of the SDS Form R and My Vocational Situation

We started using the Self-Directed Search in 1970. We had been using the Strong Vocational Interest Blank (SVIB; Campbell, 1971), but it was too complicated to manage and too expensive to use in our new self-help-oriented career services program. We didn't want to keep test files or keep track of mailed answer sheets and returned profile sheets. We didn't have enough staff to handle that. But when we switched to the SDS, some clients seemed to have questions about the power and validity of the SDS in comparison to the SVIB, which we had always described as the best interest test available. They seemed to question whether this self-scoring booklet was really a test! Was it really the best instrument available to help them sort out their vocational interests? We had to become more effective in selling the SDS as an assessment program to our clients.

To respond to these questions and concerns, we had to begin thinking in some new ways about interest assessment and about the SDS in particular. So, when clients would say, "I want to take a TEST to figure out what career I should go into, what I'm interested in," we would say something like, "Well, we have a paper and pencil simulation called the SDS that imitates an interest inventory, and I think it can help you. Would you like to take it?" Such a comment seemed to reassure the client, to add validity to the assessment activity, and to get away from the issue of taking a "test" and on to more productive activities. It also kept our clients in control of their own career assessment experience. The entire activity was played out in front of them with their full involvement. There were no mysterious scored profiles that came back after 2 weeks from the scoring service that were difficult to explain. Our clients were less likely to say, "The test told me to be a funeral director" or some other occupation.

In this chapter, we will share some of our "new" thinking about the SDS as a vocational interest assessment activity. The focus here is on the Form R (Regular) Assessment Booklet (Holland, 1994) of the SDS and the related computer-based assessment, SDS Form R: Computer Version (Reardon & PAR Staff, 1994). Chapter topics will include a review of the SDS as a simulated interest inventory, including an examination of the Daydreams section as a measure of expressed interests; a review of the five sections of the SDS; and an examination of The Occupations Finder and You and Your Career booklets as components of the SDS. We will also examine the My Vocational Situation form as an added component of the SDS because it is included in the SDS Form R computer version and because vocational identity is an important component of RIASEC theory. We also digress briefly to discuss the use of the Occupational Alternatives Question (OAQ) in conjunction with the SDS. Finally, we make some brief comments about the Myers-Briggs Type Indicator (MBTI) and the Strong Interest Inventory (SII) in comparison to the SDS.

Before getting into our views on the SDS, it is important to note several of the excellent published descriptions of the SDS and related materials. One of the best, brief descriptions is in a 1995 article by Spokane and Holland, "The Self-Directed Search: A Family of Self-Guided Career Interventions." They remind us that the SDS was developed in 1970 and revised in 1977, 1985, and 1994. Among its virtues, they list a self-administered, self-scored and, self-interpreted career exploration experience; theory-based scales; and multiple studies of its effects. Another good overview for practitioners is a chapter by Loughead and Linehan (1995), "The Basics of Using the Self-Directed Search in Business and Industry." In chapter 12 we include comments by reviewers of the SDS, which provide additional perspectives on the instrument and its place among career intervention alternatives. Finally, the *SDS Professional User's Guide* (Holland, Powell, & Fritzsche, 1994) is the best single source of information on the history and use of the SDS.

The SDS as a Simulated Career Counseling Activity

In describing the SDS as a career planning simulation to our clients, we were adopting a point of view promoted by John Holland from the earliest days of the introduction of the SDS. There are several practical points to make in this regard.

First, the SDS is not identified as a test or an inventory on any of the client materials. For us this was good because in working with our clients we wanted to remove emphasis from the *test* per se and to shift the focus to the client and his or her career problem situation. We generally wanted to keep the focus on the information clients need about themselves and their options, and not zero in on one occupation or "the choice." We wanted to de-emphasize testing and finding the "perfect" occupational match and to focus on other aspects of the career intervention process.

Second, the cover of the Assessment Booklet carries the subtitle "A Guide to Educational and Career Planning." We focused on the SDS as an intervention guide or program, not just as an assessment instrument. The SDS, as a guide or simulation, can be dissected and broken down into its component parts to more fully understand how a client's career decision making process works.

Third, the paper and pencil form of the SDS is a simulation of what might typically occur in a career counseling session. In the following sections, we will dissect the components of the SDS as a simulated career counseling session and explore how this instrument is like a career counseling interview.

A fourth point to make about the SDS is that the Daydreams section can be scored separately as a measure of *expressed* vocational interests. (We will discuss this more fully in the next section of this chapter.) The other four sections of the Assessment Booklet (Activities, Competencies, Occupations, and Self-Estimates) produce five scores that can be summed to provide a measure of *assessed* vocational interests. Both of these interest measures can be examined in terms of the RIASEC typology and the theory, which adds powerful interpretive ideas to the assessment activity.

Fifth, it is also important to note that the completed SDS Assessment Booklet "imitates" an interest inventory in several ways. For example, a person can obtain lists of occupations that match his or her interests and personality, and a person can assess or inventory his or her interests.

But the SDS does more than just imitate an interest inventory. It is also a carefully developed, standardized assessment instrument. The items in the Assessment Booklet are there because of their psychometric properties and their connection to RIASEC theory—because they function as good test items. The Self-Directed Search has been subjected to the same rigorous test development standards as other professionally published tests, and the two SDS manuals (Holland, Fritzsche, & Powell, 1994; Holland, Powell, & Fritzsche, 1994) describe a complex, sophisticated test development process begun in 1970 and leading to three editions of the SDS. The SDS is a theory-based, valid, reliable measure of RIASEC types and a client's career decision-making situation.

Finally, the SDS Assessment Booklet includes interpretive information that can help a client interpret and use the summary scores and the three-letter code. In addition, The Occupations Finder and You and Your Career booklets provide additional interpretive information to support the Assessment Booklet. Altogether, this trio of products encompass a comprehensive career assessment and intervention program that many clients can use with minimal assistance to further their educational and career planning. The numbers of clients who can use the SDS with limited counselor assistance varies by services setting, but in our case we would estimate it at 50%. In this sense, the SDS is more than a test; it is truly a career guidance diagnostic and intervention tool.

The Daydreams Section

In starting to assist a client with a career decision-making problem, a good counselor might begin by asking for a history of the occupations the client had been thinking about or had actually done. This is the Daydreams section of the SDS. To complete it, the client specifies occupations (up to eight in the paper version and five in the computer version) from among the 1,335 listed in The Occupations Finder booklet. These include occupations the client previously considered or is currently considering, as well as those occupations daydreamed about or discussed with others. In the paper version, the client is also asked to write the three-letter code for each occupation. The completed Daydreams section may be used as a measure of the client's interests and as a guidance activity.

In creating the SDS, Holland cleverly built in an "aspirations scale," the Daydreams section. What does this mean? This section of the SDS is a measure of occupational aspirations, a measure of *expressed* interests. As noted in chapter 2, aspirations are just as predictive of future occupational entry as formal, standardized interest inventory results (*assessed* interest measurement).

An important Daydreams section innovation in the measurement of aspirations is the addition of the RIASEC typology. This enables us to examine not only the occupation named, but also its RIASEC code. When the first two or three aspirations belong in the same RIASEC category, the predictive power of the first aspiration equals or exceeds the efficiency of an interest inventory (Holland, 1996a). This idea refers to the *coherence of aspirations*. Coherence will be examined more fully later in this section.

How can the expressed interests in the Daydreams section be used to help clients explore their options? There are actually two measures of expressed interests (of about equal importance) available in the Daydreams section. First, the counselor can encourage the client to simply use the code of the first career or occupation listed to search for more possibilities in occupations, fields of study, etc. Second, a counselor can create a summary code for the daydream occupations by counting the number of times each letter appears in the first, second, or third column and giving a score of 3, 2, or 1 points. For example, if the four Daydream occupations are:

Coach, professional athlete	S R E
Police officer	S E R
State highway police officer	R S E
Private investigator	E S I

then a summary code for daydreams can be created by giving each letter in the first column 3 points and each letter in the second column 2 points, etc. The scores are then:

$$R = 6\ (3 + 2 + 1) \qquad\qquad S = 10\ (6 + 4 + 0)$$
$$I = 1\ (0 + 0 + 1) \qquad\qquad E = 7\ (3 + 2 + 2)$$
$$A = 0 \qquad\qquad\qquad\qquad\quad C = 0$$

Thus the Daydreams summary code is SER. This Daydreams summary code may be used to explore additional occupational possibilities in The Occupations Finder.

The SDS computer version automatically calculates an aspirations summary code for the Daydreams section, which is reported in the Professional Summary report. Counselors may use this with clients as an alternative code to search for occupations, fields of study, and leisure activities.

In addition to being an assessment of the client's aspirations or history, the Daydreams section is also a treatment intervention. How so? In the process of recalling and reconstructing a vocational history, the client is remembering some of the occupations that may have been forgotten. Moreover, when reviewing The Occupations Finder to reconstruct a list of aspirations, the client is being exposed to an extensive list of occupational titles that might trigger recollections of interests or pinpoint current interests. This activity helps the client expand the list of options. In chapters 7 and 8, we continue this discussion of the importance of aspirations in the career problem-solving and decision-making process.

Some counselors and psychologists view the Daydreams section as an irrelevant, less valid part of the SDS. For example, they don't encourage clients to complete this section, or they think it gets in the way of the SDS scored results, the three-letter summary code. There is no mystery or expertise associated with this part of the SDS; indeed, Form CP of the SDS (Holland, 1990) doesn't even include it. When reporting SDS results for research or professional purposes, the Daydreams section is often ignored. Such practice regarding this component of the SDS is unfortunate because it negates one of the most powerful and useful aspects of the instrument.

Given that expressed interests are so important and powerful, why don't we use them more or give them more attention in our research and professional practice? Several practical reasons come to mind. First, this kind of interest measurement can't be developed and sold by test publishers like a regular test. In addition, if people can just tell a counselor what they are interested in doing and that is predictive of what they will really do in the future, why should they go to a counselor in the first place? In some of Holland's (1996a) most recent writing, he has continued to highlight the importance of aspirations in interest measurement and career assistance. (Remember to keep your eye on Holland's Artistic code at all times to fully appreciate his contributions to our field.)

The *Coherence of Aspirations*, mentioned earlier in this section and briefly in chapter 2, is another important, powerful interpretive tool for assessing a client's career situation and identifying helpful career interventions. The level of coherence may be determined from an examination of the occupations listed in the Daydreams section of the SDS. Coherence is defined as the degree to which codes for a client's occupational daydreams belong in the same RIASEC category. For example, scores of high, average, or low are determined from analysis of the first three occupational aspirations listed in the Daydreams section of the SDS.

> A *high* coherence score is defined as the first letter of the first occupation being the same as the first letter of the second and third occupations listed. For example: SEA, SAE, and SCE.

> An *average* score is defined as the first letter of the first occupation being the same as the first letter of the second or third occupation. For example: SEA, AES, and SEC.

> A *low* score is defined as the first letter of the first occupation not appearing as the first letter of either the second or third occupation. For example: SEA, ESA, and IAS.

These rules for assessing levels of coherence were taken from a study by Holland, Gottfredson, and Baker (1990), in which the level of coherence was found to be an important predictor of future occupational activity over a short time interval. The level of coherence is determined by the degree to which other aspirations match the first one. High coherence indicates future persistence in occupations with the same first-letter code as that of the first aspiration (Holland, Gottfredson, & Baker, 1990; Holland, Powell, & Fritzsche, 1994). The Self-Directed Search Form R: Computer Version scores coherence of aspirations according to these rules. Holland has indicated that coherence may become increasingly important in the research and practical implications associated with RIASEC theory.

Activities

Returning to our idea of the SDS as a simulated career counseling intervention, what happens after Daydreams? Well, a counselor might ask a client to report on any hobbies and activities that are done just for fun as well as activities he or she doesn't enjoy. This is the Activities section of the Assessment Booklet. It includes six RIASEC scales of 11 items each, which are endorsed with "like" or "dislike." In some ways, this section of the SDS is a kind of leisure assessment and represents part of the most basic thinking about career counseling. Frank Parsons and other early career counselors typically asked clients for lengthy reports of their leisure interests, their hobbies, the books they read, plays and meetings they attended, organizational memberships, etc. Early counselors realized that people basically become employed in what they like, what they are interested in.

In a practical, efficient way, the Activities section provides a counselor with a quick look at how clients might spend their free time. Inspection of the items in this section of the SDS reveals test items that are common in many interest inventories. They are included in the SDS because they effectively measure interests. It is possible that there is an important story behind many of the items, and a counselor might find it useful to explore them.

Competencies

Returning to our simulation, a counselor would also typically ask the client to describe his or her skills, the kinds of things that the client had learned to do in the past, as well as the things that he or she had never done. This kind of information is of practical importance, because a counselor would be foolish to suggest that the client totally ignore his or her personal history of skills and education- or work-related accomplishments. This list of competencies may also reflect a person's interests. People often develop skills in things that are important or interesting to them. The Competencies section of the Assessment Booklet includes the six RIASEC scales of 11 items each of self-estimated skills or proficiencies, which are marked "yes" or "no."

This section of the SDS can be especially fruitful to explore in an interview. For example, some clients may have worked in an office and developed many Conventional competencies (e.g., "I have held an office job," or "I can enter information at a computer terminal"). Sometimes, high scores in this section of the SDS Assessment Booklet will raise scores in the Conventional area. Some clients may view these competencies as skills they want to avoid in their next work situation. It is important to remember that the SDS is a simulated career counseling situation and that simulations do not always capture all of the complexity of the actual situation. The flight simulator that pilots use cannot anticipate all the actual situations that a pilot might encounter while flying. But, the simulator helps flight trainees learn more about the actual situation without spending time (and the expense) of actually flying. The SDS helps us simulate actual career counseling in a similar way.

The Social and Enterprising competencies are another possibly fruitful area to explore in this section of the SDS. Because much of career exploration and job hunting behavior takes place in human interactions (i.e., networking and informational or job interviews), clients who mark "no" to some of these items may need special assistance. For example, clients who indicate they do not feel easy "talking to all kinds of people," or are not good at "explaining things to others," "do not know how to be a successful leader," or have no "good planning or leadership skills" may need assistance in improving their S and E competencies. In contrast, clients who have high competencies in the S and E areas may be able to use these strengths in career problem solving and decision making.

Occupations

The next section of the SDS simulated career counseling activity is Occupations. It includes the six RIASEC scales with 14 items (occupational titles) each, which are endorsed "yes" or "no." Holland included this section because he wanted to make sure he obtained a good measure of the client's RIASEC typology and because he wanted to get a picture of the positive and negative feelings the client had about various occupational titles. This section of the SDS is actually a shortened form of the Vocational Preference Inventory (VPI), the assessment tool that Holland used to originally develop and evaluate the RIASEC typology and theory.

In a practical sense, this Occupations section provides the counselor with some information about the feelings and attitudes the client has toward a sample set of occupations. If the client has positive checks beside only one or two occupations, he or she may have little interest in work or in finding out about occupational life in general. A counselor can also inquire about the client's knowledge with respect to several of the occupations listed to learn about the accuracy, complexity, and depth of information he or she has about occupations and how that information was acquired.

Self-Estimates

The final section of the SDS simulation is Self-Estimates. It includes the six RIASEC scales, which are rated from 1 to 7 with respect to both ability and skill. Clients are asked to rate themselves as they really think they are and as compared with other persons their own age.

This section is particularly noteworthy. Once when Holland was asked why there were two scores produced in this section, he noted it was because he thought this section was twice as important as the other sections of the SDS. When I first heard that, I remember thinking that this matched with my experiences in career counseling college students. I remember situations where I'd look at the client's high SAT scores in math and see the low self ratings in math or science and realize that he or she was very unlikely to ever be a math major, despite the high test scores. Nowadays, we know and write about this as self-efficacy, or clients' beliefs that they can actually do particular tasks. When the SDS was first developed, some measurement psychologists viewed this section as heresy. The self-report of abilities and skills was viewed as subject to all kinds of bias and error. Clients just should not be trusted to give this kind of information. Given the current interest in topics such as self-efficacy and self-estimates of ability, it seems the inclusion of the Self-Estimates section was a fortunate step in the creation of the SDS.

As with other sections of the SDS, the counselor can use the structure of the items in this section to learn more about how the client views his or her own abilities and skills. The counselor might want to inquire about the past experiences in school or work that have shaped this self-view, as well as the kinds of stereotypes the client carries about such concepts as "artistic," "teaching," "managerial," etc. The counselor can also explore the levels of self-ratings the client marked, why extreme ratings were not used, and what it means to the client to have high abilities or skills in a specific area.

The Summary Code and What It Means

As explained in the SDS Assessment Booklet,

> Your Summary Code is a simple way of organizing information about people and jobs. It can be used to discover how your special pattern of interests, self-estimates, and competencies resembles the patterns of interests and competencies that many occupations demand. In this way, your Summary Code locates suitable groups of occupations for you to consider.

From the client's view, this is what the SDS three-letter Summary Code means, because the code is a tool to use to explore the 1,335 occupations in The Occupations Finder or the 12,000+ occupations in the *Dictionary of Holland Occupational Codes* (Gottfredson & Holland, 1996a).

Holland, Powell, and Fritzsche (1994) prescribed two "rules" that help us interpret the meaning of the SDS Summary Code: the "Rule of 8" and the "Rule of Full Exploration." The "Rule of 8" helps us remember that RIASEC summary scale differences of fewer than 8 on the SDS Form R should be regarded as trivial because they are within the limits of the standard error of measurement for the inventory. The "Rule of Full Exploration" helps us remind clients completing various forms of the SDS to use all five permutations and combinations of their three-letter summary code to generate lists of occupations and fields of study for further exploration and consideration. The computer-based reports from the SDS Form R automatically print all code combinations in the Interpretive Report for clients.

With reference to the SDS as a career counseling simulation, the calculation of the Summary Code by adding the number of "like" or "yes" responses to Activities, Competencies, and Occupations, as well as the two Self-Estimate ratings, provides a method for scoring the simulation. In other words, these calculations provide a way to move from a simulation to an assessment of interests—as we have discussed earlier, an *assessed* measure of interests.

Two problems may occur when scoring the SDS. First, some clients make errors in adding their responses across the sections. In earlier editions of the SDS, this was a bigger problem. With the most recent edition, however, Holland, Powell, and Fritzsche (1994) reported only 3.7% of a randomly selected sample of users made scoring errors involving high-point codes (first letters), and only 7.5% of this sample had derived an incorrect three-letter code. Nevertheless, counselors or peers need to recheck client codes, especially if the code is rare and unusual. Second, some summary scores result in ties (a) among the first three letters, or (b) between the third and fourth highest scores. With the former, the client should simply use the first three scores and follow the "Rule of Full Exploration." In the latter situation, the client may simply use two three-letter codes and search for options with both codes. In the computer version of the SDS, tied scores are broken by the following procedure. If scores for two or more codes are tied, comparisons are made of those code scores on the Occupations section of the SDS. The code with the highest score breaks the tie. Continued ties are resolved by comparisons on the Activities and Competencies sections, in order. This sequence of comparisons for resolving ties is based on the reliability of the section scores of the SDS (Holland, Fritzsche, & Powell, 1994). Continued tied scores are resolved in terms of the RIASEC order (i.e., R has precedence over I).

In reviewing the summary of scores across the five sections of the SDS, some counselors find it useful to examine section scores separately from the total scores. For example, they examine the three highest scores for the Activities and Occupations sections as a measure of client interests within the typology, and they look at the Competencies and Self-Estimates codes as an indication of the client's abilities or skills. The SDS:CV Professional Summary prints separate codes for the five sections of the SDS. Holland, however, has not emphasized this differential interpretation of the SDS summary scores, preferring instead to concentrate on the highest three-letter codes as indications of the best overall approximation of the client to the RIASEC models.

Clients who are not highly anxious and who are free from serious doubts about their ability to make career decisions can typically use the summary code to move ahead and explore occupational and educational options without counselor assistance. We will focus on what to do for clients for whom this is not the case later in this chapter and in chapters 7, 8, and 9.

Congruence Between Aspirations and Summary Codes

As we have noted from the beginning, there are really two interest assessment activities built into the SDS, an expressed measure in the Daydreams section and an assessed measure in the scored summary code. If the code of the first daydream occupation is closely related to or congruent with the SDS summary code, the user is probably thinking in a stable, systematic way about his or her interests and possibilities. When the level of agreement between expressed and assessed codes is relatively high, the user may need relatively less help in clarifying his or her interests and understanding life or career possibilities. Holland, Powell, and Fritzsche (1994) indicated that when first-letter codes of the current aspiration and the SDS are the same, a person is likely to maintain that aspiration over time. Further, when interest inventories and aspirations differ, the predictive validity of the aspiration exceeds that of the inventory. In a 3-year study of expressed and inventoried career choices of Australian youth, Funder, Taylor, and Kelso (1986) reported that expressed choices were usually, and increasingly over time, the better predictor of future career behavior. In research on the validity of aspirations and interest inventories, Holland, Gottfredson, and Baker (1990) found that one aspiration is as good as an interest inventory, and two or three aspirations in the same RIASEC category (high coherence of aspirations) are more efficient than any interest inventory. The SDS:CV automatically calculates a congruence level between the summary code of the Daydreams section and the SDS summary code and reports this result in the counselor's Professional Summary. This idea will be discussed more fully in chapter 7.

My Vocational Situation (MVS)

The My Vocational Situation (MVS) form, developed by Holland, Daiger, and Power (1980), is a wonderful example of Holland's creativity and attention to practical matters. This work began when Holland and his daughter Joan (Holland & Holland, 1977b) conducted research on "undecidedness," which led to the development of the Career Decision Making Difficulty scale. This effort grew out of a desire to understand more fully what "being undecided" about an occupation or career really meant. Many practitioners have sought to help students with undecided majors at the college level and have been perplexed by these clients.

Rather than finding a complex structure of characteristics associated with undecidedness, the Hollands found that one large factor or variable seemed to be most important. This was eventually labeled "Vocational Identity" in the MVS, and consists of 18 items. Two other factors seemed to be very important in undecidedness: "need for (occupational) information," and "barriers (personal limits or environmental problems in decision making)." Each of these factors consists of 4 items. The research on the development of the MVS was reported in the *Journal of Personality and Social Psychology* (Holland, D. Gottfredson, & Power, 1980).

Holland wanted to create a simple screening instrument that would enable a career counselor to quickly identify the most difficult clients, those who might not benefit from taking the SDS without counselor intervention. For this reason, all items on the MVS are scored in the same direction, and the counselor simply counts the number of "false" or "no" responses to obtain a score for vocational identity, need for information, or perceived barriers. The MVS can be completed in 10 minutes or less and scored in seconds, at a cost of about 40 cents per administration. The SDS Computer Version includes the MVS as part of the online assessment process, and the results are included in the Professional Summary Report.

The MVS is a popular measure in career research and has been reported in more than 50 published studies (Holland, Johnston, & Asama, 1993). It is a simple instrument that has enjoyed great success, even though it "violates" one of the most widely accepted principles of test development (i.e., its test items are all stated negatively).

> In short, the evidence about the Identity scale implies that it is a general measure of psychological health, although it was developed to assess only vocational decision-making difficulties and related problems. The present data provide more evidence that vocational variables are interwoven with other personal variables. (Holland, Johnston, & Asama, 1993, p. 8)

Ironically, this simple vocational assessment tool is a sensitive measure of many aspects of psychological well-being. As we are learning about much of Holland's work, apparently simple devices often have powerful effects.

Early reviews of the MVS were negative. Tinsley (1985) recommended the MVS only as a research tool (with calculated risks because of its weak validity), but did not recommend its use in applied settings. Lunneborg (1985) saw no evidence that the MVS was a good diagnostic tool but thought it might be useful in research. Westbrook (1985) did not think the MVS was ready for general use and indicated that much more research was needed before it could be used to make decisions about individuals. These reviews based on MVS data available in 1980 stand in stark contrast to the recent positive evidence reported by Holland, Johnston, and Asama (1993) and Holland (1996a, 1997) on the use of the MVS in research and applied settings. Holland (1997) now says that "the evidence for the validity of the VI [vocational identity] scale is substantial and relatively unambiguous" (p. 150).

It might be noted in passing that the MVS is still published by Consulting Psychologists Press, the former publisher of the SDS. The compilation and presentation of the wealth of accumulated data on the MVS needs to be incorporated into a revised manual for the MVS. The article by Holland, Johnston, and Asama (1993), along with the 1997 edition of *Making Vocational Choices*, provide important new information about the MVS, but they are not a substitute for a revised test manual, which is sorely needed.

How can the MVS be used in career counseling? It might be used to screen for those clients who are not likely to benefit from completing the SDS without counselor assistance (e.g., those with Identity scale scores of 6 or less). Also, MVS items marked "true" or "yes" might be explored first in career counseling. Taylor (1986) reported the use of the MVS with 213 Australian clients seeking educational and career counseling: "As expected, those with higher levels of vocational identity were more decided about their career plans and more successfully helped by brief career counseling" (p. 197). Unexpectedly, however, Taylor found that clients with low identity scores developed higher levels after career counseling, suggesting that they may have crystallized their self-concepts as they worked through the process of selecting a career.

Holland, Johnston, and Asama (1993) reported on use of the MVS in freshman orientation to screen students with the greatest needs, as part of an intake assessment in career/counseling centers, in individual counseling to examine negative self-beliefs, and as a pre- and post-measure of the effect of career interventions. Surprisingly, there is a need for more reports in the professional literature of how the MVS is being used effectively in counseling practice. These ideas and other topics related to the MVS will be discussed and explained more fully in chapters 7, 8, 9, 10, and 12. In the following section, we'll briefly explore another measure of career indecision.

The Occupational Alternatives Question (OAQ)

The Occupational Alternatives Question (OAQ) is a simple, novel measure of career indecision. The OAQ is an unpublished, well-researched measure of client career decidedness that is as old as the SDS itself. Indeed, it was initially used in validity studies of the SDS to measure the impact of the SDS on the career decision making of high school students (Zener & Schnuelle, 1972). The OAQ was revised by Slaney (1978, 1980); the concurrent validity was demonstrated with other measures of career indecision (Slaney, 1983; Slaney, Stafford, & Russell, 1981); and the test-retest reliability was reported at .93 (Redmond, 1973) and to be stable over a 6-week period (Slaney, 1978).

We have used the OAQ in our career services by imbedding it into various registration and intake forms, and we find that it is a simple, quick measure of a client's level of decidedness. We have also used it as a pre- and post-measure of the impact of career interventions in our career center. Figure 4 shows an example of a client information form that includes the OAQ. This can be used as a general purpose client intake form or it can be used for research purposes. Judging from the response of participants in our SDS workshops, the OAQ is a measurement tool that many practitioners seem to have little experience in using and might find helpful.

The OAQ consists of two parts:

Part 1. List all the occupations you are considering right now. (This first item is followed by blank lines; the format is much like the Daydreams section of the SDS)

Part 2. Circle (or write in the space provided) the occupation that is your first choice (if undecided, write undecided).

The OAQ produces four scores:

1. A first occupational choice is listed with no alternatives.
2. A first choice is listed with alternatives.
3. No first choice is listed, just alternatives.
4. Neither a first choice nor alternatives are listed.

These four scores range from higher to lower levels of career decidedness, with lower scores (1, 2) indicating more decidedness and higher scores (3, 4) indicating less career decidedness. Further discussion of career decidedness in relation to career counseling is included in chapter 8, and further discussion of screening for client readiness for career assistance is included in chapter 11.

The Occupations Finder and You and Your Career Booklets

As noted previously, the SDS as a career guidance intervention includes two additional booklets besides the Assessment Booklet, The Occupations Finder (OF) and the You and Your Career (YYC) booklets. The OF sometimes referred to as the Occupational Classification booklet, lists 1,335 occupations judged to be the fastest-growing in the 1990s, with three-letter RIASEC codes for each. A three-letter code IRA for Surgeon means that surgeons resemble people in Investigative occupations most, followed by Realistic and Artistic occupations. In this way, codes use the RIASEC theory to show how an occupation resembles these three groups.

The OF is printed in two forms, one with an alphabetical list of the occupations and one with the occupations grouped by three-letter Holland codes. The alphabetical form of the OF may be particularly useful in situations where

CLIENT INFORMATION

Name _____Age _____Sex _____Date _____

Address_____

City _____State _____Zip Code_____

Campus/Home Phone Number _____Work Phone Number_____

Currently enrolled in school? (circle)   yes no

If yes, what is your major _____and class standing?_____

Please circle the number or letters showing the highest year of formal schooling you have received:

High School 10 11 12   College 1 2 3 4 5 6 MA MS PhD Other

Ethnic Group (circle)   African-American   Asian American   Hispanic-American

                                Native American   White/Caucasian   Other_____

Disability? (circle) yes   no   If yes, what type? _____

Marital Status_____Occupation_____
                                                                                 (if other than student)

List all occupations you are considering right now.

_____   _____

_____   _____

_____   _____

What occupation is your <u>first</u> choice? (If undecided, write "undecided.")

_____

How well satisfied are you with your <u>first</u> choice? (circle the number)

    1. Well satisfied with choice   4. Dissatisfied, but intend to remain

    2. Satisfied, but have a few doubts   5. Very dissatisfied and intent to change

    3. Not sure   6. Undecided about my future career

Figure 4. Client information form including the Occupational Alternatives Question (OAQ).

clients need help quickly locating occupational alternatives and the codes for those alternatives. The entry for each occupation includes the nine-digit DOT number and a single-digit estimate (2 to 6) of the level of training required for the occupation (i.e., level 3 or 4 indicates that high school and some college, technical, or business training is necessary). Printed OFs cost about $1.25 each and can be reused. The OF is derived in part from the *Dictionary of Holland Occupation Codes* (Gottfredson & Holland, 1996a), and it can be used directly with clients who have not completed the Assessment Booklet but who have a clear idea about their three-letter code. Other uses of the OF will be explored in chapters 5 to 7.

The You and Your Career (YYC) booklet includes information about the RIASEC types, both for persons and occupations, and how to apply Holland's typological theory in career decision making. This booklet provides information that can help the client interpret the results of the SDS, by explaining how the theory may be applied to solve career decision making problems. Contents of both the OF and the YYC booklets have been incorporated into the Interpretive Reports produced by the SDS software programs.

The Myers-Briggs Type Indicator and the Strong Interest Inventory

SDS workshop participants often ask us about the SDS in relation to the Myers Briggs Type Indicator (MBTI) and Strong Interest Inventory (SII)— despite our obvious bias in favor of RIASEC theory and the SDS and our limited experience with the MBTI and SII, primarily in the context of individual counseling by appointment. The following information is typically included in our responses to these questions.

MBTI

Both the MBTI and SDS are based on personality typologies. The MBTI is based on a personality typology that specifies 16 distinct types, compared to six types for the SDS. Like most instruments based on typologies, the MBTI works better at the extremes where personality characteristics are highly differentiated and clear. Unlike the SDS, the MBTI is based on the idea that people tend towards one type or its opposite (e.g., thinking vs. feeling); a score in one area precludes a score in the opposite area. This leads to rather arbitrary judgments about a person's type, because most people actually score toward the middle rather than towards the extreme of one type or another. Walsh and Betz (1995) noted that the empirical support for this assumed dichotomy is tenuous. In contrast, a high score in one area of the SDS does not automatically produce a low rating or score in another area.

There are some research reports on the relationships between the 16 MBTI types and the six RIASEC types. Myers and McCaulley (1992) reported an association between the Sensing preference and the Realistic type; in addition, the Intuitive preference was associated with Artistic type for both men and women and with the Social type for women. Using GOT (General Occupational Theme) scores from the SII, Dillon and Weissman (1987) found both Sensing and Thinking preferences associated with the Realistic type; Intuitive and Thinking preferences associated with the Investigative type; Intuitive, Feeling, and Perceptive preferences associated with the Artistic type; Extroversion, Feeling, and Perceptive preferences associated with the Social type; Extroversion and Thinking preferences associated with the Enterprising type; and Extroversion, Sensing, and Judging preferences associated with the Conventional type. Humes (1992) reported modest relationships between MBTI types and SDS Form E (Holland, 1996b) codes with a group of learning disabled high school students. In general, the relationships among the MBTI and SDS scales are predictable and offer few surprises (Holland, 1997).

McCaulley (1990) and McCaulley and Martin (1995) described how the MBTI could be used in career counseling. For example, McCaulley reported that type preferences associated with occupations have been collected in the *MBTI Atlas of Type Tables* (Macdaid, McCaulley, & Kainz, 1987) from each completed MBTI answer sheet which listed an occupation and was scored by CAPT. She notes that "careers attract all 16 types but most careers attract more of the types whose preferences match the demands of the work" (McCaulley, 1990, p. 189). Clients could examine the extent to which their preferences match those in the *Atlas* for various occupations. McCaulley further notes that

> All types are found in all careers. Rare types in a field can become unhappy as misfits, can be happily challenged as they provide their own viewpoint to move the field ahead, or can carve a niche where their gifts are valued. Discussion of these possibilities provides the grist for good counseling. (p. 189)

The MBTI can be used in career counseling to help describe an individual's preferences regarding such things as getting information, making decisions, and internal and external orientations. Counselors can help clients explore the potential impact of these preferences on their work roles and choices. In addition to the resources available through McCaulley's CAPT and Consulting Psychologists Press, there are various resources that generate MBTI types available both in books (Keirsey & Bates, 1978) and on the Internet that might also serve this purpose.

We have found that the MBTI works best in helping clients examine work setting issues, including relationships among coworkers (e.g., the supervisor is an INFP and the client is an ESTJ). Understanding these personality characteristics can help clients (and probably the supervisor as well) appreciate differences in work styles, work values, and communication patterns. However, we think it is easier and simpler to use the RIASEC personality typology embedded in the SDS to appreciate these types of differences in work and worker relationships. For example, a C type working for an A type might experience frustrations with a lack of structure, routine, and clarity in performance expectations and procedures, and an I-type physician working for an E-type administrator might become exasperated by a constant focus on the "bottom line." An example of this use of the SDS was described by Hogan (1997). She discussed how the SDS could be incorporated into a staff development program noting: "Staff members now understand that typologies can play a role in communication patterns. The number of misinterpretations appears to have been reduced significantly" (p. 302).

Our understanding of the system by which "careers" (it is unclear whether these are also occupations and/or jobs) have been coded according to the 16 MBTI types leads us not to use this "classification" with clients wishing to explore occupational or job alternatives. The large and relatively consistent body of research supporting the classification of occupations according to RIASEC theory is superior in our judgment. In this regard, DeVito (1985) noted that the vocational information provided by the MBTI would be more persuasive if the instrument purported to be a predictor of career choice or was to be used by counselors in this way.

Thompson and Ackerman (1994) noted that the MBTI is widely used because (a) it focuses on normal variations in personality, (b) counselors have identified many creative ways to use it, and (c) many counselors find it has high "face validity" with clients (i.e., clients find the results understandable, agreeable, useful, and nonthreatening). They noted that the MBTI is especially popular in career counseling because of the MBTI data bank, but they also noted three criticisms: the use of dichotomous scoring, the fact that clients can identify their types without taking the test, and the fact that the MBTI is not grounded in all aspects of Jung's theory.

The MBTI has also been criticized in several other reviews (McCrae & Costa, 1989; Moore, 1987; Pittenger, 1993). Writing in the *Journal of Career Planning and Employment,* Pittenger noted that "there is no evidence of bimodal distributions for the MBTI. Instead, most people score between the two extremes" (p. 50). Moreover, he noted that the "data suggest that the proportion of MBTI types within each occupation is equivalent to that within a random sample of the population" (p. 52). For example, the proportion of ESTJs in the teaching profession is the same as the proportion of ESTJs in the general population.

In summary, it appears that the MBTI does not conform to many of the basic standards expected of psychological tests. Many very specific predictions about the MBTI have not been confirmed or have been proved wrong. There is no obvious evidence that there are 16 unique categories in which all people can be placed. There is no evidence that scores generated by the MBTI reflect the stable and unchanging personality traits that are claimed to be measured. (Pittenger, 1993, p. 52)

In summary, the evidence for the validity of the SDS as a career exploration tool is substantial. In contrast, the research support for the MBTI as a tool for linking personal characteristics to occupational alternatives is lacking. For this reason, we prefer the SDS.

Strong Interest Inventory (SII)

In chapter 1, we explained why and how Holland created the SDS in the early 1970s. In several important ways, he was motivated to create an alternative to the Strong Interest Inventory (SII), an inventory that could be self-scored, was based on a theory, made use of clients' aspirations, avoided separate answer sheets, and so on. Whereas Holland started with a theory, Strong started with test items that discriminated among the interests of persons in occupations.

The SII Occupational Scales (OSs) were pioneered by E. K. Strong in the 1920s and comprised the original form of the SII. Later, the Basic Interest scales (BISs) and General Occupational Theme scales (GOTs) were added. The GOT scales were based on Holland's RIASEC theory, but his name is not used with them. The 1994 edition of the SII also includes four Personal Styles scales: Work Style, Learning Environment, Leadership Style, and Risk Taking/Adventure. These Personal Style scales were developed by selecting items from the OSs, GOTs, and BISs. An article by Harmon and Borgen (1995) in the *Journal of Career Assessment* provides a brief history and description of the 1994 edition of the SII.

The OSs represent an important difference between the SII and the SDS. In creating the 1994 edition of the SII, 50 occupational groups were sampled; this led to the creation of 211 OSs, including 102 occupations represented by scales for males and females and seven occupations represented by a scale for only one sex. Clients do not know which of the 317 items scored plus or minus may have been used to develop an interest score on a particular OS. Because the OSs are statistically derived, it is sometimes difficult to know why a client may have obtained a high score on a particular occupation. A test item with a negative response might indicate a level of interest shared with members of an occupational group in the normative sample (e.g., physicians like to fly and don't like to file). "Items are included in the inventory because they 'work,' but why they are effective is unknown" (Westbrook & Norton, 1994, p. 217). The lack of obvious links between items and scales limits the face validity of the SII. In our past experience using the Strong, we often found ourselves searching for explanations about why persons scored high on occupations that seemed to have little or no connection to their views of themselves. In contrast, when interpreting SDS results to clients, it is easier to show the connection between their responses and the occupational alternatives generated. This increases the face validity of the SDS, and the test-takers' understanding of and confidence in the results. Furthermore, by following Holland's "Rule of Full Exploration" and taking into account occupational alternatives suggested by the client's day-dreams, the counselor and the client are more likely to generate options that logically connect to the client's skills, interests, and values.

The computer-generated SII profile report contains many options and features, including a summary page (the Snapshot), profiles of GOT and BIS scores, and OS scores color-coded around GOT themes; it concludes with Personal Styles scales and Administrative indexes. Two interpretive report options are also available for clients, one for general users and the other for persons pursuing professional careers. In addition to a good test manual, several counselor guides and client workbooks are available to support the SII. In particular, a book by Kummerow (1991), *New Directions in Career Planning and the Workplace*, discusses RIASEC theory in light of workplace changes. In addition, Harmon and Borgen (1995) identify the Career Beliefs Inventory (Krumboltz, 1988), the MBTI, and the Skills Confidence Inventory (SCI; Betz, Borgen, & Harmon, 1996) as materials supporting the SII. The SCI, based on Bandura's (1977) self-efficacy theory, gauges confidence for tasks in the six Holland theme areas.

Westbrook and Norton (1994) offered a critique of the SII:

> The SII is clearly impressive, and some believe that it is probably the best interest inventory available at this time. It has a long history of careful research and development, and its authors have consistently seemed willing to accept criticism and work toward improvement. (p. 217)

However, they note that there is no perfect test and the effective use of the SII is related to certain client expectations and characteristics, as well as to professional judgments by competent counselors.

In our experience, many counselors spend considerable time in SII interpretations trying to explain the meaning of Occupational Scale scores to skeptical clients. Some of the most useful counseling comes out of the discussion of the GOTs based on Holland's theory because many clients often want to expand their options beyond those listed in the OS scores of the SII. However, we think it is better to use the SDS for this, rather than the SII. Indeed, one can quickly see which items contributed to various RIASEC scores by inspection of the SDS item responses, and The Occupations Finder includes 1,335 occupations. Also, the lack of a Daydreams section reduces the usefulness of the SII, in our opinion. On the other hand, clients interested in any of the 100+ occupations included in the OSs of the SII can find it particularly useful to determine whether their interests match up well with the interests of persons already in that occupation. If they don't, however, it can be difficult and time-consuming to understand why the client's interest profile doesn't look like the profiles already there.

The MBTI and SII in Relation to the SDS

In many of our workshops and at conference presentations, we have heard practitioners suggest that counselors need to administer a variety of career assessment instruments to help individuals with career decisions. Indeed, in some settings, this is done immediately after the intake process and before the client sees the counselor; the message is that the counselor must have a large array of different types of assessments, some of which must be mailed off or require other lengthy scoring procedures, before clients can begin to resolve their career concerns. In other settings, the rationale for using several instruments is the need to confirm the information provided by the initial assessment, especially the occupational alternatives suggested.

We attended an in-house MBTI training workshop where the staff member presented university student case examples with MBTI and SDS results. Participants were asked to get into small groups, review the cases, and make suggestions about potential college majors for these undecided cases. As group members shared their suggestions, we noted that one could have reached the same conclusions simply by using the SDS results! We have seen examples from more than one career services setting where the SDS is viewed as a "light-weight" and simplistic test that anyone can give, a good start that must be followed by some "real tests," such as the SII or MBTI. Again, this goes back to the thinking that the SDS is simply about matching codes to titles. It ignores the other theoretical interpretive and diagnostic concepts available to help counselors understand clients' difficulties. Further, as we will see in later case studies, it is possible to stay within Holland's system, using not only various forms of the SDS, but also the MVS, the PCI, and the CASI to explore fully the nature of clients' career concerns.

We should be fair and say that, in our setting, we often follow the SDS with various computer-based guidance systems to encourage clients to explore options in greater detail and further clarify their knowledge about their skills, interests, and values. But the "piling on of interventions" that may take longer, cost more, and are of questionable reliability and validity is not warranted unless we are fully using all of the information provided in ones that are briefer, less expensive, psychometrically sound, and with demonstrated success. For example, Holland (1997) has noted that "It is not necessary to administer a self-efficacy measure to identify a person's beliefs about his or her vocational self-efficacy. The low points in an interest profile indicate the areas where a person lacks the self-confidence to perform well" (p. 209). As we will discuss in chapter 8, clients must be able to translate the information they're given about themselves and about their options, and Holland has provided a rich resource with the SDS and its component parts to help them do this. As practitioners, we need to make sure we're not rushing off to the next assessment unless there is a "value-added" benefit to the client in doing so.

In summarizing our reactions to the MBTI and SII, we note the following points in favor of the SDS:

1. It is based on an established theory which is fully operationalized in the test materials published by Psychological Assessment Resources, Inc.

2. The results include measures of interests and skills.

3. The results are easier for clients to understand.

4. It is less complicated to administer, score, and explain to clients because it is self-scored and uses raw scores.

5. It costs less.

6. It generates better, more detailed lists of options regarding occupations and fields of study.

7. Various forms can be used with different populations (e.g., middle school).

8. It has been favorably reviewed in the literature and has well-respected psychometric qualities.

Conclusion

As a self-guided career intervention, the Self-Directed Search is without peer. As a simulated career counseling activity, it provides a rich reservoir of interpretive information for a counselor to draw upon in helping a client. As a practical assessment tool, it can be completed and scored in 25 to 50 minutes at a cost of about $2.50 (paper and pencil form: Assessment Booklet & Occupations Finder), about $3.50 (these two forms plus the You and Your Career booklet and My Vocational Situation), or about $5.00 (SDS:CV). Together, the SDS, OF, YYC, and MVS provide the core elements in a comprehensive system of theory-based career interventions.

5

Comparing and Contrasting SDS Forms and Formats

Although the publisher of the Self-Directed Search, Psychological Assessment Resources, provides a great deal of information about the various forms and formats of the SDS in their regularly published product catalogs, our experience with users suggests that they do not always fully understand or appreciate the diversity of available SDS products. Practitioners often have questions about which SDS form or version to use with a particular population. Moreover, in reviewing a sample of journal articles and other research reports, we have found that authors often fail to specify which version of the SDS they used in a particular study or program application. More disturbing, we have found SDS evaluation reports where either all the components of the particular instrument or the most recent edition of the instrument were not used.

This chapter will provide descriptions of the four forms of the SDS: Form R (Regular; Holland, 1994), Form E (Easy; Holland, 1996b), Form CP (Career Planning; Holland, 1990), and Form Career Explorer (Holland & Powell, 1994). They were developed historically in this order. This chapter will highlight the purpose, history, and unique applications of each form and provide a basis for making cost comparisons. Note that all cost figures are based on the publisher's prices at the time this book was published. For current pricing, phone PAR, Inc. at 1-800-331-TEST, or visit the PAR website at www.parinc.com. A chart summarizing information about the various SDS forms is also included at the end of this chapter (see Table 13). Each section will also highlight facts about the particular form (e.g., number of items and sections in the Assessment Booklet) and the specific computer applications available for each. We will focus on comparing and contrasting the various versions and formats of the SDS in this chapter; critiques of the SDS by independent reviewers and by Holland himself are reported in chapter 12.

Self-Directed Search Form R

In this section, we will examine the varied array of components that comprise Form R of the SDS. In addition to the original paper and pencil versions of Form R, this section describes the computer applications associated with Form R, as well as the Canadian (French and English) and Spanish versions. The brief comments about each component are designed to help practitioners learn more about using the materials in providing career assistance.

Self-Directed Search Form R (Regular)

As noted in chapter 4, SDS Form R, now in its fourth edition, is the original paper and pencil form of the SDS and the most widely used version. The *SDS Professional User's Guide* (Holland, Powell, & Fritzsche, 1994) provides information about item content and about design changes that were incorporated into the 1977, 1985, and 1994 editions of the SDS as a result of user comments and psychometric research. Form R, along with other Holland-based interventions, was also discussed in a recent article by Spokane and Holland (1995) and a chapter by Loughead and Linehan (1996). In conducting SDS workshops around the country, we have found that practitioners working in the most varied settings imaginable have successfully used Form R with high school, college, and adult populations. Form R can be completed easily by most clients in 35 to 45 minutes, assuming no language or reading barriers.

The two basic components required for the administration of SDS Form R are the Assessment Booklet and The Occupations Finder (OF). The Assessment Booklet contains 228 items, plus the Daydreams section, and the OF lists 1,335 occupations employing about 99% of U.S. workers. (Additional information about all components of SDS Form R is included in chapter 4.) This basic administration costs about $2.50 per client. However, we believe the administration and interpretation of the SDS Form R also requires use of the You and Your Career booklet, which raises the cost to about $3.50 per client. (It should be noted that both The Occupations Finder and You and Your Career booklets can be reused, if the client does not want to keep copies of these materials.) Using all three components, Form R represents the most complete paper and pencil assessment application of Holland's theory. With respect to research and evaluation, most of what we know about the impact of the SDS has come from research with Form R, as reported in the SDS manuals.

One of the special, unique features of Form R is the inclusion of the Daydreams section, referred to in chapter 4 as an aspirations scale. To our knowledge, no other assessment instrument directly captures this kind of information from clients. Holland continues to emphasize the importance of this information in fully understanding clients' "vocational situations." Spokane and Holland (1995) noted the importance of exploring daydreams and the role of The Occupations Finder in that process. The Daydreams section helps increase the predictive validity of a client's SDS results, forms an impression of a client's goals and background, and encourages the immediate preliminary exploration of more than 1,000 occupations. In our discussions with practitioners, we have heard varied reactions to the use of the Daydreams section in the SDS. It seems useful to share some of these issues and questions here.

One of the issues most frequently raised about the Daydreams section is that it slows people down when they have to wade through the OF to find the three-letter code for each daydream. From our perspective, if the client's time or patience is an issue when completing the Daydreams section, there are other options:

1. If available, use the Alphabetized Occupations Finder (AOF) or the *Dictionary of Holland Occupation Codes* (DHOC) to facilitate the process of locating codes.

2. Ask the client to simply list his or her daydreams and skip Step 2 (using the OF to locate a three-letter code for each occupation) for the moment. (Step 2 can always be completed later with the assistance of the counselor using the OF, the AOF, or the DHOC.)

The disadvantage of this approach is that it reduces one impact of the SDS as an intervention, the "preliminary exploration of more than 1,000 occupations" (Spokane & Holland, 1995, p. 388).

Our experience is that many clients do "lose themselves" in completing this activity, but we don't necessarily view this as a bad thing. For many clients, it is their first experience with seeing so many occupations arranged in this way. For most, it is an activity that is interesting, rather than frustrating. We believe that for many clients, and for counselors as well, there is too much emphasis on the end results, or the "assessed results" as defined in chapter 4. There is value in getting clients' views of what occupations "fit them" through the use of an open ended stimulus (e.g., listing one's daydreams) before bringing in the results of a more structured assessment. Peterson, Sampson, and Reardon (1991) described this as a "tip of the iceberg" means for better understanding how individuals relate their personal characteristics to occupational alternatives.

Another issue, which we particularly see in our setting, is the tendency of individuals to list fields of study, rather than occupational titles. Several approaches could be used here:

1. Ask clients if the study area listed relates to a particular occupation they had in mind, and then either search for that occupation (or the closest thing to it) in the available resources.

2. Use the Educational Opportunities Finder (EOF; Rosen, Holmberg, & Holland, 1994) to locate a code for the option they've listed. (For a more detailed description of the EOF, see chapter 6.)

3. Use the Classification of Instructional Programs section of the DHOC to locate a code.

Practitioners often raise the issue of the validity of daydreams, especially when dealing with high school students who list such occupations as "rock star" or "professional athlete." We would argue that despite the "fantasy" nature of these aspirations, it is important not to dismiss or demean them. Practitioners are encouraged to explore the meaning a particular aspiration holds for that person. In the example of the rock star, it is possible that the client may not actually achieve this occupational goal, but what attracts the client to it? Is it being on center stage, being part of a creative process? These individuals may not be performing artists, but they may choose options that will let them be in the music industry (e.g., agent, promoter, arts manager, lyricist, etc.), or music may be part of their other life roles (e.g., they might play in a band on the weekends or perform in the community chorus).

You and Your Career (YYC)

This seven-page booklet was written by John Holland for use with the SDS Form R or the VPI. The YYC booklet discusses the scientific ideas supporting the inventories, how to use the scores and codes, the personality characteristics associated with codes, and suggestions for successful career planning. Administration costs less than $1.00 per booklet. Some practitioners have found it helpful to use portions of this booklet, before administering the SDS, to introduce users to Holland's theory and the hexagon format for organizing occupations and to help them understand what to expect from completing the SDS. This approach can be used in an individual, group, or classroom format. We consider administration of the SDS Form R paper and pencil version incomplete without the use of You and Your Career because users miss a significant part of the "treatment." Further, the seven steps included in the "Making Career Decisions" section of YYC closely mirror the kinds of activities clients should engage in after any type of assessment activity. Using these seven steps in follow-up sessions with clients can prove to be a useful checklist for monitoring the progress clients are making in their career problem solving and decision making. Finally, no research evaluation of the effects of the SDS Form R on clients should be undertaken without including this booklet as part of the intervention.

Self-Directed Search Form R: Interpretive Report (SDS Form R:IR) for Windows®

This Interpretive Report for Form R was written by Robert Reardon, first published in 1987, and revised in 1994 and 1996. The SDS Form R:IR comes with a detailed manual that includes information about the software and suggestions for program implementation and use. This program is designed for career counselors or program administrators to use in producing narrative reports for clients after they have completed the paper and pencil version of the SDS Form R. Administrators also have the option of entering up to five occupational daydreams and having this information included in the Professional Summary report.

The SDS Form R:IR computer program produces a 10- to 12-page interpretive report for the client based on SDS summary scores and a 1-page summary for the counselor. The basic interpretive report adapts material from the SDS Form R Assessment Booklet, the You and Your Career booklet, and the DHOC. It provides lists of occupational titles from The Occupations Finder according to all permutations of the three-letter summary code, the DOT number for each occupation, and the estimated education (ED) and specialized vocational preparation or on-the-job training (SVP) levels for the occupations. Additional report options available in the SDS Form R:IR include the names of fields of study from the Educational Opportunities Finder, including the CIP (Classification of Instructional Programs) number and the estimated level of training (associate, bachelors, postgraduate), and leisure options from the Leisure Activities Finder (LAF; Holmberg, Rosen, & Holland, 1990). All of this information is presented in terms of RIASEC codes. The SDS Form R:IR can be customized by the on-site administrator (i.e., adding local information about educational options or office procedures, omitting lists of options produced by the EOF and the LAF). This application requires Windows 3.1 or higher, 4MB RAM, and a Windows-compatible printer. The cost is $450.00 for unlimited uses, generating an unlimited number of interpretive reports for clients and Professional Summaries for counselors. To our knowledge, no studies have been conducted regarding outcomes or impact of the SDS Form R:IR.

Self-Directed Search (SDS) Form R: Computer Version (SDS Form R:CV) for Windows

The SDS Form R:CV (Reardon & Ona, 1996) is a computer version of the SDS that provides for on-screen administration of the complete SDS Form R Assessment Booklet, including the Daydreams section, and My Vocational Situation (MVS). It produces a 10- to 12-page interpretive report for clients and a 2- to 3-page Professional Summary for counselors that includes the seven diagnostic signs derived from Holland's theory (see chapters 2 and 4). The cost for this software application of the SDS is about $5.00 per administration (3.5" disk with 50 uses costs $250.00). With each administration of the SDS, one remaining use of the SDS is subtracted from the disk.

Very limited research has been reported with the SDS-R:CV, but Reardon (1987) wrote an article describing its original conceptual design and use considerations. A study reported by Reardon and Loughead (1988) revealed extremely high correlations between summary scores on the paper and pencil and computer versions of the SDS after 2-week intervals. Indeed, these correlations rivaled test-retest correlations on the paper and pencil version of the SDS itself. In a program evaluation study, Reardon, Lenz, and Strausberger (1996) used the SDS Form R:CV as a data collection tool to assess career needs and interests of clients in a setting. With clients' permission, the authors used results taken from clients' SDS Form R:CV Professional Summaries to develop local norms for clients using career services in their setting.

Earlier reviews of the software were done on the 1987 DOS-based version (McKee & Levinson, 1990; Urich, 1990). In his review, Urich described the computer version as a "valuable addition to the field of computer-assisted career counseling" (p. 94). McKee and Levinson described it as a time-efficient means for providing career assistance and found the program and manual detailed, yet easy to understand and use. Their criticisms focused on several issues:

1. Lack of research data related to the computer version's reliability and validity.

2. Lack of area raw scores in the Professional Summary.

3. Lack of client responses to individual items in the professional summary.

4. Options for customizing the client's report.

5. Options available to clients for altering or changing responses.

Further, because of its recent release, there have been, to our knowledge, no independent reviews of the SDS Form R Windows version. This is unfortunate because, as we noted earlier, the availability of the Professional Summary printout from the computer version makes it much easier to collect and use client data. The other criticisms by McKee and Levinson (1990) have been addressed in the latest version of the SDS:CV. Client responses in each section of the SDS are included in the Professional Summary, and the Windows version allows users to customize the reports in several ways. The Windows version is also visually more appealing and more user-friendly than previous DOS versions.

Comparison of the Computer Version (SDS Form R:CV) and Paper and Pencil Format

In this section, we will examine issues associated with the administration of the SDS in computer (SDS:CV) and paper and pencil formats. We are not focusing on the interpretive report (SDS:IR), which is produced by an administrator coding into the computer the results of a completed SDS paper and pencil version.

In both our work setting and our discussions with practitioners across the country, we have found varied reactions to use of the paper and pencil versus the computer format. In addition to the informal comments we've received in workshops over the years, we recently surveyed nine of our career advisors regarding their use of the two versions and learned about six issues that influence their practice: hardware availability, cost, time, designating daydreams, reports, and client attitudes toward computers. This section will summarize and highlight some of those comparisons.

Hardware Availability

It is clear that the paper and pencil version enjoys more widespread use than the computer version for several reasons. First, even though we often have the impression in our society that every service delivery setting has access to current technology, the reality is that in many settings where the SDS is used, computers, especially newer models, are not readily available. Even when they are available, their use is typically limited to administrative applications—making them inaccessible to the clients being served.

Cost

Second, the cost of administering the three paper and pencil booklets (about $3.50) is less than the cost of the computer version ($5.00). What do practitioners get from paying the additional $1.50 per administration for the computer version? As noted earlier, the SDS:CV has a built-in diagnostic tool in the form of the MVS. A single MVS paper and pencil administration alone would cost approximately $.50 per user. In addition to the MVS, counselors receive a Professional Summary report that includes Holland's diagnostic indicators, which saves them from having to do all the math and research by hand. In our career services setting, the career advisors report the value of this summary in enabling them to quickly assess the level of assistance needed by the client. The Professional Summary can also provide data useful in research studies, including evaluation of services and assessing the relationship between Holland concepts and those concepts assessed by other instruments.

Time

What other factors might be considered in comparing the computer version with the paper and pencil version? One variable has to do with time. Both anecdotal (authors' personal experience) and research data (Reardon & Loughead,

1988) support the notion that the computer version can be completed in less time than the paper and pencil SDS. On the other hand, clients who have a short amount of time during their visit may find the paper and pencil version more to their liking because they can take it home and complete it at their leisure. Also, in a setting with limited access to computers, there might not be a machine available at the particular time when the client is seeking help.

Daydreams

Another variable has to do with the process for capturing daydreams (i.e., occupational aspirations). This topic generates some of the livelier debates about use of the SDS-R computer version. The main issue has to do with the "source" of the daydreams. The original concept with the paper and pencil version is that the daydreams come directly from the clients, with no external stimulus to prompt them (other than the unalphabetized OF). A variation on this process emerged with the publication of the AOF. To assist clients who found it difficult to think about or list their daydreams, some counselors gave them the alphabetical list to make the process of searching for daydreams go more quickly. (Note: The introduction of the AOF coincided with the expansion of the number of occupations in the OF from about 500 to about 1,200 in the 1985 edition of the SDS.) With this list of options before them, clients suddenly "discovered" daydreams they never knew they had. An alphabetical list of occupations also appears on-screen so users of the computer version can select the ones they have daydreamed about.

Despite our best attempts to encourage clients to think of their daydreams before they review the list, we still find that they "discover" daydreams that they weren't considering before. Also, some clients must choose options from the list that don't exactly fit their stated preference. We don't think it's particularly important to label one approach as being better than the other. Some daydream purists think that the greater value is in what clients generate, apart from any external stimulus. For us, the issue is simply exploring what the daydreams represent for the client, whether they are vague or specific. As we emphasize in later chapters, the value of daydreams is the window they provide into the client's view of self and the world of work.

One additional caution should be noted related to using the alphabetical list of occupations for generating daydreams in either version: Because daydreams are used in determining coherence and congruence, and because of the significance in Holland's theory of the first daydream listed, it is important to remind clients to list their daydreams as instructed (i.e., with the most recent choice first). Not surprisingly, the tendency with alphabetical lists is to start with occupations beginning with the letter A and work through the remaining letters.

Another issue relates to clients picking options on the computer version list that only closely approximate their preferences. For instance, a client says that psychologist is his or her first daydream. The computer version lists seven options to choose from: experimental, counseling, chief, educational, school, industrial–organizational, or clinical psychologist. With the paper and pencil version, the counselor could ask the client to choose from the nine different types of psychologists. If clients' SDS results point to low levels of congruence or coherence, it may be important to check the process they used to arrive at their daydreams and the source of the code for each.

Client Attitudes

When examining clients' attitudes towards computers, consider their comfort with and expectations of computer-based career guidance. We find that even in today's technology-dominated world, some clients are still anxious about using computers, hitting the wrong key, and other related issues. They prefer the paper and pencil approach. In contrast, in a study reported by Reardon and Loughead (1988), participants used both formats, and 85% preferred the computer version. In our setting, we have access to both formats and usually allow clients to choose the version they prefer. To give them something to "see" when they're considering the computer version, we provide a brief description of the system (see Appendix B) which gives an overview of the instrument and what type of information they can expect to receive. This is typically done with all computer-based guidance interventions in our setting.

A second concern pertains to some clients' tendency to attribute "magical powers" to the computer. They may tend to see little connection between their responses and the results and, instead, sum up their experience by saying, "the computer told me to do this." When working with clients who appear to be externally focused and who are likely to give the computer too much power, it may be best to use the paper and pencil version so that they can more easily see how their responses in each section produced the end result. An alternative scenario involves clients who may lack motivation to engage in the self-assessment process or who may view sitting down to complete the paper and pencil SDS as too much like a school or work assignment. They may be more motivated and interested in completing "a computer-based simulation" (as we've described the SDS in chapter 4).

Other discussions comparing and contrasting the computer and paper and pencil versions of Form R have dealt with how ties and close scores are handled. With the paper and pencil version, counselors can quickly scan the summary scores and anticipate the need for dealing with tied scores, undifferentiated results, and rare codes. In our experience, counselors who see close scores or unusual code combinations are quick to help clients consider several combinations of codes to explore and to prevent them from being unhappy with the occupations linked to their code. When using the computer version, however, the software program simply generates the code for the three highest letters (using a series of rules explained in the SDS:CV manual to break ties, if necessary). This is the code, along with its combinations, that is used to generate the career options. Let's speculate that a client's scores on the computer version were R=8, I=15, A=25, S=19, E=33, C=20, resulting in the summary code: EAC. This would not be an uncommon code to see in our setting, where the school produces many A types who find themselves in a town (i.e., the state capital) with lots of C employment. The interpretive report for this client would list a total of three occupations, one of which is Tattoo Artist. Many clients would react negatively to this experience. A client using the paper and pencil version with the assistance of a counselor could be encouraged, in keeping with the "Rule of 8," to explore EAS as well, as the S score was only 1 point less than the C score. When we encounter this situation with the computer version, we typically give clients a copy of the paper OF along with their computer report and suggest that they review additional options using the fourth highest letter in various combinations with the first three.

SDS Form R: Professional Report Service

In some settings, career counselors (a) need to administer the SDS to a large group of people at one time (e.g., classroom setting, freshmen orientation program, employee outplacement workshop), (b) are administering a battery of tests to clients in a short period of time, or (c) do not have time to review the SDS individually with each client. This may be especially true regarding the Daydreams section, where there is no time available to complete this section or interpret it. In these instances, counselors are looking for an interest inventory, a straightforward test that will produce a report about the client's interest profile and identify training or occupational options for further consideration. In most instances, the results of the SDS administration will be incorporated into a more comprehensive report that the counselor will prepare. To meet this need, Psychological Assessment Resources developed the SDS Form R Professional Report Service, available for about $7.00 per administration. The Professional Report Service uses a version of the SDS Form R that does not include the Daydreams section. It also uses a specially designed four-page Assessment Booklet/answer sheet combination. Upon completion, the specially designed op-scan answer sheets are mailed to Psychological Assessment Resources, where they are computer-scored. The SDS results, including a client interpretive report and a Professional Summary report, are typically returned in 24 hours. The 10- to 12-page interpretive report and 1- to 2-page Professional

Summary written for each client are produced by the same SDS-R: IR program described earlier in this chapter.

We have used the SDS-R Professional Report Service for large group testing. The scannable item/response form and the absence of the Daydreams section speed up the administration process, making it especially useful for some situations. We used this version in a program intervention with a large group of student athletes at our university. After we administered the SDS and conducted a training session for the athletic academic advisors on how to interpret the results, the advisors received the results for their particular group of athletes. The advisors were particularly pleased with the linkage between SDS codes and fields of study at our university because a primary concern of many student athletes is choice of a major. There is also the "face validity" of the op-scan form, which makes the SDS look more like a real "test" for some clients.

Canadian Editions of SDS Form R

To meet the career guidance needs of Canadian career counselors, Psychological Assessment Resources developed two 1994 Canadian editions of the SDS Form R, written in both English Canadian and French Canadian. They include 1,059 occupations and provide the educational requirements and National Occupational Codes for each. Costs for using the Canadian Assessment Booklet, The Occupations Finder, and the You and Your Career booklet are less than $4.00 (U.S.) per administration.

SDS Form R Spanish Translation (1994 Edition)

In the late 1980s, Psychological Assessment Resources contracted for a Spanish translation of the SDS Form R, including the Assessment Booklet, The Occupations Finder, and the You and Your Career booklet. This has been updated for the 1994 edition of the SDS Form R materials and was done under contract with a Spanish language expert living in Puerto Rico. (A brief description of the process of developing a Spanish translation of the SDS Form E is presented in the next section of this chapter.) It is important to note that this is a Spanish translation of the SDS, not a Spanish edition, as is the case with the Canadian SDS. The cost for using this special Spanish language version of Form R is about $3.50 per administration. (Remember that the OF and YYC may be reused in some circumstances.)

Self-Directed Search Form E

Form E of the Self-Directed Search was developed almost simultaneously with Form R. Holland thought the need for Form E was self-evident, and began developing it in the early 1970s. He wanted to create a form of the SDS that was shorter, produced fewer occupational options for review, and had less complicated instructions for the client. In our review of the literature, we found several reports on the use of SDS Form E, including its use with persons who have reading disabilities and those for whom English is a second language (Cummings & Maddux, 1987; Humes, 1992; Maddux & Cummings, 1986; Taymans, 1991; Winer, Wilson, & Pierce, 1983). These reports may be of special interest to readers providing educational and career counseling to these groups. We also found two separate published reviews for the 1990 revision of Form E (Ciechalski, 1996; Diamond, 1996). Ciechalski described it as "an excellent interest instrument" (p. 314).

SDS Form E (Easy)

The fourth edition of SDS Form E (Holland, 1996b) provides career assessment for persons with limited reading skills (sixth-grade level). The most recent edition includes 57% new items, new directions including only fourth-grade words, larger print, and a revised Jobs Finder reflecting recent labor market trends and jobs of interest to Form E users. The development of the 1996 edition involved three studies of more than 1,800 persons from various settings across the U.S. In evaluating the self-scoring procedures of users, 4% made errors that resulted in an incorrect summary code. SDS Form E is intended to be similar in format and content to the other forms of the SDS; for example, 62% of Form E items also appear on Form R (Powell & Holland, 1996).

In completing Form E, test takers respond to 198 items, not including a daydreams section entitled "Jobs You Have Thought About." This is 30 fewer items than on Form R. Form E includes large-print directions written at a fourth-grade level, has a simplified scoring that produces a two-letter code, uses one set of self-ratings (Form R uses two), and has different labels for each section of the Assessment Booklet. The occupations section in the Assessment Booklet includes brief definitions of the job titles listed to help users understand the meaning of these titles, a feature unique to Form E. The Form E Jobs Finder includes 841 titles (compared to 1,335 for Form R), concentrating on jobs requiring less educational preparation across many different work settings, and a You and Your Job booklet that provides interpretive information. Form E is fully compatible with all other SDS materials (e.g., Form E Assessment Booklet results can be used with the Form R Occupations Finder for certain clients).

The use of the Assessment Booklet, the Jobs Finder, and the You and Your Job booklet costs about $3.25 per administration. For users desiring an alternative administration format, an audiotape version (1990) is available for $25.00. The alternative administration format is used along with the paper and pencil booklet to enhance reading comprehension for individuals reading below the sixth-grade level.

Canadian (English) and Spanish editions of Form E are also available, based on the 1996 and 1990 editions of the SDS, respectively. Information about the Spanish translation was provided by Susan Edwards (1997, personal communication) of Psychological Assessment Resources. The first translator translated the Form E Assessment Booklet, You and Your Job booklet, and Jobs Finder from English into Spanish. This person had lived in Spain and Mexico before coming to the U.S., and had 33 years of experience as a professional translator with expertise in medical, legal, and literary work. A second translator then translated the Spanish version back into English. This translator had learned English and Spanish simultaneously, living in Chile, Mexico, and Arizona, and had provided many psychoeducational and psychological services to Spanish-speaking persons. Her task was to examine the first translation for content accuracy, maintenance of a fourth- to sixth-grade reading level, and language that is common to all dialects of Spanish. Both translations were then sent to a bilingual psychologist with a PhD in school and clinical child psychology. After input was obtained from these three experts, the Research & Development staff at Psychological Assessment Resources published the Spanish edition of Form E.

A recent study by Glidden-Tracy and Greenwood (1997) examined the adequacy of the Spanish translation of the 1990 Form E using back-translation procedures and structural analyses. Data were collected from 145 undergraduates who completed both the Spanish translation and the back-translation of Form E at 1-week intervals. The authors concluded that SDS Form E had translation equivalence for describing men's vocational interests, but that the assumption of equivalence was equivocal for women. They noted that, whereas back-translations by expert judges are one important piece of evidence in evaluating translated tests, the actual scores from persons seeking career guidance provide even more information about the quality and validity of the translation.

Both our personal and workshop experience have confirmed the high demand for an instrument such as Form E which can be used with individuals who struggle with traditional print-based assessments due to disabilities, limited education, language barriers, or a combination of these factors. The trend of emerging community-based career resource centers or one-stop centers has expanded the clientele for many career services practitioners to include homeless individuals, immigrants, displaced homemakers, and other economically disadvantaged or nonschool-based clients. We conducted a training session on Form E for counselors in our community working with homeless individuals through the local school district's adult and community education program. A former counseling student from our institution was involved in running a career development center through the local Goodwill Industries program. The program is open to all individuals, not just those with disabilities, and has successfully used both Form E and Form R as part of its career assessment program.

Self-Directed Search Form CP

SDS Form CP (Career Planning)

The intent in developing SDS Form CP (Holland, 1990) was to create a version of the SDS designed for adult professionals or adults in transition. According to the PAR catalog, "the SDS Form CP focuses specifically on the needs of employees who have or aspire to greater levels of professional responsibility." In this version, 35% of Form R items were changed to reduce the student and adolescent focus inherent in Form R. Unlike Form R, Form CP does not include the Daydreams or Self-Estimates sections and can be self-administered in 15-25 minutes. There are 36 yes/no items covering the Activities, Competencies, and Career Titles sections of the Assessment Booklet. The components of SDS Form CP include the Assessment Booklet (216 items), the Career Options Finder (1,321 titles), and the Exploring Career Options booklet. The costs for using SDS Form CP are about $4.00 per administration in paper and pencil form.

SDS Form CP is also available in a computer format, the SDS Form CP: Computer Version, which costs about $12.00 per administration. Like Form R and the Career Explorer, SDS Form CP also has a Professional Report Service that involves the use of specially printed, scannable answer sheets. This mail-in scoring service costs less than $9.00 per client and is especially useful if large groups need to be tested in a short period of time. An SDS Form CP interpretive report program, available for $495.00, generates an unlimited number of Form CP reports. As with other forms of the SDS, the SDS Form CP:IR requires that a counselor or administrator enter the client's scores from the paper and pencil version of Form CP.

Form CP of the SDS has both fans and critics. Some praise this version because it is more in step with the needs of HRD and outplacement professionals. They report that eliminating the Daydreams and Self-Estimates sections not only makes the instrument quicker to administer, but also makes it more credible with employed adults, particularly those in professional positions. Shahnasarian (1996a) discussed the use of Form CP in several organizational settings, including using the Artistic scale to provide an additional measure of job candidates' creative interests, as a screening device before inviting job applicants for on-site interviews, as part of an organization's career management course, and as part of an agency's vocational rehabilitation process for workers injured on the job. On the other hand, some (e.g., Wheelahan, 1995) dislike Form CP because it does not include a Daydreams section, which means that an Aspirations scale is not available in this form. They have similar regrets about the missing Self-Estimates section, which eliminates a measure of self-efficacy across the six RIASEC areas. Practitioners working with adult professionals or adults in transition may wish to experiment with both Form CP and Form R, ultimately selecting the version that works most effectively with their specific adult population.

An additional review of SDS Form CP (Bauernfeind, 1992) was published in *Newsnotes*, a newsletter of the Association for Measurement and Evaluation in Counseling and Development. In a report compiled by Bauernfeind, a panel of reviewers were critical of Form CP because no norms for RIASEC scores or item data for specific subpopulations were provided for this version. However, Holland, Fritzsche, and Powell (1994) reported that an initial study of 101 working adults (59% female, 41% male) comparing Form CP and Form R (1985 edition) showed that section scale correlations were .80 or greater, and summary scale correlations were .94 or greater, indicating equivalence of the two forms.

Self-Directed Search Career Explorer

In 1994, the SDS was adapted for use with middle and junior high school students. This is the newest, most recently developed version of the SDS and has an interesting history of its own. For many years, Holland had reservations about developing a version of the SDS for 12- to 16-year-olds. His reservations had to do with the knowledge that career and personal interests are very unstable and not well-defined for younger persons, and there were philosophical, psychometric, and ethical considerations in developing an interest inventory for persons so young. Like personality, interests become better formulated, more reliable, and clearer with increasing age and life experience. However, there was a great need for an assessment tool that could be used in the schools with children in the sixth through eighth grades. For example, states increasingly require such assessments as part of the development of an educational plan for each child in the eighth grade

As evidence accumulated that practitioners were using Form E of the SDS, designed for adults with limited reading, and other less carefully standardized tests and measures, Holland and the staff at Psychological Assessment Resources undertook the development of the SDS Career Explorer. Using a pool of 373 items from earlier versions of the SDS, as well as new items, the authors administered the experimental version to 454 students from the sixth, seventh, and eighth grades (50% female, 50% male). Then, the 204-item final version was administered to a sample of 102 students (29% female, 71% male), yielding internal consistency reliabilities greater than .91 for boys and girls across all summary scales. They were pleasantly surprised to discover that the RIASEC model of interests was apparent in the test results for these young students. Although the intercorrelations were not as clear as with college students or adults using Form R, the basic elements of the hexagon were in place. To avoid inappropriate precision in specifying codes for further educational and occupational exploration, the developers decided to use two-letter codes rather than three-letter codes. Appropriate uses of the SDS Career Explorer are described in the following section.

SDS Career Explorer

The authors of this instrument are John Holland and Amy Powell, a Project Director at Psychological Assessment Resources. It was designed to help junior high and middle school students with educational and vocational planning. It includes a technical information booklet and a teacher's guide. The SDS Career Explorer includes a 216-item Self-Assessment Booklet, which produces two-letter RIASEC codes; an OF-like Careers Booklet, which includes 423 occupations; and an Exploring Your Future with the SDS booklet, which provides additional interpretive information designed for use by students, parents, and teachers. The SDS Career Explorer is packaged in sets of 35 to facilitate classroom use and can be administered and used for about $3.00 per student. We could find only one report in the professional literature regarding the use or evaluation of the SDS Career Explorer. In the Spring 1995 *Australian Journal of Career Development*, the reviewer, Ellen Gibson, noted that the SDS Career Explorer

> could well help students have a general direction in mind and to make choices with a more detailed understanding of their own skills and interests. The only area to present a problem for Australian students would be the use of American terminology and spelling. (pp. 37-38)

The Self-Assessment Booklet closely resembles the Form R format of the SDS. The booklet begins with a daydreams section called "Careers I Have Thought About," which provides four blank lines for students to list career aspirations and enter their two-letter codes. Suggestions for interpreting the two-letter summary code are provided at the end of the booklet.

The Careers Booklet lists only 423 occupations, primarily requiring at least a high school education and especially postsecondary training. The purpose in doing this was to help students understand the higher levels of training required for common occupations and to keep them from being overwhelmed with large numbers of lower-level Realistic and Conventional occupations. The

Careers Booklet is intended to stimulate exploration and realism in educational and career planning. It lists occupations using both two-letter RIASEC codes and alphabetically, to facilitate the completion of the Assessment Booklet within a typical class meeting time.

The 11-page interpretive booklet, Exploring Your Future with the SDS, provides descriptions of the six RIASEC types, the hexagonal arrangement of interests, and lists of reference materials for finding out more about occupations and training programs in schools and colleges.

The seven-page Teacher's Guide provides information to assist classroom teachers and school counselors in using the SDS Career Explorer program. It includes figures describing the six vocational personalities and work environments in terms of their defining characteristics (e.g., values, how viewed by self and others, requirements, and rewards). Brief, basic information on RIASEC theory is presented, and practical suggestions are made for dealing with tied scores and locating occupational reference materials.

SDS Career Explorer: Interpretive Report

This software, published in 1994, provides an interpretive report written by Robert Reardon. Following counselor or administrator entry of a student's SDS Career Explorer summary scores, users receive a 6- to 8-page individualized report in a question-and-answer format covering the student's educational and career interests in relation to Holland's theory using two-letter Holland codes. The contents of this report are adapted from the SDS Career Explorer paper and pencil materials, as well as the DHOC. The report is designed to be read and used by students, as well as parents and classroom teachers. The interpretive report professional manual includes information for counselors and teachers on how use of the software helps schools to meet the National Career Development Guidelines for middle/junior high school.

The sample lists of occupations printed in the interpretive report include information about GED and SVP levels. The former is an estimate of the years of formal education required, and the latter is an estimate of years of on-the-job training required. The SDS Career Explorer: Interpretive Report also includes lists of majors or fields of study for each two-letter code, including the estimated educational levels (e.g., associate, baccalaureate, postgraduate). The program is designed so that every code produces at least 10 occupations or majors for students to review. An optional list of leisure activities may be included on the interpretive report. To our knowledge, no research reports have been published in professional journals regarding the use and evaluation of the SDS Career Explorer Interpretive Report. The program allows for unlimited uses and has a batch feature for producing reports for groups. The program is designed for IBM PCs or compatibles, requires 640K RAM, two disk drives (one hard), and DOS 2.1. The cost of this unlimited-use software program is $299.00.

SDS Career Explorer: Professional Report Service

This version of the SDS Career Explorer uses special scannable answer sheets that are sent to Psychological Assessment Resources for scoring and returned within 24 hours of receipt. Students receive a 6- to 8-page personalized report, such as the one generated by the SDS Career Explorer: Interpretive Report; it includes fields of study, occupations, and leisure options for students based on two-letter codes. The cost of the SDS Career Explorer: Professional Report Service is about $5.50 per administration. The advantage of this product is that it saves staff time and personnel costs for encoding SDS Career Explorer results from the paper and pencil version into the Interpretive Report program and waiting for the reports to be printed; it also reduces the local costs for paper and computer wear. A potential disadvantage is the cost for each student report. However, this service meets the needs of school districts looking for a widescale assessment of middle school student career interests.

Conclusion

This chapter provided an overview of the various forms and formats of the Self-Directed Search and their applications in varied settings with diverse populations. The discussion of the distinctions between computer-based and paper and pencil formats may help practitioners decide which SDS application is best suited to their setting and the clients they serve. Practitioners and researchers are encouraged to continue exploring which version might work best with a particular population. In describing interventions and research results, we need to be more precise in discussing the specific SDS version used, including any Holland-based support materials used in conjunction with the instrument. This information will help readers compare and contrast approaches and develop a clearer understanding of the exact nature of the intervention. This will also help those who want to duplicate successful interventions involving Holland-based materials. In the next chapter, we will expand beyond the SDS to describe and discuss the use of other resources and tools based on Holland's theory that can help us as career services practitioners in better understanding and serving our clients.

Table 13
Comparison of SDS Forms

Feature	Form R	Form E	Form CP	Career Explorer
Paper and pencil version	Yes	Yes	Yes	Yes
Computer version	Yes	No	Yes	Yes
On-line administration	Yes	No	Yes	No
Interpretive report	Yes	No	Yes	Yes
Mail-in version	Yes	No	Yes	Yes
Pages in report	About 12	No	10-11	6-7
Target audience	High school adults	Poor readers*	Adults	Middle school
Non-English versions	Yes	Yes	No	No
Number of letters in Summary Code	3	2	3	2
Number of test items	228	198	216	216
Tests per package	25	25	25	35
Paper and pencil—cost per administration	$3.50	$3.25	$4.00	$3.00
Computer—cost per on-screen admin.	$5.00	NA	$12.00	NA
Mail-in version—cost per report	$7.00	NA	$9.00	$5.50
Number occupations listed	1,335	860	1,320	400
Daydreams section	Yes	Yes	No	Yes
Self-estimates section	Yes	Yes	No	Yes
Additional comments	Daydreams section not included in mail-in version	Some published studies of successful use with persons who have disabilities		Teacher's Guide available

Note. Pricing information is provided in this book to help the reader evaluate the relative merits of using the various SDS resources in professional practice. Although prices increase with the increasing costs of production, the relative prices among the resources remain fairly constant. For current pricing information, phone PAR, Inc. at 1-800-331-8378 or access the publisher's website at www.parinc.com.

6

Non-SDS Holland-Based
Program Materials

One of the most useful aspects of John Holland's theory and the SDS is the full array of interventions and resources that have grown out of this work. These tools enable career services practitioners to fully implement Holland's theory in their own settings and to use the RIASEC typology in a number of different ways to assist clients. This chapter will highlight some of these resources and suggest ways to use them in various settings. We will discuss the purpose, history, and unique applications of each resource, and provide readers with some information about cost based on prices listed in the publisher's Fall 1997 catalog. First, we will examine the *Dictionary of Holland Occupational Codes* (DHOC). Then we will examine Holland-based resources for exploring educational and training options, followed by sections on the Leisure Activities Finder, the Vocational Preference Inventory (VPI), the Position Classification Inventory (PCI), the Career Attitudes and Strategies Inventory (CASI), and the Vocational Exploration and Insight Kit (VEIK).

Dictionary of Holland Occupational Codes (DHOC)

The DHOC, authored by Gary Gottfredson and John Holland (1996a), provides empirically derived alphabetical and Holland code-classified indexes for all the occupations in the *Dictionary of Occupational Titles* (DOT) as well as several other major resources. The codes were updated in this third edition to reflect labor market changes. The DHOC is the fifth attempt since 1972 to extend and increase the validity of the RIASEC classification to all occupations in the U.S. economy. The DHOC is 750 pages, paperbound, and costs $45.00.

A persistent issue in the use of RIASEC theory has been the accurate coding of occupational environments. Users have complained that codes for occupations were different in the various reference resources. Three-letter codes for occupations are difficult to measure for several reasons: (a) Occupations (and their codes) change over time; (b) occupations differ from one organizational or industry setting to another; and (c) valid, reliable instruments for evaluating occupations have been lacking. The DHOC is the standard reference of codes for occupations, and all other Holland-based materials use the DHOC as the source for occupational codes.

In its initial form, the DHOC provided counselors and career information specialists with a valuable tool by assigning Holland codes to the occupations listed in one of the most widely used reference works in the career services field, the DOT. With each new edition, Gottfredson and Holland have improved on their original work. The latest edition "applies the Holland environmental classification to seven of the most widely used occupational classifications and information sources in the U.S." (Gottfredson & Holland, 1996a, p. 1). These commonly used classification systems and information sources cross-referenced in the DHOC include the *Dictionary of Occupational Titles* (DOT), *Occupational Outlook Handbook* (OOH), Occupational Employment Statistics, Standard Occupational Classification, Census Occupational Classification, Classification of Instructional Programs, and *Guide for Occupational Exploration*.

The third edition of the DHOC includes a new index of occupational level, the Complexity Level (Cx), in addition to the GED (General Educational Development Level) and SVP (Specific Vocational Preparation) levels. Gottfredson and Holland wanted to make greater use of job analysis ratings obtained by the Bureau of Labor Statistics (BLS) and to create a single measure of cognitive or substantive complexity associated with each occupation. The Cx rating of an occupation includes BLS ratings for data, GED reasoning, GED math, GED language, SVP, intelligence, verbal aptitude, and numerical aptitude. In a nutshell, the Cx rating of an occupation indicates how much cognitive skill and ability is associated with a particular occupation. For example, the Cx rating is 80 for Nuclear-Fuels Research Engineer (IRC), 37 for Shoe Shiner (CRE), and 68 for Counselor (SAE).

The DHOC provides a comprehensive cross-referencing tool that enables users to link their personal characteristics, as expressed in Holland RIASEC codes, to the major educational and occupational classifications in use today. In our experience, career services settings around the country vary greatly in the methods they used to categorize and organize occupational information. Even our own center has evolved from using DOT codes to using the Standard Occupational Classification (SOC) categories to categorize occupational information. The seven classification systems available in the DHOC allow practitioners to more easily keep their choice of a classification system congruent with Holland-based assessment and information resources used in their facility.

Exploring Educational Options

The major focus for many clients is the exploration of educational options. As with occupations, the number of options for postsecondary training can seem overwhelming. The Holland RIASEC typology is a useful tool for helping students and adults think about educational choices in relation to their own personal characteristics. Once clients have generated a three-letter (or two-letter) Holland code using one form of the SDS or the VPI, they can research educational options using either the Educational Opportunities Finder (EOF; Rosen, Holmberg, & Holland, 1994) or the DHOC.

The current edition of the EOF was published 1994, but it first appeared in 1987 as the College Majors Finder. The EOF lists more than 750 technical and college level fields of study, both alphabetically and by three-letter Holland code and level of educational degree (2-year, 4-year; postgraduate). The EOF helps users relate Holland codes to varied education options; it costs less than $2.00 per reusable booklet.

One of the more popular applications of the link between Holland codes and fields of study, particularly in educational settings, is the development of institution-specific listings of academic programs by Holland code. We have worked in conjunction with the undergraduate advising center at our university to develop such a guide to help students choose their major. Each major in this guide has been assigned a Holland RIASEC code. A sample page from this guide is reproduced in Appendix C. We have also created a more "gross" classification of majors at our institution using a single Holland category (see Appendix D). This handout is used frequently by our career advisors to introduce the link between fields of study and Holland classification.

The UMaps project at the University of Maryland (Jacoby, Rue, & Allen, 1984) is another good example of applying RIASEC theory in education. Working out of an Office of Commuter Affairs within the Division of Student Affairs, the authors reported a program to help students become aware of diverse campus opportunities, options, and resources related to RIASEC types. They created large posters displayed on bulletin boards and brochures (UMaps) distributed by advisors. Each of the six RIASEC UMaps had a standard layout, including areas of study (with office locations and phone numbers), sample career possibilities, internship and volunteer options, and student organizations and activities related to each type. Each map also had a brief description of the RIASEC type and a brief self-assessment related to interests and skills. A sample UMap is included in Spokane and Shultheis's (1996) chapter on Holland's theory.

Leisure Activities Finder (LAF)

One of the early criticisms of Holland's theory was that it was too limiting, that it tended to slot people into specific jobs, and that it did not help clients deal with broader life and career issues. Indeed, career counselors know that some persons cannot find opportunities to express their interests, values, and skills in their jobs and have to look outside paid employment to find life satisfaction. The Leisure Activities Finder (LAF; Holmberg, Rosen, & Holland, 1990) provides a link between RIASEC codes and leisure options. The LAF can be particularly useful in career, outplacement, retirement, and leisure planning. It lists more than 750 leisure activities alphabetically and by two-letter Holland codes.

One study (Miller, 1991) examined the use of the LAF with a group of 70 graduate students who completed the SDS and then listed their preferred leisure activities. These activities were coded using the LAF, and the level of congruence between the RIASEC codes of the SDS and the leisure activities were computed. The author found a moderately high level of congruence between the two sets of codes, indicating some support for using the LAF to identify possibly satisfying leisure activities. However, it might be noted that some counselors working in educational settings have been critical of the LAF because it includes leisure activities considered to be morally wrong or illegal for youth below certain ages (e.g., beer making and gambling).

The LAF costs about $1.90 per booklet, which may be reused.

Vocational Preference Inventory (VPI)

The Vocational Preference Inventory (VPI; Holland, 1985b) has a very special history of its own. Recognizing the power of occupational stereotypes and the meanings that persons attached to them, Holland created an unobtrusive, innocuous personality and interest inventory that records user responses to occupational titles. The VPI was revised eight times between 1953 and 1985, and includes 160 occupations representing RIASEC personality types. The VPI report includes scores on the six RIASEC Holland types and five other dimensions (i.e., Self-Control, Status, Masculinity/Femininity, Infrequency, and Acquiescence). It can be completed in 15-30 minutes and scored in 1 minute. VPI raw scores can be used with the SDS Occupations Finder, the EOF, the LAF, and the DHOC to explore career options in relation to the client's code. It costs about $1.00 per administration. A Vocational Preference Inventory Computer Version (Rose & Holland, 1985) is also available. The VPI Computer Version includes an administration, scoring, and interpretive program for the

1985 edition of the VPI; the interpretive report by Robert Rose includes all scores, codes, interpretive information, and lists of occupations related to codes, at a cost of about $6.00 per administration.

Drummond (1986) noted that Holland has suggested four main uses of the VPI: (a) a brief personality inventory for persons from high school through adult, (b) a helpful addition to a personality battery, (c) an interest inventory, and (d) a useful tool for career research.

Reviewers have had mixed reactions to using the VPI in these ways. Drummond (1986) seems reluctant to use the VPI as a stand-alone personality measure but thinks it can be a useful tool for career counseling, interest measurement, and research under certain circumstances and recognizing its limitations. Shepard (1989) and Vacc (1989) agreed that the VPI accomplished its stated purpose as a brief personality test and interest inventory, but they lamented the lack of information about unresolved psychometric issues and urged additional study of the test's technical properties.

Although the VPI has a long history in Holland's work, it is not as familiar as the SDS to most practitioners. The development of the VPI led to the development of RIASEC theory, which, in turn, led to the development of the SDS. As a result, the SDS and the VPI are similar in that both are measures of Holland's theory and both can be used in career counseling. Holland, Powell, and Fritzsche (1994) compared and contrasted the VPI and SDS as follows:

1. The VPI enjoys wider use in research and organizational psychology applications; it is more oriented toward traditional one-to-one interventions, whereas the SDS relies more on client initiative.

2. The VPI is a psychological inventory, whereas the SDS is a simulated career counseling activity.

3. The VPI assesses four dimensions that are not included in the SDS.

4. The SDS evaluates activities, competencies, and self-ratings in addition to occupational likes and dislikes.

5. The VPI is quicker and cheaper to administer.

In summary, the VPI provides a rapid means of generating a scientifically valid Holland code without providing the more intensive intervention that results from use of the SDS, and it allows for the assessment of additional personality factors in an unobtrusive manner. In his discussion of using the Holland typology in business settings for employee selection and development, Rose (1996) provides numerous case examples based on clients' VPI results.

Case Study Using the VPI: The Boat Yard

The following case study shows how the VPI can be used from an organizational perspective. In this example, a colleague of ours used the VPI as part of an organizational consultation and diagnostic activity in a boat yard based in the northwest. The VPI was one component of a project that assessed supervisor ratings of employees, employee job satisfaction, and the relationship between job satisfaction, work ethic, and employee work role. The worker's own VPI code was also compared to the code of the job performed by the worker. Not surprisingly, this work setting was dominated by R types, with the summary code for the group being RAI. The Realistic type contained the largest number of employees and had the highest average score of the six personality types (Leierer, 1990). The VPI results were shared with the employees and supervisors. The lack of C types in the environment contributed to some poor record-keeping procedures and problems with keeping track of work materials and tools. One of the suggestions to management was to consider instituting procedures or hiring personnel with a focus on improving the organization's attention to details (i.e., more C types), especially with regard to accounting and purchasing procedures.

Position Classification Inventory (PCI)

Earlier Holland-based instruments and resource tools focused on the classification of individuals, occupations, and educational and leisure options. The publication of the Position Classification Inventory (PCI; Gottfredson & Holland, 1991) made it possible for practitioners and workers to focus on positions within organizations and to classify positions according to the RIASEC typology. The PCI may be used with the SDS or the VPI to measure RIASEC codes for job positions and persons. It consists of 84 items and can be completed and scored in fewer than 10 minutes. Items are organized under the following headings: activities, outlooks, personal style or values, skills/abilities/personal characteristics, abilities/skills/talents and frequency of activities, and personal characteristics. The PCI costs about $2.00 per administration, and a PCI Professional Report Service costs about $2.50 per administration.

We found one review of the PCI (Austin, 1993) in *Measurement and Evaluation in Counseling and Development*. This reviewer, an industrial/organizational psychologist, concluded that the PCI was useful but that additional evidence of construct validity was needed. Austin noted that the PCI holds promise for both researchers and practitioners.

The PCI can be useful in several ways. For example, different positions within the same occupation are sometimes classified differently when the PCI is used. Also, the same occupational title may be applied to jobs that are really quite different. Helping workers and their supervisors understand the demands of particular positions and how these demands fit or don't fit with a particular employee's personality type can be valuable information in organizational career management. Organizations might choose to use the PCI to classify positions at a variety of levels throughout the organization. This information can be communicated to employees via print and electronic means to help them manage their careers within the organization.

The PCI can also be used in individual coaching sessions between employees and supervisors. The code for an employee's position can be compared to the code from the employee's SDS or VPI results. If the employee is happy in her or his present position but lacks some of the necessary skills required by the position, the supervisor can help the employee identify training and development activities that would develop skills more congruent with the demands of the position. If the employee is unhappy with the position, he or she might review information on other opportunities, classified by Holland type, that might be a better fit and explore ways with the supervisor to move into alternative positions.

In addition to individual counseling, the PCI can be used with work teams to explore perceptions of work tasks for a particular position. Organizations often have problems when employees assigned to the same position have differing perceptions of what the job demands or entails. Asking employees in the same position to complete the PCI might provide useful information for a small group discussion with the supervisor about how to work more effectively as a team. A variation on the activity might be a work team where persons actually have unique roles instead of having the same position for everyone. They could use the PCI as a "shorthand" way of describing their unique contribution to the team. This group activity might be a way of focusing on the strengths of each team member and the special set of skills, values, and perspectives he or she brings to the team.

From our perspective, the PCI has not been fully exploited for all the applications where it might provide useful. For additional information on the use of the PCI in organizational settings, readers are referred to Shahnasarian's book *The SDS in Business and Industry* (1996b) and the PCI Manual (Gottfredson & Holland, 1991).

Career Attitudes and Strategies Inventory (CASI)

One of the newest instruments in the Holland family of career intervention tools is the Career Attitudes and Strategies Inventory (CASI; Holland &

Gottfredson, 1994), designed for use with employed and unemployed adults. It went through three revisions during development, and the present version was derived from item analyses of the previous versions. The 130 items and nine scales cover a wide range of areas pertaining to a person's work situation including: Job Satisfaction, Work Involvement, Skill Development, Dominant Style, Career Worries, Interpersonal Abuse, Family Commitment, Risk-Taking Style, and Geographical Barriers.

In addition to these scales, the CASI includes a checklist of 21 career obstacles about which many persons express concerns in relation to their career development (e.g., health and finances). The CASI costs about $2.50 per administration. It is self-scored, self-profiled, and can be self-interpreted in approximately 35 minutes.

We found two reviews of the CASI in Buros' *Supplement to the Twelfth Mental Measurements Yearbook* (Impara & Conoley, 1996). Brown (1996) saw "serious drawbacks presented by the lack of adequate norms and limitations in the determination of its validity" (p. 61), but noted that he "would certainly find it useful as a preinterview survey, a device to generate discussion, or to identify potentially problematic areas that would benefit from further exploration" (p. 61). Kinnier (1996) also worried about the validity of the CASI in this early stage of development and refinement and reported that some scales had more compelling face validity and empirical support at the present time (e.g., Job Satisfaction, Skill Development, Dominant Style, Career Worries, Risk-taking Style, and Career Obstacles).

The CASI can be used as a tool in several service delivery modes. For example, in a setting where there is both brief, self-directed assistance and one-on-one counseling, it might be used as a screening tool to determine who needs more in-depth assistance. It could also be used with an adult transitions group, and the issues assessed by the CASI could be the focus of group discussions.

One of the criticisms of Holland's instruments and of his theory was that some events and issues presented by clients seeking career services are not captured or explained by the SDS and the RIASEC typology. The CASI can supplement other Holland assessments and provide further information about how individuals view their work situation and what the sources of their difficulties might be. A case example might be helpful here.

"The Case of Carol"

"Carol" is a 39-year-old training manager at a manufacturing corporation that produces educational games and toys. Except for a 3-year stint in marketing management, she has worked in varied positions related to personnel and human resource management for the last 15 years; by all accounts she has been relatively successful in this field. With each move, she has risen up the career ladder into positions with greater responsibility. A coding of her work history, including her current position, reveals a series of SEC positions, with the order of the letters ranging from ESC to SCE. Both her master's and bachelor's degrees were in education, a field which includes S and E aspects as well. Carol had come seeking career assistance, describing herself as dissatisfied with her current position. She completed SDS Form CP and had summary scores of R=3, I=7, A=15, S=23, E=22, C=18. Carol is someone whose SDS summary code (SEC) appears to match very well with her current position.

To try to understand a little bit more about Carol's situation, the counselor asked her to complete the PCI and the CASI. Here we begin to see what may be the source of some of Carol's discomfort with her present work situation. Her PCI results are reproduced below in Figure 5.

Her present job appears to demand more of an Artistic personality than Carol has. Although Training Manager is coded SEC in the latest edition of the DHOC, this particular work setting appears to place a higher value on A qualities because of the nature of the product it produces, children's games. Although A is the fourth highest letter in Carol's CP results, she has had little reinforcement for her A skills and interests over the years. She has found herself working primarily in settings where, along with S and E demands, she was forced to deal with more C tasks, repetitive procedures, and the forms and rules associated with more traditional personnel and human resource development work. Her CASI results also provide some insight into the sources of her job dissatisfaction (see Figure 6). Of particular note are her scores on the Job Satisfaction scale and the Career Worries scale. In addition, she listed "lack of self-confidence" as a career obstacle, and under "anything else?" she wrote "clear career goal."

Carol can do her job, but she has become bored with it. It has "lost its meaning." She has enjoyed E and S type tasks and has done them well, but she loses interest when the initial challenge is gone. Although her work setting is not intolerant, she feels little reinforcement for doing good work. Her "career worries," as illustrated by her raw score of 60 on this CASI scale, have kept her stuck in her present position. Carol's results illustrate how the concerns of many clients go beyond the link between personal characteristics and options, extending to broader issues in an individual's work and life situation that can quickly and easily be assessed by using additional Holland-based tools. See chapter 10 for additional case studies that illustrate the use of Holland-based resources.

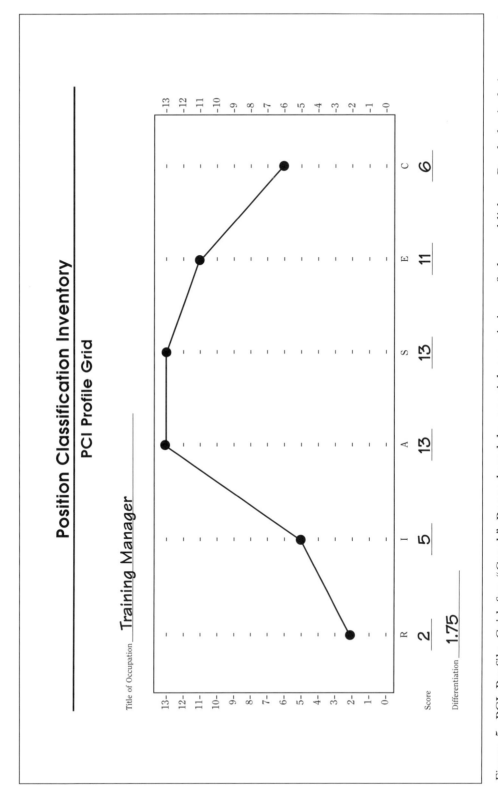

Figure 5. PCI Profile Grid for "Carol." Reproduced by special permission of the publisher, Psychological Assessment Resources, Inc., from the *Position Classification Inventory* Profile Grid, copyright © 1991 by Psychological Assessment Resources, Inc.

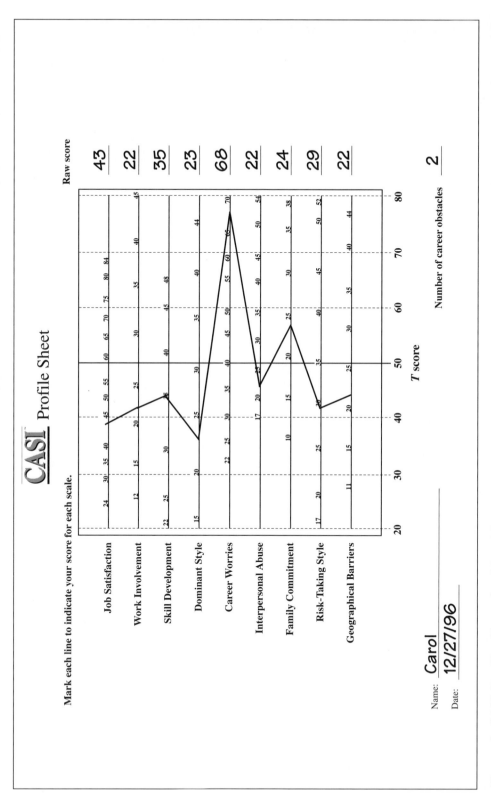

Figure 6. CASI Profile Sheet for "Carol." Reproduced by special permission of the publisher, Psychological Assessment Resources, Inc., from the *Career Attitudes and Strategies Inventory* Profile Sheet, copyright © 1992, 1993, 1994 by Psychological Assessment Resources, Inc.

Vocational Exploration and Insight Kit (VEIK)

The VEIK (Holland, 1992) was developed by John Holland with the attributed assistance of several persons, including Janice Birk, Jacqueline Cooper, Cindy Dewey, Robert Dolliver, Ricki Takai, and Leona Tyler. Holland chose to list several of these people as codevelopers because of their earlier groundbreaking pro bono work in the development of vocational card sorts. The VEIK was first reported in the professional literature in 1979 (Takai & Holland, 1979; Talbot & Birk, 1979).

The VEIK program includes an elaborate 15-step procedure built around the SDS Form R. A four-page Professional User's Guide is available. The VEIK also includes the You and Your Career booklet, an 84-item occupational card sort, and an eight-page Action Plan workbook. The first 10 steps in the VEIK revolve around use of the card sort, followed by four steps involving the SDS and a final step involving the workbook. The VEIK is designed for highly motivated clients seeking career guidance beyond that provided by the SDS alone or clients experiencing career decision making problems and desiring a more active role in career guidance. It is completed in several hours and may be done in individual or group counseling sessions. The consumable VEIK workbook costs about $1.00 per administration; the two sets of reusable card sort decks cost less than $25.00

The VEIK was reviewed by Daniels (1985) and Tittle (1985). Daniels applauded its adaptability but noted possible constraints involving staff time and budgets. Both reviewers noted that more information is needed about the value of VEIK in comparison to the SDS or Vocational Card Sort alone, as well as information about programmatic implementation of a VEIK program.

Conclusion

In this chapter we have reviewed several of the most important components of a Holland-based system of career interventions that support the Self-Directed Search. We examined the DHOC as the primary resource for information about occupations and the materials that provide information about education and training options. The chapter then moved to examine the Leisure Activities Finder, the Vocational Preference Inventory (VPI), the Position Classification Inventory (PCI), the Career Attitudes and Strategies Inventory (CASI), and the Vocational Exploration and Insight Kit (VEIK). These materials, like the SDS, are marked by their direct, straightforward presentation of information to counselors and clients. Together, they comprise a rather extensive array of materials to use in career counseling (see chapter 10) and in broader career programs (see chapter 11).

7

Interpreting the SDS

In using the SDS as counselors or helpers, we are faced with choices about how to best interpret the results to a particular client. This chapter seeks to take practitioners beyond the traditional approach to SDS interpretation. It has been our experience that all too often the focus is on a narrow, limited "end result"— the three-letter code and the occupations associated with that code. The client likes the occupations or doesn't, and that's where the interpretation ends.

Chapters 1-6 described the connection between Holland's theory and the related instruments, including the diagnostic concepts embedded in the theory. Our goal is to encourage practitioners to more fully use the variety of "diagnostic" tools contained in clients' SDS results, along with other Holland-based instruments, to expand their thinking about the complexity of their clients' situations and the best ways to intervene. This chapter reviews key concepts derived from Holland's theory that can provide a conceptual basis for interpreting a client's SDS results.

Before we discuss specific items that might be the focus of an interpretive session with a client, we will highlight several factors that may affect the nature of any SDS interpretation. Sometimes, what happens before, during, and after the SDS is administered (e.g., the office setting, the policies, and the staff involved) is more important in interpreting the results than the instrument itself. Practitioners reading this book will have to make their own judgments about which office policies and procedures might work best in their setting. The next section will examine some of these issues.

The Setting for Using the SDS

In considering how to use the SDS and related Holland instruments in your setting, you may find it helpful to consider some of the following issues and questions.

Before, During, and After Using the SDS

What are the office policies that address what happens before, during, and after the SDS is used? Policies and procedures regarding the use and interpretation of the SDS can be critical in helping clients make the best use of their SDS results.

Before the SDS is administered, counselors should understand any decisions their organization has made regarding the use of career assessments in general and the SDS in particular. Ideally, decisions about using the SDS and other guidance activities will follow a careful program development model such as the one described in chapter 11. The following questions identify issues that an organization might want to consider in designing career interventions using the SDS:

1. Is the SDS going to be used as a career guidance activity, as an assessment of interests, or both?

2. Are other career assessments or computer-based guidance systems (e.g., SIGI PLUS, Choices, MBTI) also used in the setting? Are there policies regarding which instrument is preferred for particular types of clients?

3. Do staff have complete freedom to use any career intervention with a client?

4. If prescreening instruments such as My Vocational Situation (MVS), the Career Thoughts Inventory (CTI; Sampson, Peterson, Lenz, Reardon, & Saunders, 1996a), or the Career Decision Scale (CDS; Osipow, Carney, Winer, Yanico, & Koschir, 1976) are used, are there local norms available to determine who might best benefit from an intervention such as the SDS?

5. How much time and explanation is given to the client before the SDS is administered?

6. Is the SDS completed as part of a drop-in visit, an intake, or a scheduled appointment?

7. Will an initial interpretation of the SDS be done immediately after it is completed, or will the interpretation be scheduled for a later time?

8. Will the interpretation be done by the same counselor who assigned the SDS initially?

9. Will copies of SDS results be kept in the office, given to the client, or both?

10. Do clients complete SDS materials only within the confines of the particular services setting, or are they allowed to take them home?

11. Is the You and Your Career booklet handed out at the same time as the Assessment Booklet and The Occupations Finder?

12. What criteria are used to determine whether a client uses the paper and pencil version or the computer version of the SDS?

13. Are the DHOC and other SDS-related support materials available in the office for use immediately after the SDS Assessment Booklet is completed?

Answers to these questions in the form of policies or guidelines can significantly affect the way the SDS is used and interpreted. The SDS can be used on a nonscheduled, drop-in basis; we are aware of some settings, though, that require the client to make an appointment at the testing office and come in a second time for administration of the SDS. In the latter case, the scheduled use of the SDS is no different from the Strong Interest Inventory, and the opportunity for the client to obtain immediate assessment results is lost. In some settings, only the testing office can administer tests—but is the SDS only a test? This issue was examined in chapter 4, and the answer may determine who administers and interprets the SDS and when it is administered in a particular setting.

What version of the SDS is being used? Holland designed the original Form R of the SDS to be self-administering, self-scoring, and capable of being interpreted by the user. Some alternative forms of the SDS, such as the computer version or the Professional Report Service version, require additional follow-up with regard to the client report, either printing it from the computer or waiting for the client's results to be processed and returned by mail. If the service setting is comprehensive in nature, it might be desirable to have SDS Forms CP and E as well as the Career Explorer available for adult career transitions, adults with limited English ability, and middle school youth, respectively.

Another issue to consider is how much time the client and counselor have. Does the client have enough time to complete the SDS and have a follow-up meeting with the counselor or career advisor to review the results? In our setting, clients are not required to receive a personal interpretation after completing the SDS, but they are encouraged to follow up with a career advisor if they would like help in understanding their results and making plans for next steps. We do not maintain a folder of SDS results, and client folders are maintained only for those clients served on an individual appointment basis.

Policy Options Governing Use of the SDS

There are some further questions to consider regarding policies surrounding the administration and interpretation of the SDS. Each setting will need to evaluate SDS administration options and set policies and procedures regarding its use.

1. Does the client read the You and Your Career booklet or the computer-generated interpretive report first before interacting with a counselor or other human services professional?

In general, we have found it is highly desirable for the client to read the SDS interpretation materials before talking with a counselor. In some instances, however, the client is too frustrated or too anxious to benefit from such independent work. This, in itself, is diagnostic and may help guide the interpretation of the SDS results.

2. Who is allowed to interpret SDS results with clients?

In our setting, there are clerical support personnel, a professional librarian, undergraduate student assistants, paraprofessional career advisors, and professional counseling staff. Only trained paraprofessionals and members of the professional counseling staff are allowed to provide interpretations of client SDS results. Staff SDS training activities include taking the SDS and having it interpreted by an experienced staff member, reading the *SDS Professional User's Guide*, interpreting the SDS for a client under supervision, completing the Counselor Self-Test in the Professional User's Guide, and discussing issues associated with using the SDS more effectively. An adapted version of the Counselor Self-Test has been included in Appendix E.

3. What role does the practitioner play in creating a cognitive schema to aid clients in "walking" through their SDS results?

We have found that, although the SDS materials provide interpretive information and detailed information on suggested next steps, clients often do need some encouragement and help regarding how to apply the information. In an ideal world, clients get their three-letter code, find interesting and relevant career or educational options, identify their first choice, and then take steps to implement their decision—we all know it doesn't always work that way.

4. If you are using a computer version of the SDS, how much information from the Professional Summary is shared with the client?

In some instances, the use of the technical information in the Professional Summary helps structure the interpretation of the SDS as a simulated career problem solving activity and enables clients to obtain a more complete understanding of where they are stuck in the career decision making process. This may be especially useful to clients with Investigative and Social or Artistic codes.

Practitioners need to consider how to best use the Professional Summary generated by the computer version of the SDS in their own setting. In our setting, there is no set policy related to this issue. In an informal survey of nine career advisors, six indicated that they occasionally or frequently review the Professional Summary with clients. Career advisors are allowed to make their own decisions about how much of the Professional Summary is shared with clients. We do not recommend simply providing the Professional Summary to clients as part of their printout without some intervention and interpretation by a staff member.

One of the advantages of having access to the information on the Professional Summary is that it makes it easier for practitioners to fully exploit the diagnostic indicators derived from Holland's theory, instead of simply focusing on the three-letter summary code. The next section will expand on how these concepts can be used in more fully understanding how best to assist persons with their career problem solving and decision making.

Drawing Upon RIASEC Theory

As we have noted, one of the strengths of the SDS, in comparison to other career inventories, is its grounding in Holland's theory of vocational choice. We have observed that some practitioners have a tendency to shy away from theory because they view it as not easily understood or applied (i.e., it has little relevance to practice). All too often, the focus in the interpretation of clients' SDS results has been to simply deal with a client's reaction to the occupations associated with the various combinations of his or her code. If the client is pleased (i.e., the SDS expanded the client's knowledge of options, and the options seem to be a reasonable fit, given the client's view of himself or herself), then the client and the counselor go away happy.

Consider as an alternative one of the following scenarios:

- The client was not pleased with the options related to the SDS summary code; the client was concerned that an occupation already being considered didn't come up on the list of options associated with his or her three-letter code.

- The client was overwhelmed with the number of options presented and wanted the SDS to narrow down the options and help to specify the "one occupation that is right for me."

Our experience is that when one of these three scenarios unfolds, the counselor tends to "bail out" of further use of the SDS. In these three instances, the client responses seem to suggest that the SDS did not help solve the career problem or decision. The SDS is abandoned in favor of some other activity or assessment. The client may feel that the counselor didn't help, or the counselor may be thinking, "Maybe I should have used some other instrument or intervention."

An alternative to the above sequence of events is that the counselor fully exploits all the diagnostic information embedded in the SDS and uses that information to help determine where the client may be "stuck" and what next steps might be most appropriate. Rather than abandoning the SDS, the counselor digs more deeply into the SDS itself as a career problem solving simulation and stays with RIASEC theory as a source of ideas for understanding what is happening with the client and how to be more helpful.

All too often in our workshops with practitioners, many of whom have been using the SDS for years, we find that practitioners often don't make full use of the helpful ideas in the *SDS Professional User's Guide.* Although we think practitioners can benefit from using this book to improve their practice with the SDS, it should not be considered a substitute or alternative to the *Professional User's Guide.* We realize that counseling types, usually individuals with fairly large Ss, may not relish reading manuals. Sound practice and ethical guidelines, however, dictate that use of any assessment tool be accompanied by solid grounding in the manuals that accompany that tool. The next section will draw on key concepts from Holland's theory, which have been described in his 1997 edition of *Making Vocational Choices* and the most recent edition of the *SDS Professional User's Guide,* to describe a framework practitioners can use in gaining a better picture of a client's career situation.

Applying Holland Typology Concepts in Interpreting the SDS

In chapter 2, we introduced eight basic assumptions undergirding Holland's RIASEC theory. In the following sections of this chapter, these concepts will be briefly defined and guidelines for using them in interpreting a client's SDS profile will be provided. Brief definitions of many of the terms used in the theory are provided in the Glossary (see Appendix A). These concepts have been researched and reported in the professional literature, some to a greater degree than others and with mixed results. As Holland (1996a, 1997) himself pointed out, the extent to which research supports these diagnostic constructs varies. The order in which the concepts are presented is based on our view of the level of research support they have received and the extent to which they have proven useful in helping us better assist clients with their career problem solving and decision making.

Table 14 provides a quick overview of these basic interpretive ideas. The decision rules provided in Table 15, which are used in determining whether a particular indicator is high, average, or low, are derived from the computer-based version of the SDS (Reardon & Ona, 1996). These concepts are also

Table 14
SDS Interpretive Ideas

Basic Interpretive Ideas

1. **Congruence**—degree of fit between a summary code and code of current aspiration; or agreement between codes of occupations, people, or aspirations.
2. **Personality**—general description of interests, traits, goals, and values implied by SDS Profile.

Supplementary Interpretive Ideas

3. **Qualifying Ideas**—likelihood of revising basic interpretive ideas with respect to the following six sources of information; high levels of items a-e imply stability, tenure, and persistence of personality, careers, aspirations.

   a. *Coherence of Aspirations or Work History*—level of agreement between the most recent code and earlier codes.

   b. *Vocational Identity*—level of identity as measured by the My Vocational Situation.

   c. *Consistency*—position of first two code letters on the hexagon; high levels are adjacent; medium, alternate; low, opposite.

   d. *Differentiation*—shape of the profile (i.e., flat or spiked; well-defined profiles are highly differentiated).

   e. *Commonness*—common codes are more stable, and rare codes associated with change.

   f. *Professional Judgment*—interview impressions and other test data; client's interpretive statements, along with age, race, sex, education, and socioeconomic status.

Note. From the *Self-Directed Search Professional User's Guide* (p. 42), by J. L. Holland, A. B. Powell, and B. A. Fritzsche, 1994, Odessa, FL: Psychological Assessment Resources. Copyright © 1994 by Psychological Assessment Resources, Inc. Adapted with permission.

discussed in chapters 9 and 10 to help guide readers through the case study analysis.

Basic Interpretive Ideas

The first two basic interpretive ideas that practitioners can use to begin to understand a client's career situation are congruence and the personality characteristics reflected in the client's three-letter RIASEC code.

Congruence

As discussed in chapters 2 and 3, high levels of congruence are indicative of a person maintaining the code of his or her first occupational aspiration in the future. This idea can be helpful when interpreting the SDS. When you think about congruence, think about any two codes you want to compare. You want to know the level of agreement between them, whether it is high, low, etc. Ask yourself how similar the codes are to each other. The most common interpretation of congruence in using the SDS involves comparing the client's SDS summary code with the Daydreams or Aspirations summary code. If you are

Table 15
SDS Case Study Decision Rules

	High	Average	Low
Congruence	≥86th %ile	16th–85th %ile	≤15th %ile
Codes	SE	AI	CR
Coherence	First three aspirations have same first letter	First letter of first aspiration also first letter in second or third aspiration	First letter of first aspiration not in second or third aspiration
Vocational identity (VI)	≥1 *SD* above mean	mean ±1 *SD*	≥1 *SD* below mean
Occupational information (OI)	4	2–3	0–1
Barriers (BA)	4	2–3	0–1
Consistency	First two letters adjacent	First two letters alternate	First two letters opposite
Differentiation	≥86th %ile	16th–85th %ile	≤15th %ile
Commonness	≥4.50%	0.11–4.49%	≤0.10%

Note. From the *Self-Directed Search Form R: Computer Version User's Guide* (p. 19), by R. C. Reardon and N. Ona, 1996, Odessa, FL: Psychological Assessment Resources. Copyright © 1996 by Psychological Assessment Resources, Inc. Adapted with permission.

administering the paper and pencil SDS, some minimal calculation is required. It might be tempting to simply "eyeball" two codes and speculate on their level of agreement, but Holland encourages practitioners to get into the habit of using the worksheet for congruence provided in Appendix C of the *SDS Professional User's Guide.* A portion of the worksheet and the table used to look up percentile ranks for a particular client's score are provided in Figure 7. You are encouraged to use this worksheet when working with a client's results. For the computer version of the SDS Form R, the level of congruence is calculated for you and reported in the Professional Summary.

In an ideal situation, you will have clients whose aspirations or occupational daydreams match well with how they describe themselves on the various sections of the SDS. For example, the client's Daydreams summary code and the SDS summary code are both SEC, demonstrating the highest level of congruence. When this happens, (i.e., the two measures of interests highly agree), the counselor and client may view this as a positive sign that the client will, indeed, find work satisfaction in the Social area.

But what happens if congruence is low (e.g., SEC-RSI or SEC-AIR), where the first letters are opposites or where none of the letters in the first code appear in the second? In such instances, where the signs are negative, there

Draw Xs through the number when two letters match. Sum the values of the Xed out numbers. Look up total score in the percentile ranks table to get the percentile.

Example:

	Code Two			
Code One	1. _S_	2. _A_	3. _R_	No Match
1. _S_	⊗	10	4	0
2. _A_	10	⊗	2	0
3. _E_	4	2	1	⊗
Agreement =	_22_ +	_5_ +	_0_ =	_27_
Percentile =	_94-97_			

	Code Two			
Code One	1. _____	2. _____	3. _____	No Match
1. _____	22	10	4	0
2. _____	10	5	2	0
3. _____	4	2	1	0
Agreement =	_____ +	_____ +	_____ =	_____
Percentile =	_____			

**Percentile Ranks for Iachan Agreement Index Scores
for the 1994 Normative Sample**

Agreement score	High school students		College students		Adults		Agreement score
	Males	Females	Males	Females	Males	Females	
28	99	99	99	99	99	99	28
27	97	94	95	94	97	97	27
26	90	84	85	85	92	90	26
24	87	80	80	79	89	84	24
23	76	67	65	65	75	71	23
22	71	59	60	58	72	68	22
21	65	52	52	48	62	60	21
20	59	50	49	45	59	54	20
16	54	44	45	39	53	48	16
14	51	40	41	33	51	43	14
13	43	34	37	26	44	39	13
12	41	32	36	23	44	32	12
11	34	27	29	19	38	26	11
10	29	23	26	16	34	22	10
9	23	19	21	12	30	19	9
8	18	15	18	9	25	15	8
6	16	14	17	8	24	13	6
5	13	10	12	6	16	9	5
4	12	7	10	5	15	7	4
2	6	4	4	3	8	4	2
1	2	1	1	1	5	1	1
0	1	<1	<1	<1	2	0	0
M	15.92	17.75	17.40	18.90	15.37	17.19	M
SD	8.01	8.04	8.31	7.24	8.54	7.68	SD
n	327	458	286	540	142	237	n

Note. Sample size varies slightly because not all respondents completed all items. Some agreement scores cannot occur (3, 7, 15, 17, 18, 19, 25). These anomalies are due to the particular weights used to calculate the index. Calculations of agreement for high school and college students were between obtained Summary Code and the Summary Code for their occupational daydreams. Calculations of agreement for adults were between obtained Summary Code and the Summary Code for their actual occupations.

Figure 7. Congruence worksheet for calculating the Iachan Agreement Index for the SAE code. From the *Self-Directed Search Professional User's Guide* (pp. 93 and 96), by J. L. Holland, A. B. Powell, and B. A. Fritzsche, 1985, 1987, 1994, Odessa, FL: Psychological Assessment Resources. Copyright © 1994 by Psychological Assessment Resources, Inc. Adapted with permission.

are interpretive questions to ask and issues to explore with the client related to congruence:

1. Ask the client, from his or her perspective, which of the two codes makes the most sense. Is it the Daydreams summary code or the SDS summary code? Given that they both are useful predictors of vocational interests and future occupational activity, explore both codes with the client. In comparing and contrasting the two codes, use RIASEC theory to create a possible synthesis of the codes that makes sense to the client. The client is learning to use the RIASEC typology as a new schema to think about self and, ultimately, work-related options.

2. When dealing with adult career changers, we have often found that the SDS summary code reflects where they've been and the Daydreams code reflects their aspirations for the future. One example is a client who has been in a state office job (C-type work) for many years but has A as the first letter of his or her Aspirations summary code. Practitioners can work with such a client and ask, What are you willing to do to move from your C job or to include more A activities in your life? Perhaps an A-oriented hobby could be the focus of a new business. Perhaps the client can volunteer for assignments at work that draw on A interests and skills (e.g., the agency wants to redesign its brochures and needs help designing a logo for the cover). Perhaps the person can pursue A-oriented continuing education classes. We have found that many clients readily grasp the RIASEC typology and can then use it to work around such indications of low congruence.

Low congruence may be a topic that warrants further discussion between the client and counselor, but it is often easily addressed through creative brainstorming and discussion of the client's aspirations. Holland has suggested that if congruence is low, the most productive route to follow is with the Daydreams code or the code of the client's first aspiration (Holland, Powell, & Fritzsche, 1994).

Personality Characteristics

A second basic interpretive idea has to do with the client's code itself. As we mentioned before, the tendency of most clients and many practitioners is to focus only on the three-letter code and the occupations associated with the combinations of that code.

In interpreting the SDS, however, counselors need to consider their clients' personal characteristics and how these may help or hinder them in the career problem solving and decision-making process. It is a powerful exercise to think about what can be learned from a client when one considers the interests, traits, and other qualities implied by an SDS code, particularly by the first code letter. Ask yourself, "Who is sitting in front of me? Are they a big S, I, or E? How will the characteristics associated with being an S or an I affect the client's ability to negotiate the tasks associated with making career life plans? To what extent will I, as a helper, consider the client's Holland type in prescribing interventions? What characteristics related to the client's Holland type will help or hinder him or her in the career problem solving and decision making process? How can I strengthen and capitalize on the positive characteristics and minimize the impact of the negative ones? How will my own Holland type influence my ability to help a particular client?"

There has been some research looking at the relationship between career interventions and clients' Holland type (Lenz, Reardon, & Sampson, 1993; Kivlighan & Shapiro, 1987; Mahalik, 1996). Other articles on this topic are more anecdotal or as one person noted are "untested speculation" (G. Gottfredson, personal communication, 1996). In his book *Making Vocational Choices* (1985, 1997), Holland suggested that the RIASEC types were equipped to cope with career changes in the following decreasing order: SEIACR. Think about your own experience. What qualities about R types or C types might make career problem solving and decision making more difficult? How would you approach helping an A type with career problems versus an I type? Some additional ideas about ways to intervene with different types and the qualities that might interfere with this process are provided in Table 16. Rosenberg and Smith (1985) described a similar approach in their article discussing strategies for career counseling based on Holland types (see Table 17).

You are encouraged to add your own thoughts and ideas to these tables based on your experience. Together with your clients, you can help them identify career problem-solving activities that fit with their type and personal characteristics, thus increasing the likelihood that they will follow through with the activities and ultimately resolve their career concerns.

Secondary Interpretive Ideas

Thus far, we have examined the two most powerful, robust ideas that can help enrich the interpretation of SDS results, especially in the case of negative signs. In the following sections, we will examine six other ideas that can help us interpret the SDS more fully (see Table 14). These ideas, in descending order of observed importance, were discussed in earlier chapters in a more general way; here, we will apply them directly to interpreting SDS results.

Table 16
Career Interventions by Holland Type

Realistic

Hands-on approach
Internships/Co-ops/try-out experiences
Use media—video, films, slides, etc.
Shadow experiences
Homework
Work one-on-one
Like computerized information
Use current information
Provide a clear plan of action
Likes structure/goals/objectives
Use structured forms, charts, steps
Present facts/details first
Videotaped practice job interviews
Involvement in data collection
  (current trends, salaries, time/education
  requirements, etc.)

Pitfalls:

May want "That Test"
See limited transfer of skills
See few options—careers, employers, etc.
Can get stuck in one direction
Believes must have all the skills and have done
  the job to be qualified
Finds it difficult to try something new
Not verbal in session or job interviews

Investigative

One-on-one assistance
Career library work
Computer-assisted exploration
Private contemplation
Journal writing
Written plans
Coaching
Methodical/problem-solving approach
Several 1-hour sessions
Report on career research findings
Computerized assessments
Time for personal reflection
Solving the career "puzzle"
Want to take lots of inventories
Lifeline
Written homework

Pitfalls:

May be too focused
May need to take more risks
Spends too much time thinking—not enough
  doing
May develop lengthy decision process
Cautious and conservative about career
  options
Lengthy resumes and interview responses

Artistic

Spontaneous/low-structured approach
Initial sessions, with periodic follow-up
Role plays
Projective tests/guided fantasy
Brainstorming
Verbal, free-flowing sessions
Card sorts
Future projections
Present big picture first—overall objectives
Explore possibilities/personal world of work
Write, draw, paint, act out ideal occupations
Try to find visual or auditory career
  information
Seek creative, flexible positions
Be creative

Pitfalls:

May have had several negative work
  experiences
May see too many options; too many ideas,
  difficult to focus
May not consider important details—job
  market, opportunity for advancement,
  actual job responsibilities, etc.
Impatient with details of career search—
  poor record keeping
Works in bursts of energy
Makes factual errors
May be too modest in job search
May take first "convenient" job

(continued)

Table 16 (continued)
Career Interventions by Holland Type

Social

Groups/seminars/workshops
Caring, supportive environment
Relationship with counselor
Mentor/protege
Internship/co-op/volunteer
Practice job interviews/role playing
Card sorts
Information interviewing
Verbally analyze past experiences/
 relationships
Job search clubs
Networking
Learn from others' experiences
Personal follow-up
Values clarification
Interpersonal careers
People-related data
Process oriented
Personal world of work

Pitfalls:

May want to please others with career
 decisions
Not able to deal with own strong feelings of
 fear, anxiety, inadequacy
May allow decisions to be overly influenced
 by others
May be too modest on résumé or in interviews
Difficulty in making decisions which will not
 have other's approval
Lack of positive feedback very discouraging
Has difficulty with logical analysis of options
Selective gathering of information
May take job rejection very personally and
 stop job hunting

Enterprising

Groups
Seminars/workshops
Internships/co-ops
Information interviewing
Networking
Card sorts
Practice/Role Plays
Brainstorming alternatives
Company visits
Motivated/not easily discouraged
Coaching
Challenging questions
Energetic activities
Like limited number of brief sessions
Shadowing experiences
Professional associations/conferences
Verbal interaction
Most career planning and job hunting books
 are written toward their skills

Pitfalls:

Needs help focusing/structuring
May not take enough time for personal
 reflection
Acts/talks before thinking in interviews
May move too quickly without enough
 planning
May be a"no-show" for subsequent
 appointments
Too general/lengthy résumé
May accept a job too quickly
May ignore written information

(continued)

Table 16 (continued)
Career Interventions by Holland Type

Conventional

Structure/step-by-step process	**Pitfalls:**
Behavioral objectives	May look to "authority" for answers
Computer-aided exploration	Lots of "shoulds"
Tests/inventories	May decide too quickly
Evaluate past experiences	May not "sell" themselves on résumé or in
Trait-and-factor approach	interviews
Reading brief and well organized information	Uncertainty causes anxiety/stress
Deadlines/homework/time lines	Impatient with the process
Written plans	Plans too rigid; does not allow for changes
Decision making guides	May miss opportunities because wants fast
Prioritizing/rank ordering	decisions
Organized job search	Too quiet and non-assertive in interviews
Task orientated/thorough/patient	May not develop or use networks
Set goals/objectives	

Note. From "Career Interventions by Holland Type," a workshop handout by Thom Rakes, Director of Career Services, University of North Carolina at Wilmington. Reproduced by permission.

Coherence of Aspirations

As you may recall from earlier chapters, the coherence of aspirations is defined as the degree to which codes of a person's set of vocational aspirations or occupational daydreams belong in the same Holland category. Holland (1997) has recently described coherence of aspirations as one type of consistency. Scores of high, average, or low coherence are determined from an analysis of the first three occupational aspirations listed in the Daydreams section of the SDS. In high coherence, the first letter of the first occupation is the same as the first letter of the second and third occupations. In average coherence, the first letter of the first occupation is the same as the first letter of the second or third occupation. In low coherence, the first letter of the first occupation does not appear as the first letter of either the second or third occupation.

High coherence may indicate future persistence in occupations with the same first-letter code as those of the first aspiration (Holland, Gottfredson, & Baker, 1990; Holland, Powell, & Fritzsche, 1994). Readers are urged to be cautious about overreacting to a set of client daydreams which are considered to have low coherence according to this scoring scheme. It may be useful to consider the entire pattern of codes across the daydreams, not just the first letters. For instance, the client may have a set of aspirations where none of the first letters of the first three aspirations are alike (e.g., ESA, SAE, AES), yet the combination of E and S is found throughout all five aspirations. In this case, the low coherence may be less problematic. Also, in the process of discussing aspirations with the client, there may be a very logical explanation for the unique set of aspirations listed, and the concern over low coherence may be easily resolved.

Table 17
Strategies for Career Counseling Using Holland's Typology

	General approach	Length and no. of sessions	Self-Knowledge	Occupational knowledge	Decision making and planning	Follow-up
Realistic	traditional verbal counseling may not be productive; consider hands-on; trying things first hand	generally brief; allow time for testing out interests, simulations if available	gained through hands-on experience; experiential activities; may be uncomfortable with specific questions related to self-info and insights	provide opportunities to "test" occupations to gather information; computer systems; experiential learning	may prefer knowing steps for making and implementing decisions; use forms, charts, and other structured methods	usually need little follow-up; may return to talk only when plans are not proceeding or under pressure from significant others
Investigative	methodological; problem-solving; researchable problem	several 1-hour sessions; typically enjoy reporting on the results of their "research"	enjoy self-analysis; willing to complete exercises/activities to get at self-knowledge	enjoy "researching" occupations, reading information and using CACG systems to get info; willing to spend time in career library	take great care in decision making; likely to weigh things carefully; be thorough; counselor may need to help them cope with ambiguity	generally do not request or need follow-up appointments; once they understand process can make adjustments to their plan as needed
Artistic	spontaneous; low structure; use questions and exercises in non-rigid way	may vary considerably; probably can't be held to set schedule	discuss aspirations/dream jobs; may learn what they "don't like" from past jobs; ask them to describe or write about dream job	can begin by reading, but may become bored; talk with artistic types; provide information in multimedia, interactive format	usually not a concrete activity; may be process that changes with feelings	schedule follow up only when they feel the need; do not respond well to deadlines; provide support and encouragement for their efforts
Social	verbal career counseling; talking in a friendly, open, and supportive environment	may last several sessions; tend to enjoy the counseling relationship	describe what they like about significant others; ask about their other social experience	talking to people in fields of interest; getting support from others in the field	enjoy discussing with others before making a decision; may seek support from others for decisions	appreciate periodic reassurance and knowing they can talk to a counselor as needed; brief follow-up calls or notes may be helpful

(continued)

Table 17 (continued)
Strategies for Career Counseling Using Holland's Typology

	General approach	Length and no. of sessions	Self-Knowledge	Occupational knowledge	Decision making and planning	Follow-Up
Enterprising	can challenge; enjoy verbal interaction and responding to thought provoking questions	do not have to be long or numerous	can be led to insights through probing questions	may dislike reading; encourage talking, visits to organizations, prefer "doing" rather than "analyzing"	provide assistance to balance spontaneity and impulsiveness; lead them: through process to weigh choices; make plan to implement them	scheduled follow-up meetings are likely to be canceled; prefer "doing" to "talking"; need to know counselor is available; leave scheduling to their initiative
Conventional	structured approach; may want to know what will happen, what is expected, what the outcome will likely be	30-40 minutes in length; 3-4 highly structured sessions	highly structured exercises to look at past experiences; counselor may need to offer insights and observations	reading occupational info that is brief and well organized; may prefer listening to presentations on occupations	specific decision-making guides or exercises ranking techniques	generally not necessary; can pursue action plan with little guidance; may return when unanticipated problems arise

Note. Information adapted from the Spring 1985 *Journal of College Placement* with permission of the National Association of Colleges and Employers (formerly the College Placement Council), copyright holder.

Coherence of aspirations is an interpretive idea that has recently achieved higher status among those being reviewed in this chapter. Why did this happen? One explanation is because of the overall importance of occupational aspirations in Holland's theory for providing a window into a client's vocational interests. The quality of the list of occupational aspirations is increased, from a RIASEC typology view, if the first letters of the occupations listed are the same. Second, the study by Holland, Gottfredson, and Baker (1990) reported earlier provided new information about the importance of coherence of aspirations in predicting future occupational activity and in understanding the nature of occupational interests. And finally, practical experience in using the SDS suggests to us that when there are five very dissimilar occupational aspirations listed in the Daydreams section, the client may have a confused picture of either the occupational world or his or her interests.

In interpreting the SDS with respect to coherence of aspirations, it may be fruitful to explore the following questions and issues with the client:

1. Where did these aspirations come from? What is their history?

2. In your view, how related are these aspirations to one another?

3. Do they generally share the same RIASEC codes, particularly the first letter, or are they all over the hexagon?

4. What information can the client share that might help explain this situation?

5. What are some common themes in the aspirations listed? For example, do they involve high prestige? Math or science skills? Do they require much education or on-the-job training?

6. Do some of the aspirations represent dreams that the person has since given up?

As we have emphasized throughout this book, the aspirations and the Daydreams section are very important components of the SDS. The coherence of aspirations is a powerful interpretive tool for examining SDS results with a client, especially if the SDS did not lead to immediately satisfactory results.

Vocational Identity

As discussed in chapters 2 and 4, this diagnostic indicator is taken from the Identity scale of an instrument called My Vocational Situation (MVS; Holland, Daiger, & Power, 1980). Practitioners would have access to this diagnostic sign only if they had administered a paper and pencil version of the MVS along with the SDS, or if they had used the SDS computer version, which includes the MVS as part of the on-screen assessment. In Holland's theory, vocational identity refers to both the clarity and stability of a person's goals and self-perceptions. Clients possessing high vocational identity scores on the MVS are likely to experience relatively untroubled decision making, and to have confidence in their ability to make good decisions in the face of some inevitable environmental ambiguities.

How do you use a low vocational identity score in career counseling and interpreting the SDS? If the vocational identity score is low, clients may need more follow-up after the SDS, and they may not be able to move forward with the self- and occupational knowledge gained from completing the SDS. With a low identity score, the typology just may not work very efficiently. The client's interests are potentially unstable and may not be very reliable for generating options. Also, clients with low self-esteem tend to have lower identity scores. Low self-esteem may result in unrealistically low SDS ability self-estimates or negative responses to SDS activities, competencies, or occupations where the client generally anticipates failure.

Another pattern that we have frequently observed in our setting is the tendency of some clients to have very positive indicators on the SDS and a very low vocational identity score. We refer to this as "awfulizing." What does this mean? Based on key SDS indicators (i.e., congruence, differentiation, consistency, and other information), the client seems to have a clear sense of self, has aspirations that match self-characteristics, and has interests and competencies that fit well with each other. However, the MVS results indicate that the client is saying, "Help, I'm a mess." We believe this relates quite clearly to how clients view themselves. Such clients are unlikely to think differently about themselves until the counselor helps them to see how this kind of thinking, this low vocational identity, interferes with their ability to move forward and use the knowledge gained from the SDS in their career problem solving and decision making. The concept of negative thinking is explored more fully in chapter 8.

Because the SDS is also considered an intervention, a counselor may wish to explore MVS items endorsed by clients as "true" to determine whether they still feel that way after completing the SDS. It has been our experience that even a brief intervention, lasting 45 minutes to 2 hours, can raise vocational identity scores. Clients will actually change their thinking about their career decision making situation as a result of a brief intervention.

Consistency

As we described it earlier, a personality pattern or interest profile is consistent in terms of RIASEC theory if the ideal types most resembled are closely related or adjacent according to the hexagon (e.g., IA, SE, CR). We would describe such a code as *high* in consistency. Remember, we're talking about the first two letters of the client's SDS code. A pattern is of *average* consistency if the first two types are alternate on the hexagon (e.g., RA, SC, AE). A pattern is inconsistent if the models most resembled are unrelated or opposite according to the hexagon (e.g., RS, IE, AC). We would describe this as *low* consistency. High consistency is a positive sign and correlates with more stability in work history and direction of career choice. High consistency may indicate that less interpretation of the SDS results will be required by the counselor.

As you examine the client's SDS summary code in terms of the level of consistency, focus on the first two letters, and ask yourself, Where is he or she on the hexagon? How easy is it to find occupations using that combination of skills, traits, and interests? What events in the client's life might provide a logical explanation for the inconsistency?

Even if consistency is low, think about how you can help your client creatively examine ways to use his or her diverse skills and qualities in today's work place? For example, can a client whose first two letters are I and E become a marketing specialist for a health maintenance organization? Can a client with a CA code become a bookkeeper in an art store? Or, approaching low consistency another way, could one letter emphasize paid employment and the other letter emphasize leisure pursuits? A person with an RS code might think about employment as a mechanic and coaching a children's soccer team outside of work. When consistency is low, balancing work and leisure activities across the hexagon may be particularly effective.

As noted earlier, inspection of the raw score distribution across the five sections of the SDS may reveal factors that have contributed to the low level of consistency in RIASEC scores. A rather frequent situation involves a client with considerable work history in one area (e.g., Conventional or Realistic) but interests in a different area (e.g., Investigative or Artistic). Because the SDS is a simulated career counseling situation, the counselor and client can review the responses in the Assessment Booklet to explore which competencies are associated with past work experience, determine whether those competencies are still important to consider in future occupational exploration, and evaluate what new competencies might be important or desirable to develop.

In the third edition of *Making Vocational Choices*, Holland (1997) adds two measures of consistency to the notion of profile consistency: coherence of aspirations and coherence in work history. By approaching the level of consistency in a client's SDS results in these ways, the client and counselor may jointly focus on why the level of consistency appears as it does and how this information may be used in career problem solving and decision making.

Differentiation

Differentiation refers to the level of definition or distinctness of a personality or occupational profile. A person who resembles only one type is highly differentiated, whereas someone who resembles all six RIASEC types to an equal degree is undifferentiated. One way to think about this is to think of pie slices. Someone who is undifferentiated would have six pie slices of about the same size, whereas a person who has a differentiated profile would probably have between one and three noticeably larger slices (see Figure 8).

Highly Differentiated   **Undifferentiated**

Figure 8. An illustration of highly differentiated and undifferentiated profiles.

A client with a highly differentiated code will most likely have all of the personality characteristics associated with that code. A big Enterprising type person would most likely have all the traits associated with this theoretical model. A person with an undifferentiated profile, with less resemblance to the theoretical model type, will have fewer of the personality characteristics and traits. For purposes of SDS interpretation, a code that is differentiated can be more reliably used, other things being equal (i.e., congruence, coherence, identity), than a code low in differentiation. When interpreting the SDS results for a big E or any other type, the characteristics of the type can be used in the process of interpretation. For example, big Investigative types might be more interested in learning about RIASEC theory, reviewing occupations and information in the DHOC, and researching college majors by Holland codes.

There has been much debate in the professional literature about varying ways to calculate differentiation and about the value of differentiation as a construct (Holland, 1997). It has received less research support and is viewed as a "weak" indicator compared to some of the theory's other assumptions. We still think it has useful interpretive value. A person with a "flat profile" still presents some difficult counseling issues for practitioners. These will be discussed further in chapter 9.

Commonness
This concept refers to the frequency with which a given code is observed in a particular sample of individuals. In Tables A23 through A28 of the *SDS Professional User's Guide* (Holland, Powell, & Fritzsche, 1994), various codes are given for samples of high school students, college students, and adults. Looking at these tables, one can see that there is an extremely uneven frequency of various RIASEC types. Some code combinations (e.g., AC, CA) are rare. Some persons have unusual code combinations, combinations that are

not often found in their peer group, and combinations that link to only a few occupational alternatives.

The more you work with the SDS, the easier these are to spot. One common example is SAC. Practitioners must be ready to deal with two typical scenarios in the case of uncommon codes. The first is the client's dismayed reaction to a suggested occupational alternative: "The test told me to be a fur designer... that's ridiculous." The second is the limited number of options the client has to consider. This is especially problematic if the client's goal in seeking assistance was to increase the number of options he or she might consider. Changes in the 1994 edition of The Occupations Finder now make rare codes less of a problem in interpreting the SDS because specific directions are provided on how to search other code combinations in place of those rare codes that have limited or no occupations listed.

Several solutions can help with the problem of "rare codes." The most obvious is to have the individual look at occupations using only one or two letters of the code. In keeping with Holland's "Rule of 8" (Holland, Powell, & Fritzsche, 1994, p. 20), if the score for the individual's fourth letter was within 8 points of the third letter score, consider substituting this letter for the third one and search using the newly formed code. Finally, recognizing the importance of aspirations, individuals may find it helpful to search using the code of their first aspiration or the Aspirations summary code. Any of these activities can easily produce options that clients may wish to consider after completing the SDS.

Professional Judgment

One of the things that John Holland has consistently emphasized in his advice to counselors working with the SDS is to never lose sight of their own professional judgment and observations when interpreting clients' SDS results or when using related instruments. No instrument can account for all the life factors and situations that may influence, positively and negatively, a client's career problem solving and decision making situation. Along with the SDS results, practitioners may consider impressions from client interviews, other test data, and related information. This simply reflects good career counseling practice, and it becomes even more important when the results of the SDS point to several negative signs or when the client initially seems to obtain little or no benefit from completing the SDS.

Holland has noted several sociological, biological, and economic factors that may complicate the interpretation of the SDS with a particular client. Chapters 2, 3, and 4 provide background information related to these points. Sociological factors might include ethnic group membership and race, language ability, cultural assimilation, social class, and educational background. Biological factors might include sex, unusual physical characteristics or traits (e.g., 7 feet tall, physical disability). Economic factors might include extraordinary wealth or poverty, the overall state of the economy or the economic situation in the local area, the closing of a large factory, and so forth. All of these factors are outside the bounds of Holland's RIASEC theory, and interpretation of the SDS and the use of related Holland-based instruments should take these factors into consideration.

Where Do I Go From Here in Interpreting the SDS?

Several scenarios can occur following a client's completion of the SDS. The client is satisfied with his or her results, and learning about the hexagon has increased the client's knowledge of how the world of work is organized and how personal characteristics relate to specific options. The client has increased the number of options being considered and plans to use the options generated by the SDS to conduct further personal research.

However, one problem that may arise in using the SDS is that the client is overwhelmed by the number of options generated by the various combinations of the summary code. One helpful activity we have used with clients is to ask them to review the list of options in The Occupations Finder or on their SDS computer version printout and mark the occupations as follows:

1. Cross out occupations in which he or she has no interest.

2. Put a question mark by occupations about which he or she needs more information

3. Put an asterisk by those occupations in which he or she has a definite interest.

The counselor can then process this activity with the client and get the client to share the ideas that led to marking each occupation in a particular way. For those options marked with an asterisk or question mark, the counselor can ask the client to identify themes associated with the choices in each of those categories; or, do all of the occupations the client crossed out involve working outdoors, making presentations to groups, or keeping records? This activity can help a client further clarify self-knowledge. It may also give the counselor insight into any stereotypical views about occupations that the client has. A more structured version of this activity entitled the "Career Information Exercise" can be found in Appendix F. This exercise can be adapted as needed for use with a particular client.

The media constantly bombards career counselors and their clients with the notion that the work world is becoming increasingly chaotic and that our old schemas and ways of categorizing work options are no longer useful and should be thrown out. Some suggest that we must learn to live in a completely new world of work and find new ways for understanding what it means to be a worker. A review of recent magazine and book titles provides a clue to how much this phenomenon has invaded current media. Some of these titles include *Career Transitions in Turbulent Times* (Feller & Walz, 1996) and *The End of Work* (Rifkin, 1995). One of the most common themes stressed in the career counseling literature is the need to provide clients with a means for thinking about and organizing the world of work. Processing information about educational and occupational options is a cognitively complex task.

Although researchers and others can argue about whether there are more than six types or whether the hexagon is really a hexagon, the bottom line is that clients find that the hexagon provides a useful way for them to think about themselves in terms of Holland types and about how their particular type links to occupations and fields of study. Although some would argue that in times of turbulence and confusion, we cannot rely on structured models and people need to "construct their own reality," we think that clients are better served when we give them tools and theories that are conceptually and empirically sound, have stood the test of time, and make practical sense.

Using the "RIASEC Game"

Many practitioners, regardless of whether they use the SDS, are familiar with Holland's trademark figure, the hexagon. Holland has stood firmly against throwing out the hexagon or modifying it in some way for the simple reason that both clients and practitioners can relate to it. It provides a simple, easily understandable, yet complex means for relating personal characteristics to occupational and educational alternatives. Building on this notion, we have found it useful in our setting to keep handy copies of the hexagon with brief descriptions of the six types arranged around it (see Figure 9). We have used this figure in individual sessions with clients, group activities, and as part of a career planning class exercise. This figure can be used to introduce Holland's theory to clients and as an initial check on clients' views of themselves, in both personal and vocational terms. Counselors might ask clients to read over the six types and decide which three sound most like themselves. If clients do this exercise rather quickly and decisively, the counselor may choose to review how the resulting three-letter code relates to occupations or fields of study. If the client reacts positively to this intervention, he or she may choose to proceed with career exploration of the options presented, thus eliminating the need for a more in-depth assessment. This saves time for both the counselor and the client. Alternatively, after reviewing occupations suggested by the "RIASEC Game" (described in the following section), clients can also use the SDS to confirm their interests.

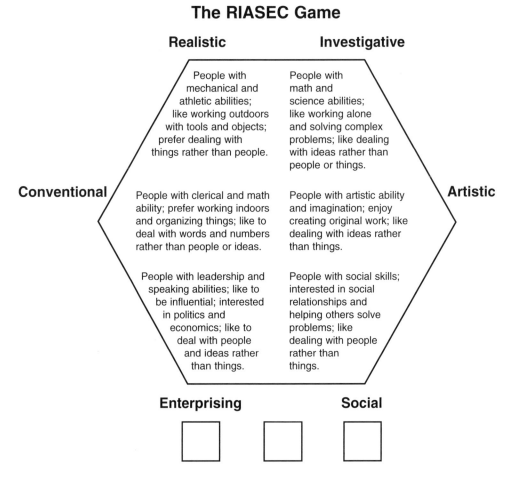

The RIASEC Game

Realistic **Investigative**

People with mechanical and athletic abilities; like working outdoors with tools and objects; prefer dealing with things rather than people.

People with math and science abilities; like working alone and solving complex problems; like dealing with ideas rather than people or things.

Conventional **Artistic**

People with clerical and math ability; prefer working indoors and organizing things; like to deal with words and numbers rather than people or ideas.

People with artistic ability and imagination; enjoy creating original work; like dealing with ideas rather than things.

People with leadership and speaking abilities; like to be influential; interested in politics and economics; like to deal with people and ideas rather than things.

People with social skills; interested in social relationships and helping others solve problems; like dealing with people rather than things.

Enterprising **Social**

Figure 9. Hexagon with RIASEC descriptions for the RIASEC Game. Adapted from *Making Vocational Choices* (2nd ed.), by J. L. Holland, 1982, Odessa, FL: Psychological Assessment Resources. Copyright © 1982, 1989, 1997 by Psychological Assessment Resources. Reproduced with permission of the publisher.

In a group setting, you might want to try a more active approach to the use of the hexagon. One procedure for structuring a group activity is described below:

1. Tape pieces of poster board, each containing one of the six RIASEC letters, around the room in RIASEC order.

2. Distribute copies of the hexagon to group members and ask them to review the six descriptions.

3. When the group leader gives a signal, all members of the group should go to the letter that represents their first choice; once gathered at a letter, group members should be asked to mingle

with the other persons gathered at that letter, interview them, find out about their interests, and so forth.

4. Repeat this process for the second and third letters.

5. Have group members share their reactions after working on the third letter. How were they able to choose each letter? What life experiences influenced their choices?

6. Next, distribute copies of The Occupations Finder and/or the Educational Opportunities Finder (depending on the needs of the group) and let group members look up their own three-letter code.

7. Ask for group member reactions to the occupations listed for the code. How well do these fit ideas that members have about occupations they wish to pursue?

This activity can be followed by a brief review of some key points from Holland's theory. Participants might be encouraged to complete the SDS if they wish a more in-depth exploration of the link between their personal characteristics and occupations, fields of study, or leisure activities.

We use an alternative group exercise that captures occupational aspirations and involves using additional resources to research occupations. It can be organized as follows:

1. Distribute a sheet that includes a place for the participants to list occupations they are considering (usually 3-5 are sufficient), and ask them to indicate which occupation is their first choice (see Appendix G for a sample format). This activity is formally known as the Occupational Alternatives Questionnaire (OAQ) and was first developed by Zener and Schnuelle (1972) and later modified by Slaney and Lewis (1986).

2. Participants then proceed with Steps 1-6 from the previous activity.

3. Ask participants to locate the codes for their aspirations (the leader may wish to keep an Alphabetized Occupations Finder or a DHOC on hand to help those who have difficulty finding their selections). The leader can then introduce a discussion of the relationship between occupational daydreams and the code that participants selected based on their review of the six Holland types.

Each of these activities can be used to introduce and explain key concepts from Holland's theory. These activities can be used to show how it is possible to bring order to some of the chaos associated with linking personal characteristics to career options, and also to demonstrate the fact that tests are not necessarily going to tell a person the one best occupation to pursue. These activities can illustrate principles of Holland's theory and help clients understand that the process of career problem solving and decision making is complex and requires some time and follow-up activities to reach a satisfying conclusion.

Conclusion

This chapter has examined many factors that are involved in the use and interpretation of the Self-Directed Search. It has reviewed some of the issues that the staff in a career services organization must examine to determine whether additional policies and procedures will need to be established. The chapter reviewed eight specific factors that might be explored with the client in interpreting the results of the SDS and offered suggestions about how to use this information for the client's benefit in career counseling. Practitioners are encouraged to look beyond the three-letter code and lists of occupations provided by the SDS so they can more fully exploit the richness of Holland's theory in providing assistance to clients.

8

Linking RIASEC and Cognitive Information Processing

The career services field is rich with assessment instruments that can help us better understand our clients' career situations, but we don't always make good use of theory to guide our practice and our use of these tools. In their desire to be helpful, practitioners sometimes place little value on theory and instead concentrate on simply providing services. Although this is understandable, we believe theory can be a road map that guides and informs practice and helps the journey more than it complicates it. Theory can make using the SDS a more productive experience.

An analogy might be using AAA, the popular motorist club, for trip planning. It might be simpler and more straightforward to just get in the car and go, hoping you'll see all the road signs and make the right choices and turns along the way. The alternative, visiting the club's offices before you start and getting trip guides, maps, suggestions about routes, and special information about road hazards and construction, means you will have more information to deal with and consider. Your journey becomes more involved. But, by being more informed, you increase the likelihood that you'll anticipate some of the bumps and roadblocks along the way, make informed choices about your routes, and successfully reach your destination. In terms of the time and effort associated with problem solving and decision making, if we don't pay the price earlier, we'll probably pay later.

This chapter links Holland's theory, the SDS, and the diagnostic concepts described in chapter 7 to an emerging career theory that has helped guide practice in our setting. We will address the question, "What's involved in career choice and how do the SDS and related Holland assessments help clients become better career problem solvers and decision makers?" Many of us have encountered clients who sum up their experience with the career counseling process by saying, "Oh, I took one of those career tests one time and it didn't help me." We think that by focusing on teaching our clients to become career problem solvers and decision makers and putting the use of assessment materials in a larger context, we will better serve our clients in the long run. This chapter provides a brief overview of cognitive information processing (CIP) theory (Peterson, Sampson, & Reardon, 1991; Peterson, Sampson, Reardon, & Lenz, 1996) as a framework for understanding what we're trying to do when we help our clients make career decisions and how the SDS relates to this framework. This chapter also describes a new tool, the Career Thoughts Inventory (CTI; Sampson, Peterson, Lenz, Reardon, & Saunders, 1996a), which can provide additional clues about where clients are stuck when assessment tools such as the SDS don't appear to help them resolve their career concerns.

Translating Theory Into Practice: The CIP Approach

Although our center had provided career services for more than 25 years and used Holland's career theory and instruments for most of that time, no single career counseling theory guided our work. A series of collaborative efforts between career center staff and faculty members in our counseling program generated a new theory that helped to tie practice and theory together and provided a context and rationale for the use of Holland's instruments, particularly the SDS and the MVS. This theory is known as the CIP approach. Persons desiring a more indepth discussion of CIP are referred to *Career Development and Services: A Cognitive Approach* (Peterson, Sampson, & Reardon, 1991), and a chapter in Brown and Brooks' career theory book (Peterson, Sampson, Reardon, & Lenz, 1996).

Using a pyramid figure (Figure 10), CIP emphasizes four aspects of the career choice process, the first three of which are very familiar to readers. Brief definitions of most terms used in the theory are provided in the Glossary (see Appendix A).

1. The first component is labeled *self-knowledge*. Self-knowledge refers to "individuals' perceptions of their own values, interests, skills, and so forth" (Sampson, Peterson, Lenz, Reardon, & Saunders, 1996b, p. 6).

2. The second component is knowledge about options, *occupational knowledge*, including educational and occupational alternatives and knowledge about how occupations are organized.

3. The third area is the *decision making* process. CIP uses a generic problem solving process referred to as the CASVE cycle, the steps of which will be described in more detail in a later section.

4. We refer to the last component of the CIP model as the *executive processing domain*, or more simply "thinking about thinking," which may be less familiar to readers. This focus on how individuals think and feel about their career choices has received increasing attention in the career literature. In our experience,

individuals' views of themselves as career problem solvers and the "conversations" they have with themselves about their career decisions have a huge impact on their ability to make good use of knowledge about themselves and their options in making career decisions. In a later section, we will explore how negative thoughts can impact the career problem solving and decision making process and how signs from the SDS and MVS can help shed some light on client needs in this area. Now that we've briefly described the CIP approach, let's look at how Holland's instruments and concepts help us better understand a person's "pyramid."

What's Involved in Career Choice

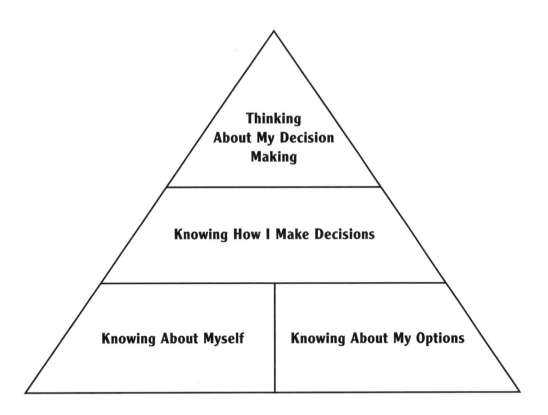

Figure 10. The CIP pyramid. From "A Cognitive Approach to Career Services: Translating Concepts into Practice," by J. P. Sampson, Jr., G. W. Peterson, J. G. Lenz, and R. C. Reardon, 1992, *The Career Development Quarterly, 41,* pp. 67-72. Copyright 1992 by the National Career Development Association. Reprinted with permission.

Knowledge About Self

An essential component of the career counseling process is helping clients gain a clearer understanding of themselves, including their skills, values, and interests. The SDS has proven to be a valuable tool in this regard for many years. Numerous studies support the notion that clients report understanding themselves better after completing the SDS. The SDS and Holland's typology give them a clear and concise way to think about their personal characteristics and provide a framework for describing themselves that is easily understood. The SDS does this in several ways.

As we've noted, the SDS Daydreams section is often minimized or under-used. This list of daydreams is the first "window" into a client's view of self. The client's daydreams may represent both a realistic view of self (i.e., clients list options they could actually see themselves doing) and a "flight of fantasy" (i.e., occupational dreams clients may still hold or ones they've abandoned). In either case, these daydreams provide an initial means for clients to project their view of themselves onto career choices. Discussion of these daydreams can reveal important aspects of self-knowledge. Do they represent things the client likes and enjoys doing? Do they represent some important values the client holds (e.g., a need to make a difference in the world or a need for power, prestige, or money)? Do they capture some skills the person has or wants to develop? Daydreams often contain important information that is not always captured by more structured assessments.

Further, practitioners can examine clients' "expressed" view of themselves (Daydreams code) in relation to their assessed view of themselves (three-letter SDS summary code) by examining the level of congruence between the two codes. (These ideas were initially discussed in chapter 4). How big a gap exists between the skills, interests, and personality characteristics of the clients and what they say they want to do? We all know from experience that our work is made easier when what clients can see themselves doing matches their self-perceptions. The SDS can provide some valuable clues about the clarity and accuracy of a person's self-knowledge. Lack of self-knowledge is also reflected in lower vocational identity scores. Several of the items on the MVS Vocational Identity scale reflect issues related to self-knowledge (e.g., "I don't know what my major strengths and weaknesses are," or "My estimates of my abilities and talents vary a lot from year to year.").

The other SDS sections also provide a quick and simple means for counselors to gather information about how clients see a variety of their personal characteristics. As we noted in chapter 4, the sections of the SDS Assessment Booklet mirror the kinds of things counselors might do when sitting down to interview clients. The counselor would ask about things clients enjoy doing

(Activities), the kinds of things they do well (Competencies), the kinds of occupations they've considered, and their estimates about their strengths in various areas. Although the Occupations scale deals with clients' views about particular options, their endorsement or rejection of those items provides clues to their self-perceptions (e.g., they reject R occupations that seem to lack prestige), and how well their view of themselves matches or doesn't match with a particular occupation.

Clients' reactions to both the occupations listed in the Occupations scale and the occupations associated with various combinations of their three-letter code are also an important link to self-knowledge. As we mentioned in chapter 7, discussing with clients their reasons for liking or disliking the options presented can reveal important themes about personal preferences and self-knowledge. They reject an option presumably because it is not consistent with how they see themselves, either now or in the future. For example, clients might utter such phrases as "I can't see myself doing that," or "None of these options fit me." Further exploration and elaboration of the thoughts and feelings behind these statements can help fill in the self-knowledge side of a client's pyramid.

A link also exists between self-knowledge and Holland's concepts of differentiation and consistency. Persons with flat profiles or low levels of differentiation may have had "insufficient experience to acquire well-defined interests, competencies, and self-perceptions" (Holland, 1992, p. 137). Clients who think they don't know themselves very well may have trouble rating themselves in the various sections of the SDS. With regard to consistency, a counselor can explore how well clients' personal characteristics "hang together." Do their patterns of skills, interests, and values form a consistent pattern (e.g., do they work well with people, enjoy working with people, value working with people, and have high scores on the E and S scales)? This pattern can be contrasted with clients who have had ambiguous or conflicting life experiences which in turn may produce inconsistent codes on the SDS (e.g., a person with a code of CA who works in a clerical position for a state agency but sings in a choral group on the weekends).

This section has helped us see how a number of concepts embedded in Holland's theory and the SDS can help us work with clients in exploring their self-knowledge. Next we'll examine how these same concepts can help us examine the client's knowledge of occupational and educational options.

Knowledge About Options

An essential aspect of many career interventions is helping clients to think about options. For some clients, the goal is to narrow down the number of options they're considering; for others, the goal is to increase the number of options they might consider. In CIP theory, occupational knowledge refers to knowing about specific occupations, as well as understanding how the world of work is organized (Sampson, Peterson, Lenz, Reardon, & Saunders, 1996b). Some might argue that it is futile in today's changing work environment to think about and explore specific options, but the reality is that our school and work organizations still force people to identify specific options they are considering. Suggestions by some theorists and practitioners that clients "construct their own reality" or stay unfocused don't really match the realities clients face when they're confronted with making educational and occupational choices.

For example, many school districts have instituted career planning programs in the eighth grade, where students are encouraged to identify specific occupational choices to use in planning their high school curriculum. High school students must consider career choices because such choices influence their preparation for post-high school options, be it work, military, or additional schooling. Adults seeking jobs in organizations must list the position for which they are applying on an application form or specify the career path they hope to follow as part of their personal career management plan. Clients in rehabilitation programs must not only specify how the course of training they're pursuing relates to the career field they seek to enter, but must also provide evidence of specific jobs that they can enter after completing training.

In settings where the SDS Form R computer version is used, practitioners can also explore My Vocational Situation items that provide a window into clients' knowledge about options. This is easily seen when clients endorse items on the Occupational Information scale (e.g., "I need...information about employment opportunities.") The concept of identity also comes into play with respect to exploring options. The Vocational Identity scale includes items that reveal clients' lack of knowledge about options (e.g., "I would like to increase the number of occupations I could consider," or "I don't know enough about what workers do in various occupations.").

It should be fairly clear by now that the SDS helps clients explore options in several ways. First, by including the Daydreams section as the initial activity, the SDS recognizes that clients have some useful and interesting ideas about options, and these options are often very predictive of the career fields they eventually enter. Letting clients list options without any external stimulus can give practitioners insight into the clarity or complexity of clients' "occupational maps" (i.e., what views of work do they carry around in their heads?). Some clients can quite easily fill up all of the slots in the Daydreams section with very specific occupational alternatives, whereas others have trouble listing more than a few, and often the items they do list are vague in nature (e.g., management, psychology, sales). The concept of coherence might also be considered here. Have clients selected alternatives from the same job family or do their aspirations reflect options that are quite different from one another with respect to RIASEC types? If clients' daydreams are quite varied and distinct from one another, exploring this may provide important information about how they view options or, in CIP terminology, their occupational map or schema.

Second, if clients complete the Daydreams section as directed and look up the codes for their daydreams in The Occupations Finder, they are immediately involved in an activity that expands their knowledge about "what's out there." As we've noted, clients can easily get "lost" in this task, but from our perspective, that's not necessarily bad. It may become problematic for some people who are already overwhelmed by the number of options they have to consider, but for most clients it is an interesting and eye-opening experience.

Third, the SDS provides clients with an opportunity to consider and evaluate options through their responses on the instrument's Occupations scale and in their review of options associated with their three-letter summary code. Client reactions to occupational titles provide important counseling information in two forms:

1. Their discussion of options may reveal the clarity of their thinking about the world of work, the nature of work, and their view of themselves in relation to particular types of work.

2. Their discussion of options may reveal occupational stereotypes that could potentially interfere with their ability to make good career choices. An example might be a female student who dismisses Architect as a career option because she believes that there is too much math involved or that Architecture is a field primarily for men. Or a counselor is working with an unemployed auto industry worker who dismisses Radiation Technology as a retraining option because it's a "woman's job" and "the pay is low."

Exploration of options is also affected by the "commonness" of the codes. Clients with rare codes may be frustrated by the few or unusual options listed for their code and may need help in exploring additional alternatives. (See the discussion in chapter 7 for strategies to use in dealing with rare codes.) An alternative scenario is that of a client who has a very common code, one that is associated with a variety of occupations (e.g., SEC). In the latest Form R Occupations Finder, the code SEC and all its combinations generate a total of 175 options for a client to consider. Further, using these code combinations to explore options in the DHOC produces more than 700 alternatives to consider. For some clients, if their goal was to expand the number of options they might consider, this may be more than they bargained for! For clients trying to narrow their options, it is potentially overwhelming and frustrating.

Clients who specifically state that they're trying to narrow their choices and are determined to take an interest test to help them do this may benefit from a "sneak preview" of their potential SDS results. For example, if they reviewed descriptions of the six types and identified their code as ESA, we might pull out a copy of The Occupations Finder and show them the lists of alternatives for this code combination. This lets them know that their experience with the SDS may produce the opposite result (i.e., more choices instead of fewer). They can still proceed with that activity, or they may choose to simply explore some of the options they already have in mind.

Finally, in defining occupational knowledge, we noted that this aspect of the pyramid comprises not just knowledge about specific alternatives, but also refers to having a way of thinking about how work options are organized. With the thousands of alternatives that exist for clients to choose from, having a way to think about more manageable groups of options becomes extremely important. We are referring to a cognitive schema, a map or method for classifying and organizing facts and ideas. As we noted in previous chapters, one of the most important outcomes of Holland's theory and the development of his instruments is the RIASEC typology and the accompanying hexagon figure. Although the number of letters, the descriptions of the types, and the shape of the hexagon have been widely debated and researched, there is no denying the fact that both clients and counselors find this figure extremely helpful. People understand it and relate to it easily. The RIASEC typology has been incorporated into many other career intervention resources because of its practicality and usefulness. Appendix L gives a sampling of additional resources that use the RIASEC classification.

As your clients talk to you about options in relation to their SDS results, both the ones they've generated and the ones presented to them in the Assessment Booklet and The Occupations Finder, use this information to help them fill in the right side of their pyramid. Taking the self- and occupational knowledge gained from the SDS and translating it into a choice leads us to our next topic, the CASVE cycle.

Decision Making: The CASVE Cycle

Most practitioners have worked with one or more decision making models to help their clients in the career choice process. The CASVE cycle (pronounced Ca SA' Veh) is one such model. We like to use it because it represents a process that clients can understand and apply. It appears to emphasize a logical, rational approach to decision making, but it recognizes the role that feelings and intuition play in this process. The model also recognizes the role that significant others play in some clients' career problem solving and decision making.

The simplest way to think about the CASVE cycle is as the means by which clients recognize and solve a career problem; they need to resolve the "gap" between where they are now and where they'd like to be. An example of this is a college sophomore who is undecided about her major and would like to select a satisfying major by the start of her junior year. Another example is a downsized computer industry worker whose unemployment benefits run out in 3 months and who wants to make a decision about enrolling in a training program.

This initial phase of the CASVE cycle is labeled *Communication* (C). In the Communication phase, people may become aware that they need to make a career decision through their own thoughts and feelings (internal cues), as well as through communication from other persons in their life (external cues). At this phase of the career intervention process, counselors may need to assess the readiness level of clients to engage in self- and occupational assessment activities (Peterson, Sampson, Reardon, & Lenz, 1997). Such tools as the MVS and the Career Thoughts Inventory can help in this process. The "Guidelines..." presented in chapter 9 may also help in determining a client's ability to benefit from a career assessment intervention.

In the *Analysis* (A) phase of the CASVE cycle, clients try to gather and fully understand all the relevant information associated with their choice. This includes information about themselves, their options, how they like to make decisions, and how their career thoughts are influencing the process. The SDS represents a structured means for helping clients quickly pull together information about themselves and information about possible options. RIASEC theory is a typological matching scheme for linking persons with environmental options.

In the *Synthesis* (S) phase of the CASVE cycle, clients engage in activities that help them expand (elaboration) and narrow (crystallization) their options. By *Synthesis elaboration* we mean encouraging clients to just "consider the possibilities" for a moment, "freeing the mind to consider as many potential solutions as possible" (Sampson, Peterson, Lenz, Reardon, & Saunders, 1996c, p. 9). Most clients using The Occupations Finder, either as part of the Daydreams activity or as part of exploring alternatives associated with their SDS summary code, will find their options increase. The "Rule of Full Exploration" described in chapter 4 also assures Synthesis elaboration by identifying all five permutations of a client's three-letter summary code. *Synthesis crystallization*, on the other hand, occurs after clients have researched and processed information about options and are ready to narrow their list to a more manageable number. The goal in the crystallization phase is to learn about options and reduce them to a number that is not overwhelming. The idea is to carry forward three to five options into the next phase of the CASVE cycle. Once clients have created a list of options, how do they get to a point where they are able to commit to a first choice and execute a plan for implementing that choice? This is where the *Valuing* and *Execution* phases of the CASVE model come into play.

In the *Valuing* phase, clients consider the three to five options that have been generated and weigh the pros and cons of each. They may weigh these alternatives in terms of the costs and benefits of each option to "themselves, significant others, their cultural group, and the community or society in general" (Sampson, Peterson, Lenz, Reardon, & Saunders, 1996b, p. 9). Ideally, this process results in *ranking* the client's options so that the person has a first choice and a "Plan B" or "Plan C" in case the first choice doesn't work out.

At this stage, choices are still considered tentative because further exploration through training programs, short-term experience (e.g., internships, or job hunting) may reveal that a choice is unattainable or inappropriate (Sampson, Peterson, Lenz, Reardon, & Saunders, 1996b). These activities are accomplished in the next step in the CASVE cycle, *Execution*. In this phase, "clients formulate and commit to a plan of action for implementing their tentative choice" (Sampson, Peterson, Lenz, Reardon, & Saunders, 1996b, p. 9).

How then do counselors work with clients in the Valuing and Execution phases, and what role can the SDS play in helping them through these parts of the process? In our experience, these steps are probably the most neglected aspect of the career intervention process. This is particularly the case when counselors work in settings that do not have any "outside world" links (e.g., information resources on occupations and educational programs, opportunities for reality testing such as internships and volunteer opportunities, employer information, job listings, and so forth). By fully using all the components of the SDS as an intervention, however, counselors can begin to help clients successfully negotiate this step into the "real world." Holland has, in effect, built "Valuing" and "Execution" activities into the SDS Assessment Booklet and its companion booklet, You and Your Career.

The Assessment Booklet section entitled "Some Next Steps" encourages clients to engage in such activities as investigating options more thoroughly, learning about educational requirements, and weighing personal factors that may affect choices (e.g., physical limitations, gender, family history). The You and Your Career booklet also speaks to this process of exploring, prioritizing, and implementing choices. The YYC section entitled "Making Career Decisions," provides seven steps designed to help clients improve the quality of their career decisions. Examples of these include, "Talk with a few people who do the kind of work you are interested in" and "Consider volunteer and part-time work activities." This booklet also includes lists of resource books that further support activities of the Valuing and Execution type.

In an ideal world, where clients are completely self-directed, they would faithfully follow these next steps. However, we know from experience that this is often not the case. Practitioners may want to consider making these next steps a more explicit part of the "contract" with their clients. They could be a weekly "homework assignment" and be included on an Individual Learning Plan (see Appendix H). These items might also be the basis for counselor-client discussions in ongoing sessions. The Assessment Booklet and the You and Your Career booklet, when used in the intended manner, provide a strategy for clients to use in fully exploring, evaluating, and choosing among options. In our experience, these SDS components are often overlooked or at least underused and can play an important role in moving clients through the Valuing and Execution phases of the career decision-making process.

Taxonomy of Decision Making

Before we end this section on the decision making component of the CIP model, we want to briefly address the issue of decision making states. Considerable career research has examined how clients differ with respect to their levels of career decidedness (Holland & Holland, 1977b). In addition, writers such as Peterson, Sampson, and Reardon (1991) have suggested that the amount and type of counseling assistance provided should take into account differences in clients' decision making status. This "needs assessment taxonomy" was first described by Peterson, Sampson, and Reardon and further refined in Peterson, Sampson, Reardon, and Lenz (1996). We have found it useful to look at how these three categories used to describe clients' decision-making status can be linked to use of Holland tools and assessments. Figure 11 lists the three categories and their subcategories.

Decided individuals are described as having "made a private or public commitment to a specific individual choice" (Peterson, Sampson, Reardon, & Lenz, 1996, p. 446). If clients are decided, why would they present themselves for assistance in our various career services settings? In our experience, many of these clients do present themselves on our doorsteps for reasons that relate to the subtypes within this category. Some clients have identified an occupational goal and simply want to confirm it (*Decided-confirmation*). The SDS has long been recognized as a tool that can help clients feel confident in a tentative choice they have made (Holland, Powell, & Fritzsche, 1994). For clients, this is the "Aha! experience." Their Daydreams code matches their SDS summary code, and the occupation they're considering appears on their list of alternatives in The Occupations Finder. Skeptics might say, "It told them what they wanted to hear," or "They answered the questions in a way that would produce this result." This may be the case for some clients, but for many, this "external validation" gives them the confidence they need to move forward with their choice.

Decided Individuals

Decided-confirmation
Decided-implementation
Decided-conflict avoidance

Undecided Individuals

Undecided-deferred
Undecided-developmental
Undecided-multipotential

Indecisive Individuals

Figure 11. Three levels of client decision-making status. From "A cognitive information approach to career problem solving and decision making," by G. P. Peterson, J. P. Sampson, Jr., R. C. Reardon, and J. G. Lenz, 1996, in D. Brown and L. Brooks (Eds.), *Career choice and development* (3rd ed., p. 446). Copyright © 1996 by Jossey-Bass, San Francisco: CA. Reprinted with permission.

Other individuals have made a choice, but they need help taking the next step (*Decided-implementation*). As we discussed earlier, this is similar to the Execution phase of the CASVE cycle. The activities outlined in the Next Steps section of the Assessment Booklet and the Making Career Decisions section of You and Your Career could help a motivated and self-directed individual begin to implement a choice. Other clients would likely require the assistance of a helping professional to encourage and support them in proceeding. These clients may benefit from the use of an Individual Action Plan (Sampson, Peterson, Lenz, Reardon, & Saunders, 1996c) as a means of structuring their next steps.

Some individuals present themselves as having already made a choice, but this choice may reflect external pressures (e.g., "My parents told me I had to declare my major or they weren't paying for school anymore.") and may have been made with little or no information. Persons who fall into this category (*Decided-conflict avoidance*) typically make a public commitment to a specific choice as a strategy for avoiding conflict with significant others. In reality, they may be undecided or indecisive. Several of the diagnostic signs on the SDS may provide clues that point to this decision making status. One example has to do with aspirations. You may find clients who listed aspirations that do not reflect their interests, skills, dreams, and values, but rather reflect those of a significant other. The lack of agreement (congruence) between these aspirations and how clients describe themselves on the SDS may further highlight this conflict. Persons with a flat profile (low differentiation) may be sending a message about their lack of investment in any particular choice, suggesting that the push for that choice is coming from a source other than themselves. Another source of information for understanding clients falling in this category may be the MVS Vocational Identity items they endorsed as true (e.g., "I am not sure that my present occupational choice or job is right for me."). In developing a sense of how to help these persons, practitioners can use information drawn from several different Holland-based tools. We will elaborate on this further in chapter 9 when we look at these diagnostic signs and how they might be used in developing a career assistance plan.

More commonly seen by career services practitioners are those clients who can be categorized as *Undecided* (see Figure 11). Even though we've used three subtypes to help describe differences in types of undecided clients, we share the view that it's important to avoid labeling clients in this category. There may be very good reasons that an individual has not made a commitment to a specific career choice (Krumboltz, 1996). Clients categorized as *Undecided-deferred* have no pressing need to make a choice at the present time. For these clients, the emphasis is on exploration and information gathering. They feel no pressure from themselves or others to commit to a specific option, and they should be exposed to Holland's hexagon as a means of organizing their exploration. Rather than actually completing the SDS at this point, they may find it helpful to simply browse The Occupations Finder, Educational Opportunities Finder, or DHOC, with some preliminary ideas about how they see themselves, based on a review of descriptions of the six types.

A second group of undecided clients, *Undecided-developmental*, include those who are beginning to feel the need to make a choice but remain undecided because they may lack information about themselves, their options, and decision making strategies. The SDS has a clear role to play with these clients because it addresses all three of these aspects of the pyramid and provides a series of diagnostic indicators to let practitioners know of more complex issues that may be interfering with the decision-making process.

The third type under this category is probably one of the most challenging for career services practitioners. *Undecided-multipotential* individuals typically have an overabundance of talents, interests, and options. They may be overwhelmed with the choices available to them and may experience pressure from significant others to be high achievers. These are the clients who say such things as "There are so many things I like to do," "My interests are so varied," or "I'm having trouble picking one thing." Several issues associated with using the SDS with these clients should be considered.

First, a client who is overwhelmed with options may not benefit from an expanded list of options generated by SDS results but may instead benefit from the application of Holland's typology to the options they're already considering. Exploring their aspirations by using the DHOC to assign Holland codes may provide some useful information for the counselor and client to process. We've had experience with clients who say, "I've got so many different things I'm thinking about," but as we've listened to them describe these options, we see they're actually in very similar Holland categories. When we use the hexagon and The Occupations Finder to show them that the options actually tend to fall into the same job family, the response often is, "I'm not as confused as I thought I was," thus reducing their anxiety. The next step with these clients may be to use career information resources to help them better define the similarities and differences between options and to further narrow their choices based on criteria important to them. The "Career Information Exercise," described in chapter 7, might be useful for this purpose.

Even when practitioners suspect they are dealing with a multipotential individual, they may still decide to administer the SDS. Part of the goal in proceeding with the SDS may be to gather more concrete evidence of the multipotentiality. In this instance, it may be important to explain to the client that the "danger" of taking the SDS is that more options may appear. With some of these clients, we will actually ask them to stop after they've added up their scores, instead of looking up occupations related to their code. The counselor would intervene at this point to talk about their experience with completing the SDS before adding more information for them to process. (On the other hand, a positive outcome may be that the SDS results reinforce or confirm a client's first choice.)

Practitioners can inspect SDS results for signs of multipotentiality, including flat profiles (lack of differentiation), high self-estimates across all areas, and an unusually large number of Yes responses on the Occupations scale. In our experience, SDS results can be used with multipotential clients to reassure them—in effect to say, "No wonder you're having a tough time making a choice, you seem to like a lot of things and do a lot of things well." The task then becomes one of engaging clients in steps that will help them explore and narrow their options and deal with the thoughts and feelings associated with committing to a first choice. At this point, counselors may find it helpful to share biographies or minivignettes of how peoples' life and career paths have allowed them to explore various combinations of their Holland codes. One of our favorite examples is the best-selling writer (AES) John Grisham, who is an attorney (ESA) by training. These types of stories seem to provide some reassurance that it's possible to follow several dreams in making career choices.

In some cases, however, these first levels of intervention seem to produce no progress on the client's part with respect to being closer to a career choice. These clients appear to be completely stuck, and despite practitioners' best efforts, they declare themselves, often with great emotion and despair, hopelessly undecided. In the career counseling literature, these clients are often described as *Indecisive*. They not only lack information about themselves and their options, but their thoughts and feelings totally overwhelm their attempts to resolve their career indecision. In the next section, we will talk about how the executive processing domain may contribute to clients' indecisiveness, but first we want to briefly look at indecisiveness in relation to the SDS and the interpretive ideas outlined in chapter 7. In our experience, which has been further supported by research, indecisiveness is clearly linked to lower vocational identity levels. One item on the MVS Vocational Identity scale that seems to get at this issue most clearly is the one that reads, "I am not sure of myself in many areas of life." Clients who endorse this item typically need more intensive, one-on-one assistance over an extended period of time. Their inability to make career decisions and the negative emotions they experience related to this issue may be just the "tip of the iceberg." In addition to MVS results, counselors may be alert to other indicators from SDS results, including low coherence, lack of differentiation, low congruence, and a low level of consistency.

Counselors who suspect a client may be indecisive, but who choose to use the SDS to get more information about the client's situation may wish to modify their instructions to the client concerning completion of the SDS. For instance, some indecisive clients are paralyzed by the simple act of having to list their aspirations. They may say or write such things as, "I have no clue." When asked to complete an activity, they respond by saying, "If I knew what I wanted to do, I wouldn't be here." These clients may benefit from having access to the Alphabetized Occupations Finder to make the search process a little less intimidating. The counselor might also allow them to skip this step all together or at least the step where the client searches for codes.

Similar to these suggestions, counselors may ask indecisive clients to stop after adding their scores before proceeding to the section, What Your Summary Score Means. Counselors can check to see what thoughts and feelings clients experienced while completing the SDS and deal with any negative reactions before encouraging clients to pursue additional self- and occupational exploration. Indecisive clients may have a harder time dealing with an uncommon code. The lack of interesting or attractive options may make them feel worse about their situation. Conversely, those with a code associated with large numbers of options may experience anxiety when faced with so many choices. This notion of "getting inside clients' heads" to explore the impact of their thoughts and feelings on their ability to successfully engage the career decision making and problem solving process takes us to the final component of the CIP model: executive processing or thinking about thinking.

Executive Processing or Thinking About Thinking

As we noted earlier, a topic that has received increasing attention in both the counseling and career counseling field is the impact of thoughts on both feelings and behaviors. In other words, how we think affects our emotions and how we behave. Sometimes, despite our best efforts to assist clients in obtaining self-knowledge, knowledge about options, and developing a decision making strategy, they are still stuck. What accounts for this? Why didn't the intervention work?

We have come to believe that part of the answer could be found by "looking inside our clients' heads," or asking, "What are they thinking? How do they view themselves in this process? How are those thoughts influencing their ability to make progress in solving their career problems?" Our early experiences using the SDS and the MVS in our center also confirmed some of our ideas along these lines. On the one hand, we would see very positive signs on clients' SDS results. They seemed to know themselves and were considering options that fit well with their personal characteristics. On the other hand, they had very low vocational identity scores on the MVS. In chapter 7 we referred to this as "awfulizing," meaning that despite the fact that they had options and seemed to know themselves, these clients presented themselves as needing a great deal of help They came for services using such phrases as "I'm really confused," "I have no idea what I want to do," and "I need lots of help." Or they would comment after completing the SDS, "This really didn't help me." You may have heard one or more variations on these themes in your own practice. Our work on the CIP model led us to identify this aspect of the career problem solving process as an important missing piece.

As clients "process the process" of making career choices, several cognitive activities may enhance or impede their ability to successfully resolve their career concern. Sampson, Peterson, Lenz, Reardon and Saunders (1996b) described several ways clients experience difficulty in this area. First, they may not view themselves as being able to do this task well (e.g., "I'm not confident I can make a good choice."). They lack confidence as a career problem solver and decision maker. Second, they overwhelm themselves with shoulds, oughts, and musts (e.g., "I must make the right career choice."). Third, they may be depressed or anxious about ever finding a satisfactory solution to their career concern. Fourth, they seem unable to persist in the activities required to complete the problem solving task, and they cannot maintain their focus and energy. Finally, they may be overly reliant on external forces to solve their problems (e.g., a significant other in their lives).

Similar to indecisive clients, those experiencing difficulty in the executive processing domain would be expected to exhibit low levels of vocational identity and to have a number of negative indicators on SDS interpretive factors. Our observations of clients with these patterns of negative thoughts led us to develop an instrument known as the Career Thoughts Inventory (CTI) that could provide a brief objective measure of the impact of these thoughts on their career problem solving and decision making process.

Career Thoughts Inventory

The Career Thoughts Inventory (CTI) is a "theory-based assessment and intervention resource intended to improve the quality of career decisions made by adults, college students, and high school students, and the quality of career services delivered to these clients" (Sampson, Peterson, Lenz, Reardon, & Saunders, 1996c, p. 1). Consisting of 48 items covering each area of the pyramid and the CASVE cycle, the CTI provides a total score and scores on Decision-making Confusion, Commitment Anxiety, and External Conflict. It can be used as both a screening and a needs assessment measure, and when accompanied by the CTI workbook, can be used as a learning resource to help clients identify, challenge, and alter their negative thoughts.

Preliminary screening of clients using an instrument such as the CTI may help practitioners assess their ability to benefit from an intervention such as the SDS. It may also help identify where in the career choice process clients may be having trouble. Practitioners can use both CTI and SDS results to help clients see where they may be stuck and what activities may be needed to get them unstuck, and to enable them to learn and apply the skills needed for successfully engaging and solving their career problems. In addition, it may be noted that the MVS Identity scale and the CTI total score are highly negatively correlated (i.e., low identity scores are highly correlated with high CTI scores). This relationship between the CTI and the MVS provides another link between RIASEC and CIP theories. Other research (Sampson, et al., 1996b; Saunders, 1996; Saunders, Sampson, Peterson, Lenz, & Reardon, 1993) has supported the notion that lower scores on the vocational identity scale are associated with negative career thoughts.

Readers wanting a more detailed description of the CTI are referred to the CTI Professional Manual (Sampson, Peterson, Lenz, Reardon, & Saunders, 1996b), to a chapter by Peterson, Sampson, Reardon, and Lenz (1996) in the third edition of Brown and Brooks' *Career Choice and Development*, and to the chapter on "Negative Thinking and Career Choice" by Sampson, Peterson, Lenz, Reardon, and Saunders (1996d) in Feller and Walz's *Career Transitions in Turbulent Times*.

Connecting RIASEC and CIP Theories

Holland's RIASEC theory is especially strong in connecting the self- and occupational-knowledge domains, and CIP theory is strong in describing the metacognitions, the thoughts, and the beliefs in the executive processing domain that govern the career decision making and problem solving processes. Together, these two theories help counselors unravel the "personal career theory" (PCT) (Holland, 1997) that clients bring to the career services process. In the following paragraphs, we will explore the idea of a PCT and the role it plays in career services, including counseling.

Partly in response to the criticism that RIASEC theory was silent about career counseling processes, Holland (1997) has suggested that everyone has a PCT about careers or work, which can range from weak and invalid to complex and good. When a PCT fails, a person seeks outside career assistance, and a successful career intervention helps a person revise or implement his or her PCT. Holland (1997) views most PCTs as having elements of the RIASEC typology (e.g., personal characteristics related to occupational structures, as well as beliefs and strategies for achieving work and nonwork aspirations that flow from a special life history).

Counselors can become informed about a client's PCT by using card sorts, by completing the Daydreams section of the SDS, by listening to the client's career history, and by understanding the client's present career difficulty. The typology may be assessed with the SDS, and the beliefs and strategies (career thoughts) can be measured with the CTI. Holland (1997) speculates that one reason for the popularity of RIASEC theory is that it helps clients improve the typologies in their own PCT. We believe that the CTI may come to be popular because it helps clients learn more about the negative thoughts that interfere with their successful career decision making. PCTs can be improved by using the SDS and related Holland-based interventions, particularly the MVS and CASI, and by using the CTI and the CTI workbook.

Holland (1997) suggests that most career interventions are successful because the average client has a PCT with a moderate degree of validity. As a result, clients need relatively little help to implement their PCTs. On the other hand, clients with flawed, dysfunctional PCTs may need more extensive assistance. Holland thinks that problems stem from the three parts of the PCT: personal characteristics, occupational knowledge, and translation units. In

CIP terms, these are defined as the knowledge domains and the decision skills domain. Holland believes that persons having a PCT with a weak translation unit (i.e., poor CASVE decision-making skills) or pervasive weaknesses (i.e., many negative career thoughts on the CTI) require more intensive career assistance.

In summary, counselors can use a client's PCT to help determine how to provide career assistance. "The active and sensitive pursuit of a person's PCT may foster some of the counseling qualities that usually lead to effective individual counseling: respect for the client, genuineness, and empathic understanding" (Holland, 1997, p. 208). And the ideas, instruments, and materials provided by RIASEC and CIP theories can help clients improve their PCTs.

Conclusion

This chapter has provided a link between an emerging career theory, cognitive information processing (CIP), and the use of Holland-based tools and concepts. The marriage of these ideas and interventions provides practitioners with a powerful set of tools to use with their clients. Holland's RIASEC typology works especially well in linking self- and occupational knowledge, and other Holland instruments such as the MVS and the CASI enable us to learn more about how a client might be approaching the career decision-making process. CIP theory, represented by the pyramid of information processing domains and the Career Thoughts Inventory (CTI), help improve our understanding of the cognitive processes at work in career problem solving and decision making, including the CASVE cycle and the executive processing domain. Finally, the taxonomy of decision making examined the varied characteristics of the decided, undecided, and indecisive decision makers seeking career services. For each of these groups, suggestions were made for using the SDS and other Holland-based interventions in career assistance.

9

Using Diagnostic Signs
in Career Assistance

This book assumes that practitioners are working in settings where they have several Holland-based tools at their disposal. In our setting, we found that our paraprofessional staff members were often too quick to assume that administering the SDS was the most appropriate intervention for a client. We are obviously big fans of the SDS and do not think anyone will be "hurt" by taking it, but cost considerations, as well as client need factors, led us to develop guidelines that would help our staff make more informed judgments about which Holland tool might meet a particular client's needs. We begin this chapter by sharing some guidelines we developed. Following these guidelines, we will review how counselors might use the diagnostic information provided by RIASEC theory and the SDS, as well as CIP theory, to make decisions about how to best assist a client. We demonstrate these ideas by walking readers through a case study illustration. Information in this chapter can also be readily applied to the six case studies in chapter 10.

Guidelines for Using the Self-Directed Search and Related Holland-Based Interventions

Various forms of the SDS can be used both as diagnostic screening tools and interest assessments, but we suggest that a complete administration of the SDS not be automatic in every case. Some of the other Holland-based tools described in chapters 4, 6, and 7 can be used as a preliminary activity before administering the SDS or as an alternative to the use of another structured intervention. Some of these tools include My Vocational Situation (MVS), the *Dictionary of Holland Occupational Codes* (DHOC), the Educational Opportunities Finder, the Leisure Activities Finder, the hexagon figure, The Occupations Finder, and the You and Your Career booklet.

The purpose of these guidelines (see Table 18) is to identify situations where non-SDS, as well as SDS interventions might be indicated. The guidelines follow from the use of a brief screening interview which is designed to determine the client's readiness for career assistance. As we explain later in chapter 11, this assistance may be in the form of self-help, brief staff assistance, or individual case management, providing a range of career counseling assistance from less to more. The guidelines provide the counselor with client information along a series of markers or decision points that can be used to suggest alternative intervention activities.

Deciding on a career intervention can be based on several considerations that are explored in a brief screening interview following either a client request to "take a test to find out what I should be," or a client's expressed need to learn more about career interests. The choice of an intervention may also be based on the traffic flow in the office or center, the time that a staff member has

Table 18
Suggested Guidelines for Assigning the SDS Form R,
SDS Form R:CV, and Related Holland Interventions

Given the condition(s) in the left column below, the counselor may choose one or more of the non-SDS interventions in the right column.

Conditions	Non-SDS alternatives
If the client can confidently describe himself or herself in terms of Holland types and wants to translate this into compatible work settings...	Use the hexagon to explain Holland types and their interrelationships (i.e., consistency); provide a copy of The Occupations Finder for use in exploring options.
If the client can identify an occupational aspiration(s), but wants to expand the number of options...	Use the hexagon and The Occupations Finder and/or the DHOC to explore occupational alternatives.
If the client can identify aspirations and needs to explore majors...	Use the hexagon, academic program guides, or the Educational Opportunities Finder to explore fields of study.
If the client would benefit from a clearer understanding of the structure of the occupational worlds...	Use the hexagon, The Occupations Finder, the Educational Opportunities Finder, or the You and Your Career booklet to explain Holland's theory.
If the client lacks self- or occupational knowledge...	Use the You and Your Career booklet to illustrate how persons use the theory to relate self-knowledge to occupational or educational options.

If the client does not respond to the above activities and appears to benefit little from them, the counselor may consider the conditions outlined below.

Conditions	SDS interventions
If the client has noncoherent aspirations, suspected noncongruence between aspirations and Summary code, a discrepancy between interests and skills, or suspected low vocational identity or negative career thoughts, or if the staff member is uncertain and needs more information...	Use the SDS Form R, SDS Form R:CV, or another version appropriate to the client being assisted.

available to talk, and the career intervention policies of the office (e.g., get the client started on something quickly in order to reward the client for seeking career assistance).

In a nutshell, we view diagnosing career problems as a collaborative activity between the counselor and the client to understand and improve the client's Personal Career Theory (PCT), discussed earlier in chapter 8. The PCT has two basic components, one represented by the RIASEC hexagon and the other by the CIP pyramid. Diagnosing a client's career situation involves focusing on his or her hexagon and asking, "What does it look like?" In other words, How good a matching typology does the client have to work with? Does the client know where he or she is on the hexagon? Does the client know what fields of study or occupations exist and where they fit on the hexagon? Does the client understand how different kinds of persons or careers relate to one another? Similarly, what does the client's pyramid look like? What do the self- and option knowledge domains look like? What kinds of facts and experience does the client have about work situations? What kind of decision making and problem solving strategies does the client use? And, finally, what about the client's executive processing domain, the metacognitions? Is there evidence of negative thinking about career decision making? We believe increased knowledge and understanding about the client's hexagon and pyramid can help improve a PCT that is not enabling the client to solve career problems and make career decisions effectively.

A Brief Screening Interview

Many of us have encountered clients who came in asking to "take the test." Some are even quite adamant in their demand that they receive this type of assistance from a counselor. In our setting, we encourage our staff not to "cave in" immediately to such requests but to take some time to gather additional information from the client by exploring one or more of the following questions:

1. Did someone tell the client to do this?
2. What outcomes does the client expect?
3. How much time does the client have?
4. Does the client want to explore options, narrow options, or confirm a previous option?
5. Has the client taken interest and/or aptitude tests before?
6. How confused or anxious does the client appear to be?

Based on client responses to these topics, counselors might choose to explain alternative activities to the SDS that could be used to help clients solve their career and educational planning problems. In other instances, a referral to another agency might be needed or services could be withheld. For example, if the client does not appear self-motivated to work on a career problem (e.g., "My parents told me to come in.") or if the client has only a brief, insufficient period of time available, career services might be delayed until these matters are resolved.

With clients who are more vague or uncertain, but who appear to be self-motivated with sufficient time and energy to engage in career decision making, counselors may wish to explore the following 11 topics in the brief screening interview:

1. The client's history of occupational aspirations and whether these are coherent (e.g., shape of the hexagon).

2. Whether interests are congruent with skills (e.g., nature of hexagon).

3. Whether the problem involves primarily fields of study and training or occupations.

4. How much structure the client seems to need regarding career assistance.

5. What has been done in the past to solve the problem.

6. How much time is presently available (both for the client and the staff member).

7. The client's anxiety level (e.g., nature of the pyramid).

8. The client's estimated or assessed degree of negative thinking (e.g., nature of the pyramid).

9. The estimated or assessed level of vocational identity (e.g., nature of the pyramid).

10. The client's readiness to examine educational or occupational information (e.g., nature of the pyramid).

11. The extent to which intensive educational counseling or academic advising might be needed.

Exploration of these topics may provide some clues for counselors to use in deciding whether interventions other than the SDS may be more appropriate. Obtaining information related to these topics will also clarify the nature of the client's PCT and illuminate the nature of the client's hexagon and pyramid using RIASEC and CIP theories, respectively.

When the SDS Is Not Indicated

In our judgment, the SDS may not be the most appropriate intervention if (a) the client primarily needs occupational information; (b) the client needs educational planning information; (c) the client is highly agitated, depressed, or anxious; (d) the client's negative thinking and/or low vocational identity seem to overwhelm his or her ability to make good use of self- and occupational information; or (e) the client appears intent on having a test or some other external device or outside authority make a vocational choice.

Table 18 summarizes some of our ideas on this subject. A counselor might be able to immediately refer to information resources such as the DHOC, EOF, YYC, and other Holland-based materials, but in some cases may need to engage in mental health counseling or make a referral for personal counseling before proceeding with career assistance. Depending on the agency policies and the training of the counselor, it may be possible to combine mental health and career assistance using the Career Thoughts Inventory (Sampson, Peterson, Lenz, Reardon, & Saunders, 1996a) and a cognitive information processing approach to career counseling (Peterson, Sampson, & Reardon, 1991; Peterson, Sampson, Reardon, & Lenz, 1996).

Assigning the SDS

If a counselor opts to use the SDS and the client agrees (see Table 20), several structuring statements at the end of the brief screening interview may increase the likelihood of a positive experience. These statements should emphasize the use of the SDS to meet the client's need for self-assessment information and to meet the client's need to make career decisions. The focus is not on taking the SDS to simply obtain a list of occupations to enter. In our setting, we often use the pyramid figure, described in chapter 8, as a way of linking the SDS to the career choice process. We can use the pyramid to talk about where the SDS fits and what "knowledge gaps" in the pyramid it can fill. The SDS can also be presented as a means for learning more about the client's PCT.

First, the counselor should discuss with the client the use of the SDS as an appropriate intervention given the client's situation. In other words, the use of the SDS is not automatic, but the result of an informed judgment by both the counselor and client. In our setting, staff members list the SDS on an Individual Learning Plan (Appendix H) and explain the purpose of this activity in relation to information obtained in the brief screening interview regarding the client's goals.

Second, the SDS is distinguished from a test or inventory. As noted in chapter 4, it is technically an educational and career planning guide which simulates an interest inventory. Highly test-oriented clients may find it useful to have the SDS described as a paper and pencil or computer-based career planning simulation. Research and experience has taught us that the SDS is effective with 50-75% of users through increased self-knowledge, number of occupational alternatives considered, satisfaction with present aspiration, and knowledge of the theory.

Third, the counselor can briefly review with the client the components of the SDS, especially the assessment sections (including the MVS with the SDS Form R:CV) and The Occupations Finder (or the alphabetical listing of occupations in the computer version), and underscore the importance of the Daydreams section. The counselor can also remind clients to make sure they start with their most recent daydream and work backwards, avoiding the temptation (especially if using an alphabetical listing) of starting with the As and just working through the alphabet. For the paper and pencil SDS, counselors should note the scoring procedures at the end and emphasize the importance of carefully transferring and adding the numbers for each scale.

Fourth, the counselor should explain that the SDS may take 45 to 60 minutes (paper and pencil) or 40 to 50 minutes (computer) to complete, and that the client should allow at least 20 minutes to discuss the results with a counselor or an appropriate staff member following the administration. This procedure can vary in the particular setting where the SDS is being administered. If both computer and paper versions of the SDS are readily available in a setting, practitioners may want to check with clients regarding the format they would prefer.

This section has presented guidelines for counselors to consider in deciding whether to use the paper and pencil or computer-based version of the SDS or some other Holland-based intervention. Consideration of these issues and use of these guidelines can potentially lead to more discriminating use of the SDS, more responsive and efficient client services, and more satisfied clients.

Using and Interpreting SDS Results

After the decision is made to administer the SDS, the next issue is how to use the SDS results to most fully assist the individual needing assistance. One of the aims of this book is to encourage counselors to make full use of the information embedded in an individual's SDS results. If using the paper and pencil version of Form R, some simple calculations will be required, along with review of selected tables in the *SDS Professional User's Guide* (Holland, Powell, & Fritzsche, 1994). Users are encouraged to adapt the worksheet in Appendix I to facilitate use of the secondary constructs. Counselors using the computer version of the SDS Form R will be able to quickly review the secondary constructs and other interpretive information by printing a copy of the Professional Summary from their client's completed SDS results. Figure 12 shows a sample of a Professional Summary from the SDS Form R Computer Version.

The Self-Directed Search Professional Summary

```
Client Name : Jane Doe          Age : 19
ID Number : 042                 Sex : Female
Reference Group : College       Education : 13
Test Date :  3/27/97
```

SDS Scores:	R	I	A	S	E	C	Code
Activities	3	5	4	5	5	0	ISE
Competencies	7	11	4	11	8	8	ISE
Occupations	0	6	3	4	6	1	IES
Self-Estimates I	4	6	5	6	5	5	ISA
Self-Estimates II	4	5	3	5	5	5	ISE
Summary Scores	18	33	19	31	29	19	ISE
Percentiles	74	89	44	37	65	45	

OF Selection Codes: ISE, IES, SIE, SEI, EIS, ESI

Diagnostic Signs:

Congruence	Average (Iachan Index = 6)
Summary Code	ISE
Aspirations Summary Code	REI
Coherence of Aspirations	Average
Vocational Identity	Average
Consistency	Average
Differentiation	Average (Iachan Index = 4.00)
Commonness	Average

MVS Scores:

Vocational Identity	11
(Need for) Information	1
(Decision) Barriers	4

Aspirations Listed:

Biologist	IRE
Chemist	IRE
Jeweler	REC
Photographer, Still	AES
Teacher, Secondary School	SAE
Aspirations Summary Code:	REI

Figure 12. The Self-Directed Search Form R Professional Summary. From the SDS Form R: Computer Version, 1996, by R. C. Reardon and N. Ona, Odessa, FL: Psychological Assessment Resources. Copyright © 1996 by Psychological Assessment Resources, Inc. Reprinted with permission.

Dealing With Flat Profiles

Differentiation of a client's profile may provide additional insight into the source of career problems. As explained in chapters 2, 4, and 7, differentiation is the extent to which a client's profile has clearly defined highs and lows or peaks and valleys, as opposed to a profile that is flat or undifferentiated. A flat profile may be undifferentiated high or low. Let's explore the practical implications of a so-called flat profile and possible ways to intervene.

Clients with flat profiles may lack self- and occupational knowledge and may need more life experiences, including training and exposure to different fields of work. They may need to review occupational information resources to narrow their thinking about options (i.e., they may need to engage the Synthesis phase of the CASVE cycle). These clients should be encouraged to pursue experiential learning opportunities, such as volunteer activities, internships, and cooperative education assignments. The counselor may encourage these activities in one or more of the service delivery formats mentioned in chapter 8, including individual counseling, self-directed activities, groups, or curricular interventions.

Individuals with high flat profiles often represent a special case of career indecision. In the career decision making taxonomy described in chapter 8, we noted that these individuals might be classified as "multipotential." They often have multiple talents and interests, as well as high levels of energy. To gather additional information about the client's situation and help pinpoint what may be contributing to the flat profile, the counselor may wish to administer a diagnostic instrument such as the Career Thoughts Inventory (CTI) or the My Vocational Situation (MVS). One would expect to see elevated scores on the Decision-making Confusion and Commitment Anxiety scales of the CTI.

Counselors need to be particularly alert to low flat profiles that result from other more complex and serious emotional and psychological issues. Clients who are thinking in negative ways about themselves, who are experiencing low self-esteem or depression, and who lack self-efficacy would be expected to have low flat profiles. Again, counselors may want to explore these issues more fully by administering additional assessments and scheduling extended individual interviews with the client. These clients may need to examine the extent to which personal and career counseling issues overlap. They may want to consider a support group that deals with particular issues (e.g., a woman who is reentering the work force following a divorce may find it helpful to participate in a divorce support group while she is exploring her future career options).

Using these concepts and the interpretive ideas outlined in chapter 7, the following case analysis example illustrates how this information might be used in developing ideas about a client's PCT, including the shape of the hexagon and pyramid. This example also specifies positive and negative signs in the PCT, accompanied by strategies for assisting that client; these are outlined on a sample Individual Learning Plan.

College Student Case Study: "Inez"

Inez is a 19-year-old Hispanic female seeking assistance regarding her choice of major. Inez is attending a public 4-year university, and she came into the career center wanting to "find out what you do here." She completed the Career Thoughts Inventory (CTI). Her total score was 66 (82nd percentile); her scores on the Construct scales were as follows: Decision-making Confusion, 20 (90th percentile); Commitment Anxiety, 20 (90th percentile); and External Conflict, 5 (79th percentile). Inez indicated that she was good in math and science in high school, but expressed some concern about her ability to do college-level work in these areas. She expressed interest in both business- and science-related fields. She indicated that she is somewhat reluctant to pursue a science major because she's heard that it's hard. Her father is retired and her mother is working in a clerical position with a government agency. She is the first one in her family to attend college. Inez's previous work experience was in grocery stores and fast food restaurants, and currently she's employed as a student assistant in a student services office. She has completed most of her college prerequisite courses and wants to decide her major before registering for next semester's classes. Inez indicated that she had not completed any type of interest inventory in high school, but she had explored occupations on her high school's computer-based guidance system. She indicated that she had at least 2 hours to spend in the center, and after the counselor described the Self-Directed Search Form R, Inez expressed an interest in completing it.

The results of Inez's paper and pencil SDS are as follows:

Occupational Daydreams

Pediatrician	(ISE)
Nursing	(SIA)
Physical therapist	(SIE)
Sports therapy	(SEC)
Business administration	(ESC)
International business	(ESR)
Business management	(ESC)

Because some of Inez's aspirations were not found in The Occupations Finder, the counselor assisted her in using the DHOC to locate codes for some of the options she had listed.

Before we focus on Inez's assessed results, let's examine her aspirations and walk through how we calculate an Aspirations summary code as described in chapter 2. As you may recall, we assigned a 3 to each letter in the first position, a 2 to each letter in the second position, and a 1 to each letter in the third position, and then added the total for each. Our results for Inez were:

R=1, I=7, A=1, S=17, E=13, C=3.

Calculating the Aspirations summary code using all of Inez's daydreams produces a code of SEI. The results of her paper and pencil SDS are shown in Figure 13.

Table 19 summarizes the key diagnostic information from Inez's results on a worksheet. Before reviewing our analysis of this case, readers might want to think about strategies for assisting this individual. Some issues and questions to consider might include the following:

1. What are the important elements in her PCT?

2. How would you describe her pyramid in terms of her decision-making status?

3. Apply the "Rule of 8" in considering her S and I summary scores.

4. What about the influence of her C-oriented work history?

5. What about her aspirations toward more prestigious S occupations that also pay fairly well and offer some degree of job security, compared to her rejection of all S occupations listed in the SDS Occupations section?

6. What do you suspect is making it hard for her to commit to a first choice? How would you help her deal with her anxiety over this decision?

Authors' Case Analysis of Inez

Inez appeared to have a workable PCT, in that her self-knowledge and information about options were based on a good approximation of RIASEC theory. She readily acknowledged her "people-oriented nature," and this was evident in the prominence of the Social and Enterprising types in her expressed and assessed interests. Regarding her pyramid, she appeared to be "undecided" as opposed to "indecisive" and seemed to need some help learning more about the relationship between her personal characteristics and her options. Her decision making process was also being overwhelmed by her tendency toward negative thinking. She lacked confidence in her ability to solve her career problems and seemed overwhelmed by the choices available to her. Although her parents were supportive, she still felt some pressure to make a choice that would please them. Inez's negative thinking may cause her to underestimate her abilities, anticipate failure, or limit her exploratory behaviors.

How To Organize Your Answers _____

Start on page 4. Count how many times you said **L** for "Like." Record the number of **Ls** or **Ys** for each group of Activities, Competencies, or Occupations on the lines below.

Activities (pp. 4-5)

0	5	1	5	9	8
R	I	A	S	E	C

Competencies (pp. 6-7)

8	3	1	8	7	8
R	I	A	S	E	C

Occupations (p. 8)

0	1	1	0	4	4
R	I	A	S	E	C

Self-Estimates (p. 9)
(What number did you circle?)

2	3	4	4	5	4
R	I	A	S	E	C

4	6	2	4	6	6
R	I	A	S	E	C

Total Scores
(Add the five R scores, the five I scores, the five A scores, etc.)

14	18	9	21	31	30
R	I	A	S	E	C

The letters with the three highest numbers indicate your Summary Code. Write your Summary Code below. (If two scores are the same or tied, put both letters in the same box.)

Summary Code

E	C	S
Highest	2nd	3rd

10

Figure 13. SDS summary sheet for "Inez." From the Self-Directed Search Form R Assessment Booklet (p. 10), by J. L. Holland, 1994, Odessa, FL: Psychological Assessment Resources. Copyright © 1970, 1977, 1985, 1990, 1994 by Psychological Assessment Resources, Inc. Reprinted with permission.

Table 19
SDS Case Worksheet for Inez

Indicators	Information about Inez
Summary code	ECS
Aspirations summary code	SEI
Code of first aspiration	ISE
Congruence	Average
Coherence	Low
My Vocational Situation	N/A
Vocational identity	N/A
Occupational information	N/A
Barriers	N/A
Consistency	High
Differentiation	Average
Commonness	Average

Additional assessment information	CTI Scores
	    Total Score: 66 (82nd %ile)
	    Decision Making Confusion: 20 (90th %ile)
	    Commit. Anxiety: 20 (90th %ile)
	    External Conflict: 5 (79th %ile)

Additional notes	First generation college student C-oriented work experience Self-efficacy regarding math and science
Possible interventions	Correct negative self-talk
	Learn more about high level S options in relation to E and I supporting areas
	Obtain more tryout experience in science courses and health occupations
	Build on the positive qualities of Inez's present PCT and encourage her to build upon what she already knows about herself and her options

Inez acknowledged that she was torn between the helping professions and something more secure, such as business. The counselor raised the issue of the discrepancy between the S orientation in the aspirations, in contrast to her score of 0 for S on the SDS Occupations scale. She had eliminated those alternatives because she viewed them as lacking in prestige, job security, and income potential. She preferred to use her S competencies in a field like health care, which for both her and her family was viewed as offering a good future and an acceptable level of prestige and income. Inez was pleased with some of the options that appeared when various combinations of her Aspirations summary code, SEI, were used to identify options.

The counselor explored with Inez the possibility of a volunteer position or internship in a health care setting to gain occupational information and help boost her confidence about her ability to do this work. She planned to begin taking the prerequisites for admission to the School of Nursing beginning the next semester. To help Inez work on her tendency to think negatively about her career decisions, the counselor gave her a copy of the Career Thoughts Inventory Workbook (Sampson, Peterson, Lenz, Reardon, & Saunders, 1996c). Inez had 20 items on the CTI that she endorsed "Agree" or "Strongly Agree." The counselor used one of these as an example of how a person can identify, challenge, and alter negative thinking. Inez agreed to work on at least two more items during the next week and report on that process at her next appointment. Inez hasn't given up the goal of considering a career as a pediatrician some day, but she wants to prove that she can do the science coursework before she actively pursues that goal. Inez felt good that she could please herself and her family and benefit society by her choice of occupation. She acknowledged that doubts about her ability to be successful sometimes creep in, but she felt better about being able to handle that negative thinking when it occurs.

Conclusion

This chapter provided a transition between earlier discussions about the various tools that comprise the Holland family of resources, as well as those coming from cognitive information processing theory, and the way these tools might be interpreted and used. It provided a link to practice by discussing how someone might intervene with clients, by not only using the RIASEC theory and SDS, but also considering the use of other Holland-based interventions as a first step. The idea of unraveling clients' Personal Career Theory (PCT), including the nature of their RIASEC hexagon and their CIP pyramid, was presented. Guidelines were provided to improve counselors' decision making about how to match Holland tools with client needs and how to introduce the SDS to clients to achieve maximum benefit from the intervention. This was followed by a case study designed to illustrate how the various diagnostic and interpretive signs from both Holland and CIP theory could be applied. The next chapter will provide additional case study examples and encourage practitioners to directly apply what they have learned in the preceding chapters.

10

Six Case Studies

This chapter presents six case studies that vary from the one examined in the preceding chapter. Major points and concepts explained in earlier chapters will be illustrated using cases involving two older workers, a college student, a community college student, a high school student, and a prison inmate seeking career assistance. Readers are encouraged to use the concepts discussed in chapters 7, 8, and 9 to analyze the cases and think about interventions that might be helpful for each client. Readers can then review the authors' analysis and suggestions for these cases in Appendix J.

Case 1: "Martha"

Case Notes

Martha is a 47-year-old, single White female who has been employed for several years with a government agency. She has had a continuous work history in various human services positions, except for a brief period when she was terminated from her job after a new board of directors took over and wanted to place their own person in the agency's senior position. During this period, Martha did part-time administrative work for a legislative committee. Martha completed her bachelor's degree in psychology and some graduate-level courses in religious education. She expressed some interest in church-related positions if she were to change jobs. In her leisure time, Martha is an avid reader. She subscribes to magazines related to crafts and cooking and has redone some furniture in her house. She is active in a local church and has held leadership roles in a civic organization.

Martha has been unhappy in her current job as a management analyst for a state agency and is concerned that she may be downsized due to reorganizations in the agency. She had been hesitant to leave her job because of her seniority and the stable income it provided, but acknowledged that she had become increasingly frustrated because of new supervisors who didn't recognize or appreciate her contributions. The possibility of being downsized has prompted her to consider other work alternatives.

Martha sought assistance at a university-based career center that served community adults. Although she admitted that she is sometimes angry at the treatment she has received from her employer, Martha did not present herself as being overly distraught or depressed, and she indicated she was looking forward to exploring some other options. Following her initial interview and to assist the counselor in better understanding her present situation, Martha completed the SDS Form R, the Position Classification Inventory (PCI), and the Career Attitudes and Strategies Inventory (CASI). The results of these assessments follow.

Using the information provided, readers are asked to complete the worksheet at the end of the chapter. After determining the diagnostic signs involved in her case and the extent to which Martha has positive and negative factors working for her, readers should make recommendations about how to intervene with Martha. How can we best help her? To compare your results with those of the authors, see Appendix J.

Case Data

SDS

Occupational Daydreams

Minister	SAI
Religious education director	SEA
Psychologist	SIA
Education and training manager	EIS
Desktop publisher	CSE

Code for current occupation based on the third edition of the DHOC: ICR

Our Comments

Martha's case is a good illustration of a situation experienced by many adults who seek career counseling. Her SDS and PCI results indicate that she is an S working in an S job, and the PCI code is one combination of her SDS summary code. Although the DHOC code for her current occupation of Management Analyst is ICR, the fact that it is located in a government human services agency may account for S being the highest letter for the position based on her PCI scores. This discrepancy between the DHOC code and Martha's PCI code reaffirms the importance of developing "local norms" for occupational codes using the PCI. The unique demands of a particular work setting may have a significance influence on a person's view of his or her occupation. A review of the data in Martha's case suggests that she seems to be working in a job that is congruent with her skills and interests, yet she's not happy. What might be the source of her career difficulties?

How To Organize Your Answers _____

Start on page 4. Count how many times you said **L** for "Like." Record the number of **Ls** or **Ys** for each group of Activities, Competencies, or Occupations on the lines below.

Activities (pp. 4-5)

3	1	11	8	10	2
R	I	A	S	E	C

Competencies (pp. 6-7)

8	0	6	10	8	10
R	I	A	S	E	C

Occupations (p. 8)

2	2	10	7	8	1
R	I	A	S	E	C

Self-Estimates (p. 9)
(What number did you circle?)

2	1	5	6	4	4
R	I	A	S	E	C

4	1	4	7	6	5
R	I	A	S	E	C

Total Scores
(Add the five R scores, the five I scores, the five A scores, etc.)

19	5	36	38	36	22
R	I	A	S	E	C

The letters with the three highest numbers indicate your Summary Code. Write your Summary Code below. (If two scores are the same or tied, put both letters in the same box.)

Summary Code

S	A	E
Highest	2nd	3rd

10

Figure 14. SDS summary sheet for "Martha." From the Self-Directed Search Form R Assessment Booklet (p. 10), by J. L. Holland, 1994, Odessa, FL: Psychological Assessment Resources. Copyright © 1970, 1977, 1985, 1990, 1994 by Psychological Assessment Resources, Inc. Reprinted with permission.

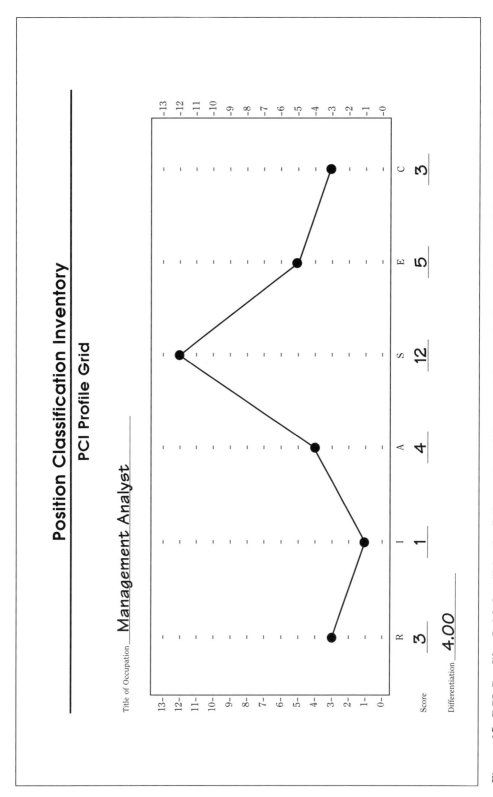

Figure 15. PCI Profile Grid for "Martha." Reproduced by special permission of the publisher, Psychological Assessment Resources, Inc., from the *Position Classification Inventory* Profile Grid, copyright © 1991 by Psychological Assessment Resources, Inc.

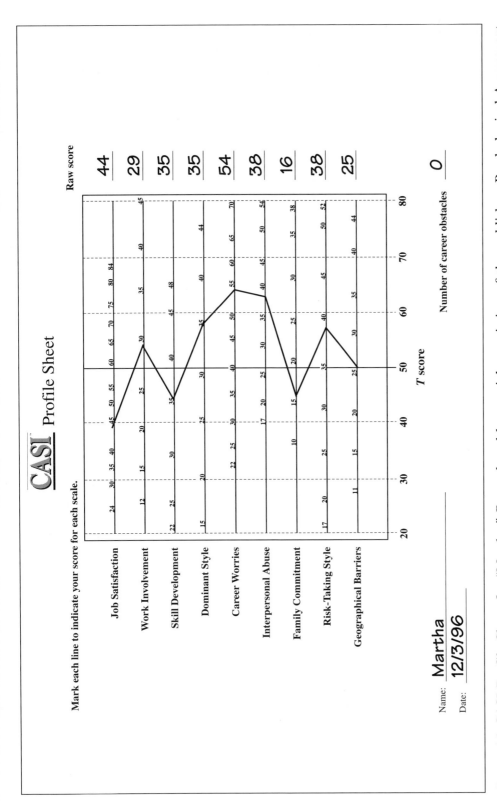

Figure 16. CASI Profile Sheet for "Martha." Reproduced by special permission of the publisher, Psychological Assessment Resources, Inc., from the *Career Attitudes and Strategies Inventory* Profile Sheet, copyright © 1992, 1993, 1994 by Psychological Assessment Resources, Inc.

This is a case where the CASI provides us with some clues, particularly the Job Satisfaction, Career Worries, and Interpersonal Abuse scales. Martha is concerned about finding another job if she leaves her present one, and she is at a point in her life where she is very dependent on her income to meet her living expenses. She is, however, aggravated enough by her present work situation to consider making some kind of change. Much of her dissatisfaction comes from her personal feelings toward her work ("I am bored with my job.") and the treatment she has received from others ("One or more persons about my level at work have treated me in a degrading way.").

Despite these factors, Martha felt good enough about her skills and her accomplishments to want to explore other alternatives. Martha worked with the counselor to develop a functional resume that highlighted her accomplishments. She identified contacts at consulting firms she had dealt with in her current work with whom she could network regarding future opportunities. Many of the government services Martha had been involved with were being privatized, and she was willing to consider using her knowledge of these services in a consulting role. Because of her interest in religious education work, she planned to pursue opportunities for part-time or full-time work in church settings or with other religious education agencies. She was excited about the possibility of developing training materials that could be used in single adult ministries. In subsequent sessions, the counselor also worked with Martha to help her deal more effectively with her anger and occasional bouts of low self-esteem and depression. Six months later, Martha was able to locate employment with a private consulting firm, where she develops training materials and conducts training sessions for government agencies who are implementing a new software system used to manage employee health care benefits. She is also being paid by a local church to work with its single adult ministries.

Case 2: "Kisha"

Case Notes

Kisha is a 20-year-old African-American female enrolled in a career planning class at a local community college. She was completing her general education courses and was planning to transfer to the university to complete her 4-year degree. She had been undecided about her major but was considering something in the social sciences where she could help people. She had had a part-time job on campus working in the office that serves students with disabilities; as a result of this experience she had thought about becoming a rehabilitation counselor. Kisha had done some volunteer work at a nursing home where her grandmother was living and had also considered some type of work with the elderly. She said she planned to go on to graduate school, but wanted to be sure about her career choice before pursuing additional education.

As part of the career planning class assignments, Kisha completed the Career Thoughts Inventory and the computer version of the SDS Form R (which includes My Vocational Situation). The results of these assessments follow.

Using this information on Kisha, complete the Case 2 section of the Case Analysis Worksheet at the end of this chapter and think about how you might assist Kisha with her career situation. To compare your results with ours, review Appendix J.

Case Data

Occupational Daydreams

Alcohol-drug abuse program administrator	ESR
Rehabilitation counselor	SEC
Aging program administrator	EAS
Equal opportunity representative	ESA
Social welfare administrator	ESA

My Vocational Situation

Vocational Identity	0
(Need for) Information	0
(Decision) Barriers	1

Career Thoughts Inventory (CTI)

CTI Total Score:	61 (76th percentile)
Decision-Making Confusion (DMC):	13 (62nd percentile)
Commitment Anxiety (CA):	26 (99th percentile)
External Conflict (EC):	1 (14th percentile)

Our Comments

The good news for Kisha is that she was considering several options that fit well with the S and E aspects of her Holland code. The bad news is that she was experiencing a great deal of anxiety about choosing the "right" occupation, as evidenced by her CTI Commitment Anxiety score. Her inability to make a choice was also affected by her lack of vocational identity. Although she had ideas about occupations, she portrayed herself as being completely stuck when it came to arriving at a first choice. Her lack of detailed knowledge about the options she was considering made it difficult to prioritize her choices. Kisha had C competencies from her office work, but, as evidenced by her C score on the Occupations scale, she clearly was not considering options in this area, despite it being the second letter in her summary code. In contrast, Kisha

The Self-Directed Search Professional Summary

Client Name : **Kisha**   Age : **20**
ID Number :   Sex : **Female**
Reference Group : **College**   Education : **14**
Prepared for : FSU Career Center   Test Date : **2/18/97**

SDS Scores:	R	I	A	S	E	C	Code
Activities	1	1	2	9	5	2	SEA
Competencies	0	3	4	9	2	9	SCA
Occupations	0	2	0	12	3	0	SEI
Self-Estimates I	3	4	3	4	5	5	ECI
Self-Estimates II	5	2	5	7	5	6	SCR
Summary Scores	9	12	14	41	20	22	SCE
Percentiles	36	27	27	80	24	54	

OF Selection Codes: SCE, SEC, CSE, CES, ESC, ECS

Diagnostic Signs:

Congruence	Average (Iachan Index = 14)
Summary Code	SCE
Aspirations Summary Code	ESA
Coherence of Aspirations	Average
Vocational Identity	Low
Consistency	Average
Differentiation	High (Iachan Index = 11.50)
Commonness	High

MVS Scores:

Vocational Identity	0
(Need for) Information	0
(Decision) Barriers	1

Aspirations Listed:

Alcohol/Drug Abuse Administrator	ESR
Coordinator of Rehabilitation Services	SEI
Council on Aging Director	EAS
Equal-Opportunity Director	ESA
Social Welfare Administrator	ESA
Aspirations Summary Code:	ESA

Figure 17. The Self-Directed Search Form R Professional Summary for "Kisha." From the SDS Form R: Computer Version, 1996, by R. C. Reardon and N. Ona, Odessa, FL: Psychological Assessment Resources. Copyright © 1996 by Psychological Assessment Resources, Inc. Reprinted with permission.

identified only two competencies in the E scale, yet this code appeared as the first letter in her aspirations.

As part of her class assignment, Kisha was required to do three informational interviews with people in occupations she was considering. The class instructor referred her to a counselor working at a local rehabilitation hospital who had graduated from the university with a degree in rehabilitation services. Kisha also agreed to ask the administrator at her grandmother's nursing home if he would talk with her about his job, and she decided to interview a guidance counselor in her old high school. Kisha reported that these interviews helped her think more about the kinds of settings where she might work, and that she had felt best in the educational setting. This setting seemed to be a more positive place for her to work than the medical setting. Kisha used the information section of the career resource center's computer-assisted career guidance system to get printouts on several of the alternatives she was considering. The instructor explained to Kisha that she could use both of these activities as reference materials for the occupational analysis paper required in the class.

In addition to the assistance Kisha received from her instructor, she met with a career counselor in the college career counseling center and shared the results of her class assignments. In reviewing Kisha's SDS results, the counselor observed the low score on the E Competency scale. Together, they reviewed the section on the SDS Form R interpretive report that describes E types, and then the counselor asked Kisha to say a little bit more about what she was thinking as she responded to the items on this scale. In the process, Kisha reported an incident where her work supervisor had fired a crew because of missing money, and those fired were high school age, African-Americans. Although she felt terribly wronged, she did not confront this injustice or provide leadership to the other persons involved. She reported still being very angry about that incident. The counselor noted that Kisha had listed four occupational daydreams with E as their first letter. Together, they brainstormed ways that Kisha might develop her E competencies, through involvement in campus organizations, class activities, and additional volunteer work. One big difficulty for Kisha was speaking in front of groups. Kisha acknowledged that if she had exercised more of her E in that job layoff situation years ago, she might feel better about herself today.

Finally, after reviewing Kisha's CTI results, the counselor provided Kisha with a copy of the Career Thoughts Inventory Workbook and discussed with her how she might begin to take steps to challenge her thinking about her ability to make career choices and to alter some of her negative thoughts. Kisha noted that she had been vaguely aware of having a problem taking charge of situations that affected her, of needing to be more proactive rather than reactive, and seeing her high CA score on the CTI had really made her aware of how passive she had become. She expressed a desire to become more assertive and direct in her dealings with other people. In this case, the low E Competency scores on the SDS and the high CA score on the CTI were part of the same problem that Kisha wanted to correct. The Individual Action Plan developed by Kisha and her counselor is shown in Figure 18.

As a final project in the class, Kisha was required to write a Strategic Career Plan using the CASVE cycle described in chapter 8 and incorporating the results of her other class assignments. In this paper, Kisha noted how much she had learned about herself from taking the SDS and the CTI. She truly wanted to become a helping person, and becoming a professional counselor was really what she wanted to pursue. Becoming a career counselor was now her first occupational preference, followed by school counseling and rehabilitation counseling. She also reported recognizing how being a helping person meant making presentations to groups of people in some cases, especially if one was going to be a school counselor. Kisha reported having completed the CTI Workbook and how she had taken some specific steps to become more assertive and clear in voicing her preferences. She had begun a specific plan for getting work experience in schools and community agencies and applying to graduate school to become a counselor.

Case 3: "Ariel"

Case Notes

Ariel is a senior in high school who plans to attend the local university next year. He came into the career center with a friend and indicated that he needed "career planning assistance" and "occupational and academic information." He said, "I just want to find out the kind of job I'd be right for." He reported feeling pressure from his father to major in a field where there is a demand for employees and where he will have a practical skill, such as engineering or business. His father is currently employed as a semiconductor engineer. Ariel plans to attend the local university because he was not admitted to his first-choice school, which had an architecture program. His interest in architecture had been peaked through a high school career explorer program that allowed him to shadow an architect for 3 days. Ariel had a good SAT math score, but he did not do well on the verbal portion. He has been in honors courses in high school. He is uncomfortable making presentations in front of large groups. He likes to write and sees this as something he does well, despite his scores on the verbal portion of the SAT. He indicated that he had talked to people in architecture and had visited them at their worksites, but thought he wouldn't really know if he could succeed at this unless he actually tried it full-time. He acknowledged that he was concerned with pleasing his father. He described himself as

Individual Action Plan

Name **Kisha**   Date __2/6/97__

Goal **To learn more about my career**
       options and make some decisions

Activities to help me reach my goal	People or information resources needed	Activity order	Date	Activity complete (✓)
Talk to advisor	Alisa Lopez	5	3/97	
Work on computer system	Career Center	3	2/97	
Learn about occupations	career library resources	4	2/97	
Talk with people in occupations	Kathy Harris Ginger Murphy	7	3/97	
Research certificate program in OT	career library	6	3/97	
Learn more about my skills, interests, and values	career planning class activities	1	2/97	
Obtain a job in field to get experience	internship coordinator	8	4/97	
Talk with my instructor	Dr. Wright	2	2/97	

Figure 18. Individual Action Plan for "Kisha." From the Career Thoughts Inventory (p. 77), 1994, by J. P. Sampson, G. W. Peterson, J. G. Lenz, R. C. Reardon, and D. E. Saunders, Odessa, FL: Psychological Assessment Resources. Copyright © 1994, 1996 by Psychological Assessment Resources, Inc. Reprinted with permission.

a good student, but said he has to work really hard at school. He feels like he needs to know what he plans to study before he enrolls in classes for the fall.

Case Data

As part of the initial intake process, the career advisor administered the My Vocational Situation (MVS). Ariel's MVS scores were as follows:

Vocational Identity   3
Occupational Information   0
Barriers   2

Because of Ariel's low scores on the MVS, the career advisor decided to administer the paper and pencil version of the SDS to learn more about his view of himself and his options, and use the diagnostic concepts imbedded in the SDS to decide how to further assist him. Ariel's Form R results are presented in the following section and in Figure 19.

Occupational Daydreams

Architect	AIR
Financial analyst	CSI
International business manager	ESC
Newspaper editor/journalist	AES
Free-lance writer	AES

Using this information, complete the section for Case 3 at the end of this chapter. Before reviewing our comments, think about the issues facing Ariel and how you might help him in your setting. Our case notes are presented in Appendix J.

Our Comments

Ariel is feeling some pressure because of his upcoming enrollment at the university and the perceived "messages" he is receiving from his father. He doesn't want to waste time taking courses that don't relate to what he will major in. It will be important to get him to identify a reasonable timeline for making his decision, noting that it is unlikely that this decision will be resolved during his visit to the career center today. Capitalizing on the Investigative aspect of Ariel's personality and his interest in architecture, the counselor can use the hexagon and a diagram of the CASVE cycle to help him understand the nature of his Personal Career Theory (PCT). He may be willing to approach this as a "researchable problem." As a good student, he may be willing to follow through on homework assignments designed to help him resolve his career concern.

Full exploration of Ariel's code is important because he needs to expand his alternatives beyond his first choice. Because of the fewer options in the A and

How To Organize Your Answers _____

Start on page 4. Count how many times you said **L** for "Like." Record the number of **Ls** or **Ys** for each group of Activities, Competencies, or Occupations on the lines below.

Activities (pp. 4-5)

4	8	8	8	7	3
R	I	A	S	E	C

Competencies (pp. 6-7)

4	10	7	6	2	3
R	I	A	S	E	C

Occupations (p. 8)

0	2	8	3	6	1
R	I	A	S	E	C

Self-Estimates (p. 9)
(What number did you circle?)

2	6	6	4	1	4
R	I	A	S	E	C

3	6	5	5	4	3
R	I	A	S	E	C

Total Scores
(Add the five R scores, the five I scores, the five A scores, etc.)

13	32	34	26	20	14
R	I	A	S	E	C

The letters with the three highest numbers indicate your Summary Code. Write your Summary Code below. (If two scores are the same or tied, put both letters in the same box.)

Summary Code

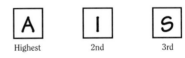

A	I	S
Highest	2nd	3rd

10

Figure 19. SDS summary sheet for "Ariel." From the *Self-Directed Search Form R Assessment Booklet* (p. 10), by J. L. Holland, 1994, Odessa, FL: Psychological Assessment Resources. Copyright © 1970, 1977, 1985, 1990, 1994 by Psychological Assessment Resources, Inc. Reprinted with permission.

I areas, he may want to explore S jobs requiring high levels of education. The counselor can explore how much Ariel wants the S aspects of his personality to be reflected in his work. It may be useful to discuss the interest/values/skills differences between Es and Is. Enterprising shows up in his aspirations and on the Occupations scale, but not in his competencies or in the self-estimate rating for sales ability. His high rating on I competencies is in contrast to his lack of interest in I occupations. Ariel might benefit from some creative brainstorming about how he could work in the business world, but be involved primarily in "symbolic-analytic" roles, as opposed to roles that require "in-person services," public speaking, or sales ability. Given his low MVS score on occupational information, he will need to spend some time learning about other options, beyond architecture, that reflect his interests, skills, and values. As an A type, it may be important to explore his style of decision making. He may base his decision making on his direct experience and the feelings that follow from that experience. Ariel can use RIASEC and CIP theory to improve his PCT and provide some guidelines for his decision making. In follow-up sessions, the counselor can review specific MVS items to determine whether Ariel believes he is making progress on issues associated with those items.

Case 4: "Linda"

Case Notes

Linda is a 44-year-old White female. She was born in Ireland and moved to the U.S. when she was 18. She is divorced and has two children, one daughter, age 15, and one son, age 18. Linda attended a community college and a vocational training program. She has been working as a licensed practical nurse in a variety of settings for the last 20 years. She came into the career center because of dissatisfaction with the working conditions in the field of nursing. She likes some of the specific duties she performs as a nurse, but dislikes the hours, the lack of prestige, and the fact that she deals with supervisors who are generally not supportive and sometimes even abusive. Linda described herself as being anxious about her future. Her parents are not in a position to support her. They are retired and are living on a small of amount of savings. She receives a minimal amount of child support from her former husband. She views her options as somewhat restricted because she still bears primary responsibility for the children. Presently, she lacks the resources to return to school for any type of retraining. She worries about whether it is too late to make a change and finds the thought of changing careers a bit overwhelming.

Case Data

As part of the initial screening process, Linda completed the Career Thoughts Inventory (CTI) and the Career Attitudes and Strategies Inventory (CASI). Linda's CASI results are presented in Figure 20. Her scores on the CTI were as follows:

Career Thoughts Inventory (CTI)

CTI Total Score:	59 (84th percentile)
Decision-making Confusion (DMC):	17 (90th percentile)
Commitment Anxiety (CA):	17 (92nd percentile)
External Conflict (EC):	6 (92nd percentile)

In a follow-up session, Linda completed the SDS Form R. Her SDS results are provided in the following section and in Figure 21.

Occupational Daydreams

Writer	AES
Buyer	ESA
Columnist	EAS
Actor	AES

Our Comments

In Linda's case, several of the assessment tools used helped to pinpoint the source of her difficulties. Her CTI construct scale scores (i.e., Decision-making Confusion, Commitment Anxiety, and External Conflict) were all at the 90th percentile or higher. In addition, she has low scores on the Vocational Identity and Occupational Information sections of the MVS. Several issues and obstacles were also identified by the CASI. Although her SDS summary score and the PCI code for her current occupation share the same first letter, the other letters do not match up well. She perceives herself as being in a job that has R and C elements, but these two letters do not appear anywhere in either her summary code or her aspirations summary code. Of some concern is the fact that no health-related occupation appears at all in her aspirations, despite her lengthy work history in this field. In a follow-up session with Linda, the counselor learned that Linda, for the most part, views her aspirations as "true daydreams." She doesn't feel she can realistically pursue these options, and she also noted that although she endorsed several A occupations on the SDS Occupations scale, she described this as mostly "wishful thinking." The counselor explored with her the extent to which negative or stereotypical thinking might be interfering with her ability to consider A occupations. The counselor also discussed other roles that might allow Linda to exercise some of her A interests.

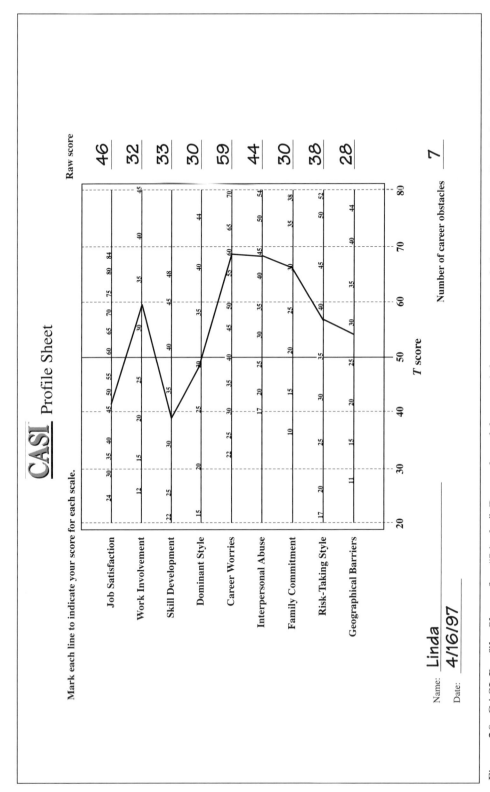

Figure 20. CASI Profile Sheet for "Linda." Reproduced by special permission of the publisher, Psychological Assessment Resources, Inc., from the *Career Attitudes and Strategies Inventory* Profile Sheet, copyright © 1992, 1993, 1994 by Psychological Assessment Resources, Inc.

How To Organize Your Answers _____

Start on page 4. Count how many times you said **L** for "Like." Record the number of **Ls** or **Ys** for each group of Activities, Competencies, or Occupations on the lines below.

	R	I	A	S	E	C
Activities (pp. 4-5)	3	3	7	6	2	1
Competencies (pp. 6-7)	1	3	1	6	4	1
Occupations (p. 8)	1	7	10	3	3	1
Self-Estimates (p. 9) (What number did you circle?)	1	2	3	5	1	1
	5	3	2	6	3	1

Total Scores
(Add the five R scores, the five I scores, the five A scores, etc.)

R	I	A	S	E	C
11	18	23	26	13	5

The letters with the three highest numbers indicate your Summary Code. Write your Summary Code below. (If two scores are the same or tied, put both letters in the same box.)

Summary Code

S	A	I
Highest	2nd	3rd

10

Figure 21. SDS summary sheet for "Linda." From the Self-Directed Search Form R Assessment Booklet (p. 10), by J. L. Holland, 1970, 1977, 1985, 1990, 1994, Odessa, FL: Psychological Assessment Resources. Copyright © 1994 by Psychological Assessment Resources, Inc. Reprinted with permission.

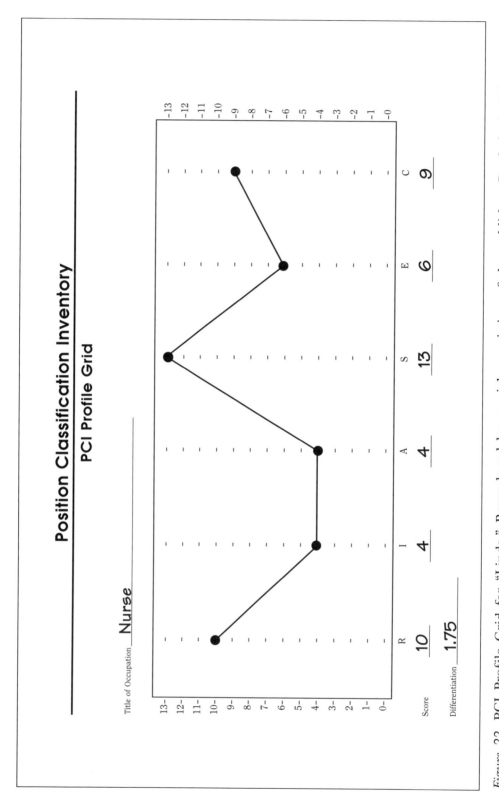

Figure 22. PCI Profile Grid for "Linda." Reproduced by special permission of the publisher, Psychological Assessment Resources, Inc., from the *Position Classification Inventory* Profile Grid, copyright © 1991 by Psychological Assessment Resources, Inc.

The counselor discussed Linda's desire to explore other health-related occupations and gave her a sheet listing health occupations. Linda agreed to spend some time in the career library researching occupations in this area. Linda clearly wants to avoid anything that involves C-type work, given her low SDS score in this area. The counselor provided Linda with some information about resources for returning adult students that might help her view returning to school as a more manageable task. Linda is a client who is likely to require individual case-managed counseling over an extended period of time. She thinks she can remain in her present position, but doesn't want to waste any more time. She also thinks she will have more freedom to consider her options once her children are older. Linda benefited from cognitive restructuring exercises, including use of the Career Thoughts Inventory Workbook, as a means of helping her think differently about her career situation. At the time of this writing, she was continuing to work on her career change process.

Case 5: "Susana"

Case Notes

Susana is a 28-year-old Hispanic female who is serving prison time for credit card fraud. She is married for the second time and has three children. She dropped out of school in the eighth grade and is now working toward her GED. Susana is participating in an in-house program for prisoners close to their release date that helps them prepare for reentry into the world of work. As part of this process, Susana completed the SDS Form R and attended a follow-up interpretation session with the prison psychologist. She told the psychologist in this session that she wants to try and make a better life and be a better role model for her children. She disclosed that she had a very underprivileged upbringing and was exposed to illicit drugs by her parents. She was also a victim of domestic violence in her first marriage. At one point in her life, Susana developed a dependence on crack cocaine, and during this time she had one child out of wedlock. Susana worked sporadically in the cosmetology field and also was involved in some drug dealing, but was not ever arrested for this activity.

Case Data

Susana's SDS results are presented below and in Figure 23. Use the worksheet for Case 5 at the back of this chapter to analyze Susana's situation and determine how best to help her.

How To Organize Your Answers _____

Start on page 4. Count how many times you said **L** for "Like." Record the number of **L**s or **Y**s for each group of Activities, Competencies, or Occupations on the lines below.

Activities (pp. 4-5)	3	4	4	8	10	10
	R	I	A	S	E	C

Competencies (pp. 6-7)	8	4	6	11	8	9
	R	I	A	S	E	C

Occupations (p. 8)	6	3	5	8	9	9
	R	I	A	S	E	C

Self-Estimates (p. 9) (What number did you circle?)	6	1	2	5	7	7
	R	I	A	S	E	C

	1	3	1	7	6	6
	R	I	A	S	E	C

Total Scores (Add the five R scores, the five I scores, the five A scores, etc.)	24	15	18	39	40	41
	R	I	A	S	E	C

The letters with the three highest numbers indicate your Summary Code. Write your Summary Code below. (If two scores are the same or tied, put both letters in the same box.)

Summary Code

C	E	S
Highest	2nd	3rd

10

Figure 23. SDS summary sheet for "Susana." From the Self-Directed Search Form R Assessment Booklet (p. 10), by J. L. Holland, 1994, Odessa, FL: Psychological Assessment Resources. Copyright © 1970, 1977, 1985, 1990, 1994 by Psychological Assessment Resources, Inc. Reprinted with permission.

Occupational Daydreams

Cosmetologist	SEA
Bricklayer	RSE
Welder	RIS
Cashier	CES
Daycare worker	SER

Our Comments

Susana's SDS results have been influenced both by her prior work history and her exposure to vocational training programs in the prison setting. Prisoners are allowed to put in a request for placement in one of seven vocational training programs, and Susana has applied for enrollment in the brick masonry program. She is open to returning to her work in cosmetology, but would need to complete some continuing education to update her license. Unfortunately, some of her E, C, and S qualities were developed during the course of illegal activities. Reviewing The Occupations Finder helped to expand Susana's thinking (Synthesis-Elaboration) about legal occupations where she could use these skills and interests. She is currently participating in a prison support group to deal with her substance abuse issues. The counselor explored her current feelings about this, and she indicated she was committed to not using drugs. The counselor worked with Susana to affirm her positive accomplishments thus far: working on her GED and an unblemished track record during her incarceration. Susana was referred to prison workshops designed to help her prepare a resume and learn effective interview skills. She was allowed to use prison library resources to research several of her occupational alternatives. Prisoners are also allowed to write to agencies and organizations to obtain more information for use in their career planning. The counselor helped Susana locate the contact information for the local cosmetology licensing board, and then helped her draft a letter to inquire about procedures for updating her cosmetology license. Susana is still preparing for her transition back into society and to the work force, but she thinks she has some realistic alternatives and is taking positive steps to execute her plan.

Case 6: "Frank"

Case Notes

Frank is a 48-year-old African-American male who was referred to the career center by a job hunt support group. For the last 10 years, he has managed his own business which involves the resale of rental cars. He recently sold the business because he was "feeling stressed and burned out." He enjoyed the people aspect of the business, but did not enjoy the pressure of constantly having to bring in business to support himself, his family, and his two other employees. He is married and has one son, a freshman in college. His wife is employed as an account representative with a local telecommunications company. She is supportive of Frank's desire to change careers, but thinks they need two steady incomes to maintain their current middle-class lifestyle. Frank has some money from the sale of the business that can support them while he explores other alternatives. He completed a bachelor's degree in business management 26 years ago, and since then he has completed some additional training by attending sales and management seminars sponsored by a professional association to which he belongs. During college, Frank worked part-time for a rental car company, checking in rental car returns and doing some detailing work to prepare the car for the next rental. Frank has experienced some high blood pressure in recent months, which he attributes partly to his career situation. Frank is active in a local church, where he serves on several committees and sings in the choir. Now that his son is in college, Frank thinks he has a little more geographic flexibility in where he looks for work.

Case Data

Frank indicated that he had completed the SDS Form R as part of the job hunt group activities. To gather additional intake information, the counselor asked Frank to complete the Career Thoughts Inventory (CTI). Frank's CTI and SDS results are reproduced below.

Career Thoughts Inventory (CTI)

CTI Total Score:	51 (76th percentile)
Decision-making Confusion (DMC):	15 (84th percentile)
Commitment Anxiety (CA):	13 (76th percentile)
External Conflict (EC):	3 (50th percentile)

Occupational Daydreams

School administrator	SEI
Adult education teacher	SER
Entertainer	AES
Human resource manager	ESR
Sales analyst	ISC

Frank's SDS summary sheet is presented in Figure 24. Review Frank's results and make your notes on the Case 6 worksheet section at the end of this chapter. Compare your results with the authors' comments and the worksheet in Appendix J.

How To Organize Your Answers _____

Start on page 4. Count how many times you said **L** for "Like." Record the number of **Ls** or **Ys** for each group of Activities, Competencies, or Occupations on the lines below.

Activities (pp. 4-5)	5	2	8	9	8	5
	R	I	A	S	E	C

Competencies (pp. 6-7)	4	5	8	7	8	9
	R	I	A	S	E	C

Occupations (p. 8)	4	4	5	4	12	4
	R	I	A	S	E	C

Self-Estimates (p. 9) (What number did you circle?)	4	5	7	7	6	6
	R	I	A	S	E	C
	5	3	7	6	7	6
	R	I	A	S	E	C

Total Scores (Add the five R scores, the five I scores, the five A scores, etc.)	22	19	35	33	41	30
	R	I	A	S	E	C

The letters with the three highest numbers indicate your Summary Code. Write your Summary Code below. (If two scores are the same or tied, put both letters in the same box.)

Summary Code

E	A	S
Highest	2nd	3rd

10

Figure 24. SDS summary sheet for "Frank." From the Self-Directed Search Form R Assessment Booklet (p. 10), by J. L. Holland, 1994, Odessa, FL: Psychological Assessment Resources. Copyright © 1970, 1977, 1985, 1990, 1994 by Psychological Assessment Resources, Inc. Reprinted with permission.

Our Comments

Frank's CTI results suggested that he felt uncomfortable at this point in his life being uncertain about his future work direction. His work had been a significant part of his identity and he was embarrassed to be involved in this process at this point in his life. He had several ideas about what he might enjoy doing, but it was not clear in his mind how he would begin to pursue these. He noted that he had a hard time getting enthusiastic about going back to school at this point in his life. The indicators on Frank's SDS results were fairly positive overall, with only one low category. The E and S categories were a predominant theme in both his SDS results and aspirations. Although A was the second letter in his summary code, it appeared only once in his aspirations. Of particular interest is the fact that Frank checked Yes for 12 occupations on the Enterprising Occupations scale. Frank agreed that even though he had thought about occupations in the field of education, he wasn't really committed to pursuing additional education to enter that field, and he thought his chances were better for finding employment in business settings. Frank acknowledged that he could use volunteer activities through the church and his local community to meet some of his needs for "helping others." He also thought that without the pressure of running his own business, he would have more free time to devote to his A interests. He has thought of trying out for plays at the community theater, but his previous work schedule prevented him from pursuing that idea further.

After consulting with the counselor, Frank decided to use a computer-based guidance system to further clarify his self-knowledge and to research specific options he was considering. His computer results confirmed his interest in the business field and his skills and interests in training and education. With the help of the counselor, Frank brainstormed about how to combine his work history in the auto industry, his people and persuasion skills, and his desire to have a stable income, through some means other than running his own business. Frank spent additional sessions, with brief assistance from a career advisor, using employer directories in the career library to research work settings. The career advisor helped Frank update his resume and highlight the skills he had developed in running his own business. Using information from the Internet and library resources, Frank began contacting auto dealerships and manufacturers. His efforts paid off with several interviews, and he eventually accepted a position as a training manager for a regional automobile dealership.

Conclusion

These six cases have helped to highlight the richness of information that can be gathered using a Holland- and CIP-based framework. The diagnostic indicators provided give us more than enough "clues" to begin to help clients investigate their personal career theories and further, how to help them begin to understand and resolve their career problems. Readers are encouraged to adapt the case study formats provided as needed in their own settings. For us, the strength of the approach presented in this chapter is that the counselor can gather a great deal of information in a short period of time, using only simple calculations or summing of scores. The instruments are easily administered, scored, and interpreted, making the counselor's job easier and assistance more readily available to clients. Ongoing practice and application of this approach, or one similar to it, will foster a more thorough, yet practical method for the delivery of career interventions.

SDS Case Analysis Worksheet

Indicators	Case 1: Martha	Case 2: Kisha	Case 3: Ariel
Summary Code			
Aspirations Summary Code			
Code of first aspiration			
Congruence			
Coherence			
My Vocational Situation Vocational Identity Occupational Information Barriers			
Consistency			
Differentiation			
Commonness			
Additional Assessment Information			
Additional notes			
Possible interventions			

SDS Case Analysis Worksheet

Indicators	Case 4: Linda	Case 5: Susana	Case 6: Frank
Summary Code			
Aspirations Summary Code			
Code of first aspiration			
Congruence			
Coherence			
My Vocational Situation Vocational Identity Occupational Information Barriers			
Consistency			
Differentiation			
Commonness			
Additional Assessment Information			
Additional notes			
Possible interventions			

11

Program Development Strategies

In previous chapters, we examined Holland's career and his RIASEC theory, and described how and why the "crown jewel" of Holland's work is the Self-Directed Search. Holland and his theory provide career counselors with a comprehensive range of materials and ideas to help clients who are experiencing varied career problems. We have examined assumptions of the RIASEC theory that may be used to more fully understand how to provide career counseling to clients (chapters 2, 4, and 5), and we examined the contributions of Cognitive Information Processing (CIP) theory (chapter 8) in career counseling using the SDS. Chapter 11 builds upon this understanding of RIASEC theory and focuses on strategies for the development of career services programs.

But how do counselors or program developers (in this chapter we will refer to them as developers) get involved in organizing an array of materials and resources into a comprehensive program of career services? Perhaps RIASEC theory can provide us with some clues. The code for counselor is SAE, project director is ESI, department manager is ESA, training and education manager is EIS, grant coordinator is SEI, and program manager is EIR. Given these occupational titles and codes, the summary code for developer is EIS. For career counselors to become successful program developers and managers, it seems clear that they must draw heavily on skills and interests in the Enterprising and Investigative areas.

So how does a developer go about incorporating the SDS or other Holland-based materials into a career guidance program? What guidelines might assist a counselor in this process? How does a developer determine which clients might be able to use the SDS on their own with little assistance and which ones will need more help? How do RIASEC and CIP theory help us design better career services programs?

It strikes us as ironic that there is very little information available in the professional literature, even in the documents supporting the SDS, regarding the programmatic use of the SDS and Holland-based materials. Because the SDS is both an assessment instrument and a self-guided career intervention (Spokane, 1990), it might be expected that demonstration models would be available to describe how the SDS could be incorporated into comprehensive career guidance services. But this does not seem to be the case. This chapter seeks to begin to fill this gap.

It begins with a review of the contributions of CIP theory in career program development and then connects this work to RIASEC theory. The outcome is a model for guiding career counselors in thinking about how to use the SDS and related materials in assisting clients in a programmatic way (e.g., a regular class, individual counseling programs, small group counseling, brief workshops, and/or self-directed use). The application of the model in a middle school setting is demonstrated, followed by brief scenarios of the programmatic use of the SDS in a military transition program and in a university-based employment office setting. This chapter includes a brief examination of the National Career Development Guidelines (Kobylarz, 1996) in relation to Holland-based career interventions and illustrates how these guidelines may be used in program development. It concludes with a summary of Holland's (1997) most recent ideas for improving career programs.

Career Services Program Options

In developing career services programs, the following factors might be considered: (a) the complexity level of the client's presenting problems, (b) the number and complexity of career interventions available, and (c) the range of staff skills.

In previous chapters, we identified an array of Holland-based materials and diagnostic indicators of career problems (e.g., SDS, MVS, coherence of aspirations, congruence between aspirations code and SDS summary code, and differentiation) that provide indications of the first factor identified above. In other chapters, we have identified a range of Holland-based career interventions that are published or have been reported in the literature (e.g., OF, DHOC, EOF). And in your present work setting, you can assess the range and quality of skills possessed by the staff for conducting career interventions (e.g., degrees held, workshops attended, career classes taken, and years of experience in career services).

In some of our earlier writing (Peterson, Sampson, & Reardon, 1991), we pictured these three factors as a cube (see Figure 25). As the figure shows, some interventions require more time and staff expertise and are best suited for more complex client problems. Other interventions require less staff time and can be used by clients in a self-help way. In general, career services programs should be designed to assure that the most expensive career materials and staff resources are applied to the most complex, difficult client problems. In this chapter, we will show how RIASEC and CIP theory can help us figure out the

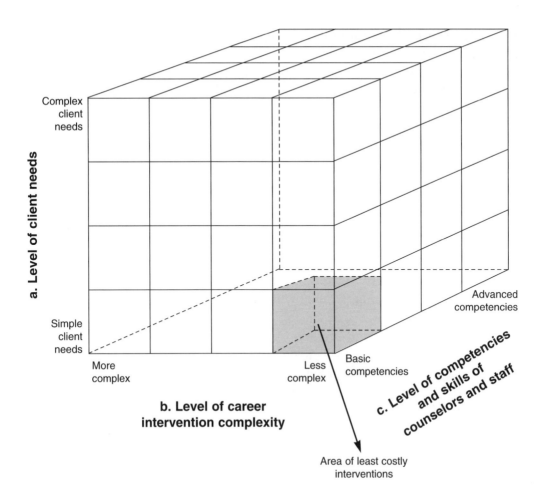

Figure 25. A synthesis of three guidance dimensions: Client needs, intervention complexity, and staff competencies. From *Career development and services: A cognitive approach* (p. 319), by G. W. Peterson, J. P. Sampson, and R. C. Reardon. Copyright © 1991 by Brooks/Cole Publishing Company, Pacific Grove, CA 93950, a division of International Thomson Publishing, Inc. Reproduced by permission. All rights reserved.

appropriate level of services for clients in varying states of readiness and with different kinds of barriers in career decision making.

In designing career services programs, developers can use the three dimensions of this cube to determine where to focus program efforts. If the developer is required or seeks to address complex client concerns, has highly trained staff available, and has the time and resources to provide extensive interventions, the program will operate in a different part of the cube than if the developer is required or seeks to provide direct information services, has less staff intensive interventions, and expects clients to use self-help materials. The focus of career services programs may grow out of policy directives from supervisors or philosophical, values-based preferences of the staff. Either way, the cube helps us focus on options in conceptualizing career services programs.

Three Levels of Career Intervention

Following up on this way of thinking, Sampson and Reardon (1997) described three levels of service delivery: (a) Self-help services, (b) brief staff-assisted services, and (c) individual case-managed services. This idea was developed for a research project examining ways to make maximum use of staff resources in One-Stop Centers, the new comprehensive centers designed to provide employment and social services in community settings. We think it can be applied to the design of programs using Holland-based materials. You may also recall the decision making taxonomy introduced in chapter 8 that used the categories of decided, undecided, and indecisive. Decided and undecided clients can generally benefit from self-help and brief staff-assisted services, whereas indecisive clients will more likely need individual case-managed services. These three approaches are more fully described below.

Self-Help Services

Self-help services include answering client questions upon initial contact at the career service office or on the telephone. Examples include the following:

1. "I would like to use a computer program to see what other kinds of jobs might be related to my interest in biology."
2. "What are some different jobs involving computers?"
3. "What occupations involve working with children?"
4. "Do you have addresses of law schools?"
5. "I need some information about the Internal Revenue Service."
6. "Do you have a tape or booklet on job interviewing?"
7. "My SDS code was CAS. Can you help me find the names of more occupations related to this code?"

Depending on the resources and design of the career service setting, clients could be immediately referred to a computer terminal, a videotape, books, filed materials, or special publications to answer these kinds of concerns. For example, the You and Your Career booklet (YYC) and the DHOC might be given to a client asking the seventh question. Career services would most likely be provided in a career resource center or other library-type, resource-rich setting. In addition, Sampson and Reardon (1997) noted that self-help services could increasingly be obtained from remote locations using a telephone or the Internet (i.e., labor market trends and information). Information and materials provided in the self-help mode should have been designed with this purpose in mind. The Self-Directed Search is an example of an interest inventory that was purposefully designed to be used in self-help situations.

Clients most likely to benefit from a self-help approach would have several positive indications of their readiness to use career materials (e.g., good reading skills, high vocational identity, coherent aspirations and work histories, strong personal motivation to engage in career decision making, less debilitating anxiety and/or time pressure to conclude the task, and a highly differentiated RIASEC code). Clients best suited for self-help services would most likely be decided, but might possibly be undecided. Indecisive clients might not benefit from such services. We will discuss screening more fully in a later section of this chapter.

Brief Staff-Assisted Services

If it is apparent that self-help services may not be the most helpful, and that intensive individual case-managed services are not necessary, then brief staff-assisted services may be used. Brief staff-assisted services are similar to self-help services in many ways (e.g., use the same materials and resources and are conducted in the same kind of setting), but they differ in that more staff time is spent in specifying the nature of the client's problem, client goals are set in collaboration with the counselor, a written plan is created that outlines the sequence of materials and resources to be used by the client, and time is provided to review client progress in achieving the specified goals. This idea was discussed more fully in chapter 8 in terms of the Individual Learning Plan.

Brief staff-assisted services are enhanced through group counseling, workshops, and self-directed career decision making. In the latter, the client directs his or her personal use of materials and resources with staff providing assistance as requested (Peterson, Sampson, & Reardon, 1991). Brief staff-assisted services would most likely be provided in a career resource center setting which would be marked by several features:

1. Clients would use services at any time (i.e., appointments would not be needed in most cases).
2. Staff would model good information-seeking behavior and work collaboratively with clients to solve career problems.
3. Different staff might assist the same client over a period of time.
4. Staff could work with several clients during a 1-hour period.
5. Staff are constantly available to assist clients.

6. Differentiated staffing would be used (i.e., at any one time, a range of staff skills would be available).

7. Career counseling and other helping skills would be used in service delivery.

8. Responsibility rests with the client to initiate and manage career services in the brief staff-assisted approach.

Additional information about this approach to career services is provided in Reardon (1996), Reardon, Domkowski, and Jackson (1980), and Reardon and Minor (1975).

Individual Case-Managed Services

If an initial screening indicates that neither self-help nor brief staff-assisted services are likely to be appropriate, then individual case-managed services are provided. In general, this approach might be described as career counseling by appointment in an individual office, where the client receives the undivided attention of a professional career counselor or service provider.

Clients most appropriate for individual case-managed services include those who are indecisive and anxious, have low vocational identity and negative career thoughts, have mental health issues, experience interpersonal conflict involved in their career decisions, have low coherence in work histories and aspirations, have been expelled from school, have undifferentiated RIASEC interest profiles, and have other related career issues (e.g., poverty, poor language skills, disabling conditions, criminal records). In general, these clients have signs that are the opposite of clients ready for self-help services. For such clients, human contact may be wanted and needed, and the presence of a therapeutic counseling relationship is essential in providing effective career assistance.

However, it is important to note that all three services approaches—self-help, brief staff-assisted, and individual case-managed—use the same assessment resources and materials (e.g., SDS, DHOC). The difference in the three approaches involves the degree of staff assistance provided to clients while using these materials, the setting of the service (e.g., information resource room vs. individual office), the degree of staff collaboration in service delivery, and the amount of responsibility for service delivery given to clients themselves. The latter is a policy decision made by the staff at the agency. Setting policies about career services programs involves setting program goals, choosing among alternative kinds of interventions, allocating resources, and deciding which clients should be served and how they should be served. We have to make these policy decisions in program development because there never seem to be enough resources (i.e., staff, money, materials, space) to do everything needed. In the following section, we will describe the application of a systematic procedure for developing a career services program proposal.

A Systems Approach to Program Development

In chapter 8, we introduced the CASVE cycle as a 5-step sequence for making a career decision or solving a career problem. Our focus in that chapter was on individual client situations. The 5 steps of the CASVE cycle were Communication, Analysis, Synthesis, Valuing, and Execution (Figure 26). In this chapter, we are changing the focus to program development. These same 5 steps can be used in program development—they outline a logical, rational, systems approach to program development. By going through these 5 steps, the developer of a career guidance program is more likely to consider all the issues involved in successful program development. Interested readers might want to refer to chapter 12, "Developing and Implementing a Career Service Center: A Personal Case History," in the book by Peterson, Sampson, and Reardon (1991). This chapter provides a detailed review of the 20-year development of a career services program from a CASVE perspective.

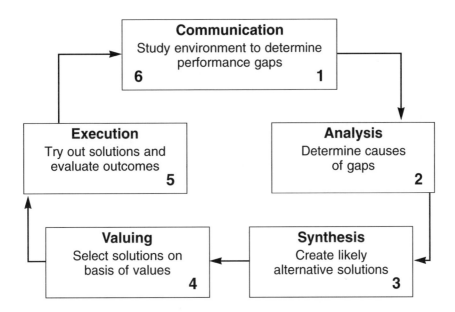

Figure 26. CASVE process of program development. Adapted from *Career development and services: A cognitive approach,* by G. W. Peterson, J. P. Sampson, and R. C. Reardon. Copyright © 1991 by Brooks/Cole Publishing Company, Pacific Grove, CA 93950, a division of International Thomson Publishing, Inc. Reproduced by permission. All rights reserved.

In the following sections, we will briefly describe the issues and topics included in each step in the CASVE process of program development. We will do this by raising questions that a program developer might want to answer in a program proposal, a written document typically used to obtain funds for a career program. (Sometimes, a career program proposal may be written in response to an RFP, a Request for Proposal, issued by a foundation, agency, or other group.) And, in keeping with the purpose of this book, we will focus on issues from a RIASEC or CIP perspective wherever possible.

Communication

The need for a program arises from several possible situations, each of which involves a need to remove the gap between the present situation and a more ideal situation. This gap may have been identified by a higher level administrator in the organization, by an outside study group or advisory council, by the collective wisdom of the counseling staff, or by the felt need of one staff person. Whatever the origin, this gap carries emotion, energy, and motivation to make things better, to reduce the gaps in performance between the "real" and the "ideal." For example, the middle school counselor is aware that 60% of the seventh-grade students cannot name five occupations related to their career interests, or 75% of middle school parents want their children to be able to name five postsecondary fields of study related to their career interests.

In the Communication phase of program development, this gap between the present and the more desirable state of affairs creates emotional energy to do something, to change the present state of affairs. This energy is channeled into efforts to fully understand the nature of the gap, and in the process the following questions may be addressed in a written report produced by a developer:

1. Can it be reasonably assumed that the gap can be removed? Does RIASEC or CIP theory provide some logical solutions to the gap?

2. What is the history of the gap in this setting? How long has it existed?

3. Does this gap exist at other places? What has been done in other places to remove the gap?

4. Who in the organization or community is concerned about this gap? How badly do they want it removed?

5. What resources (e.g., consultants, proven programs, space, funds) are available to remove the gap? Are these resources readily available on-site or do they have to be obtained from elsewhere?

6. What data are available (e.g., survey results, auditor reports, accountability findings), that provide specific information about the nature and extent of the gap?

In the process of reviewing the answers to these and similar questions, a developer begins to understand what is needed to resolve a gap between the present and a more ideal situation. In the following section, we undertake an analysis of the information collected in the first step, Communication.

Analysis

In analyzing all of the causal elements involved in creating the gap, a developer begins to look for relationships between problems and possible solutions. In effect, the developer engages in an intuitive process of generating tentative hypotheses about how to remove gaps. In our experience, Holland's RIASEC theory and CIP theory are especially useful here because these theories help us explain how gaps occur in career problem solving and decision making, and they provide insights for us in thinking about developing strategies for removing these gaps. For example, in considering methods for improving student use of a career resource center, we might note that students who are Realistic or Investigative types are using the center less often, and we might focus our program marketing efforts on making the center more attractive to R and I types. As another example, in helping retired persons think about leisure options, we might use the code of their last job or their first occupational aspiration to locate suitable options in the Leisure Activities Finder (LAF).

In the Analysis phase of program development, a developer begins to convert statements of gaps or needs into statements of program goals. These statements of goals usually are of two kinds: process goals and learner outcome goals. Process goals could include the following: "Administer the SDS Career Explorer to 250 middle school students and provide interpretive reports to students, parents, and teachers" or "Lead three classroom discussions of SDS Career Explorer interpretive reports in middle school social studies classes examining RIASEC theory, how codes are translated into occupations/fields of study, and how to obtain more information about occupations of interest."

Learner outcome goals could include the following: "Middle school students will be able to identify the two RIASEC codes of most and least career interest" or "Students can describe the relationship among interests for each of the six RIASEC types." These goal statements describe how things will be different as a result of the introduction of a proposed program of career services, how the gap identified in the Communication phase of the CASVE cycle has been removed or reduced.

The process of conceptualizing program goals involves the developer in a process of critical thinking and analysis of all the possible options and solutions available to remove a gap. Every possible solution has strengths, weaknesses, costs, and problems, and the developer goes through a process of examining every option in a critical way. What are the advantages and disadvantages of each option? What are the immediate and long-term costs and benefits associated with each option? Who in the organization is interested in supporting various approaches?

In the Analysis phase of the CASVE cycle, the developer begins to shape and form a set of goal statements that describe how a program might remove the gaps identified in Communication. These goals will not address everything that might possibly be done to remove a gap, but only those things that meet the policy objectives of the service organization and are congruent with the philosophy of the developer. As this information is written and disseminated among other staff and stakeholders in the organization, the developer begins to obtain feedback about whether the gaps are really important ones and whether the possible solutions have support from other important people outside and inside the organization (i.e., stakeholders).

Synthesis

In the Synthesis phase of the CASVE cycle, the developer begins to specify the solutions that will remove the gap, synthesizing information obtained from Communication and Analysis to identify old and/or new resources and activities to remove gaps. The developer may specify doing familiar things in similar or new ways or creating completely new activities. As in the case of individual application of the CASVE cycle, the developer might go through a process of brainstorming to make sure every possible solution is considered and reviewed. But over time, as trial balloons are floated by an advisory committee or the staff, the new program begins to crystallize. The important point to remember in this CASVE approach to program development is that the developer did not start with Synthesis, but started with the specification of a gap in the Communication phase and then expanded understanding of the gap in the Analysis phase. This helps to keep the developer focused on the needs of the clients being served and the needs of the organization.

As the proposed program and a written proposal begin to take shape, some of the practical aspects of the Synthesis phase of the CASVE cycle include the following:

1. Does the proposal specify the roles of all staff involved in the program (e.g., secretary/receptionist, counselor, student assistant, public relations specialist, records clerk, senior manager)?

2. Are procedures explained regarding staff selection and training? Does everyone need to be trained? Do different types of staff receive different types of training? Can some staff opt out of the program?

3. What space and equipment will be needed for the program?

4. How will the program be introduced to staff and clients?

5. Is a flowchart provided, showing how clients, staff, and materials are used in the program activities?

6. What are the decision points regarding client continuation or termination from the program?

7. How will it be supervised and managed on a daily basis?

8. Is the program reflected in the unit organizational chart? Have job descriptions been changed if needed?

9. Will there be costs associated with the program? What is the nature of these costs (e.g., materials, personnel, postage), and how will they be paid?

10. How will the proposed program change the current procedures and related programs?

11. What consultation, technical assistance, and human resources support are needed by the proposed program?

12. What are the daily, weekly, monthly, and quarterly timeframes for program operation? Will it operate during breaks and holidays? In the evenings or weekends?

13. Will endorsements for the proposed program be sought from important people in the organization, community, and profession?

14. How will the program be evaluated? Who will do this? When will they do it? How will clients and staff provide feedback to the program developer?

15. What special forms and materials will be needed to evaluate the program?

16. Will the information collected by the program and in the evaluation enable the developer to determine whether the original gaps identified in the Communication phase have been removed or reduced?

17. How and when will information about the success of the program be shared with others in the organization (e.g., potential future clients, staff, top administrators)? In the larger community? In the profession (e.g., journal articles, conference presentations)?

This list of questions specifies the kinds of information that the developer reviews during the Synthesis phase of the CASVE cycle. Work in this phase of program development requires the developer to become quite specific regarding who will be involved in the program, when they will be doing things, how they will be operating, what they will be doing, and why they will be doing it. Addressing these questions in the program proposal means that the program will more likely operate smoothly when introduced and will more likely be effective. If these questions are not addressed in the proposal before actual program operations begin, staff confusion and resistance may cause the program to fail.

Valuing

In the Valuing phase of the CASVE cycle of program development, basic questions about the worth and merit of the proposed program are raised and answered. The basic issue in this phase boils down to one question: Is this program worth doing, given the costs? A positive response from all the stakeholders in the organization, including the managers, staff, and client representatives, means that the organization wishes to make a commitment to establishing the program as it has been proposed by the developer. A positive response might mean any or all of the following:

1. The philosophy of the proposed program is the right one.
2. It is more important to do this proposed program than some other one.
3. The costs are reasonable.
4. The likely outcomes of the program are desirable.
5. Most stakeholders favor the proposed program.
6. The organization will be more effective as a result of implementation of the proposed program.

In the process of going through the Valuing phase of the program development process, the developer and/or development team make choices from among the program options initially raised in the Analysis phase and elaborated in the Synthesis phase. A program based on Holland's theory might be marked by the following characteristics:

1. A desire to maximize self-help approaches by clients who are likely to benefit from this approach.

2. Recognition of the power and acceptance of RIASEC theory among career professionals.

3. The efficiency of the RIASEC typology in organizing information about persons and options which facilitates searches for congruence that are easily understood by clients.

4. The existence of four forms of the SDS for clients of different ages, abilities, and situations.

5. The existence of computer-based SDS interpretive reports that reduce staff time in providing reports to clients.

6. The cost-effectiveness of Holland-based career materials.

When commitments to the proposed program have been obtained from all the stakeholders (i.e., administrators and staff), the developer proceeds to the Execution phase of the CASVE cycle.

Execution

In the Execution phase of the CASVE program development process, the developer takes the program on the road. It is the time to try the program in a real-life setting, to see how it works with real clients. In the entertainment world, this might be called the "dress rehearsal." If the program has a "name," then client reactions to that name will be important. If the developer is considering several program names (perhaps only a "working title" has been given to the program at this point), then those alternative names can be evaluated in the Execution phase of the program development. It is particularly important to specify how the program will be introduced into the organization. How will the opening of the program be handled? Will a "grand opening" follow a period of trial operation?

The Execution phase might first involve a limited pilot run with a select group of clients to determine whether the procedures and materials work as expected. This period of testing a prototype or limited version of the proposed program provides one additional opportunity to collect information about the program procedures and possibly to return to an earlier phase of the CASVE process if necessary to rethink and redesign some program activities.

The Execution phase may be likened to a process evaluation of the proposed program. This means that all of the processes needed to implement and operate the program are evaluated. For example, what do clients say about each aspect of the program? Brief interviews or simple, open-ended evaluation forms might be used to obtain this feedback. The same procedure could be used with each member of the staff involved in delivering the program to clients. How could the program be improved with respect to advertising, staff training, hours of services, room arrangements, signs directing clients to and within the program, and so forth? A daily log or journal might be used to obtain this feedback from all program participants.

Execution, then, involves the behavioral tryout and implementation of the program in real time and in a real world setting. After the program has been operating for a period of time, it will be desirable to determine whether the goals and objectives specified in the Analysis phase have been achieved. This eventually takes us back to Communication.

Communication

In returning to the Communication phase of the CASVE cycle, the developer returns to the original problems and needs, the "gaps," that led to the development of the program in the first place. In this phase of the process, however, the issue is whether the program as implemented has removed or reduced the gaps.

Depending on how the program goals were written, information about the impact of the program on gaps could be provided in any of the following forms:

- Case study materials of former clients using the new program could show the beneficial effects of the program.

- Tables and charts can be produced showing the numbers of clients impacted by the program, including their demographic characteristics and number of program contacts.

- Reports from staff involved in the program could explain the impact of the new program on client services.

- Participant observations, including rating forms and open-ended reports, might be tabulated and reported in relation to the program goals.

- Formal reports or program manuals can be printed and shared with all stakeholders in the program to inform them of all project activities and outcomes.

- Changes in test scores can be analyzed for statistical significance, or graphs can be prepared showing changes in objective data. This might include increased Vocational Identity scores on the My Vocational Situation, lower scores on the Career Thoughts Inventory, or other change scores obtained from the more than 10 instruments and procedures described in the next section of this chapter.

- Reports from consultants or other experts who made visits to the program and observed program operations could be shared with stakeholders.

These data and reports provided by the developer in the final Communication phase of the CASVE program development process conclude the cycle. The decision makers in charge of the program will then decide whether to continue the program and on what basis it might operate in the future. The CASVE cycle of program development can be used in any kind of program development activity. In the remainder of this chapter, we will show how it might be applied to the operation of Holland-based programs. First, however, we need to address an important issue that is critical to all career services programs: deciding which clients are ready for particular program activities. We refer to this as screening for client readiness.

Screening for Client Readiness

In the *SDS Professional User's Guide*, Holland, Powell, and Fritzsche (1994, p. 1) note that the SDS "serves a large proportion (perhaps 50%) of students and adults whose need for vocational assistance is minimal. The confirmation or reassurance they receive from taking the SDS, or the alternatives generated by that experience, provide all the help or information they desire." However, the basic question remains, Which 50% of clients can use the SDS in a self-help way? Secondary questions include the following: Are some forms of the SDS (e.g., computer versions, Form E, Career Explorer) and related materials (e.g., DHOC, EOF, PCI) more useful in self-help approaches?

Use of the CASVE cycle in program development would help developers provide answers to these questions. For example, the SDS could probably be used in a self-help way by more clients than ordinary *if* a comprehensive program directed to this purpose had been put in place. Whether 50% of clients can use the SDS in a self-help format depends on the organizational context in which the SDS is being used and the kinds of procedures established in the organization to support self-help approaches to career decision making.

A key factor in using the SDS in a self-help way has to do with client screening, determining which clients could most likely benefit from a self-help approach. Sampson and Reardon (1997) proposed a two-dimensional model for determining the support necessary to make effective use of assessment results and information resources in career services (Figure 27). The two dimensions are readiness and barriers. Clients lacking readiness for decision making and experiencing many barriers to implementing their decision require a higher degree of counseling assistance. This would include individual case-managed services, as described earlier. Clients who are ready for career decision making and are experiencing few barriers for implementing their choice, require less counseling assistance and can benefit immediately from self-help services. Combinations of high readiness and high barriers, or low readiness and low barriers, require moderate degrees of counseling in the form of brief staff-assisted services. As we discussed earlier, decided and undecided clients would tend toward high readiness, whereas indecisive clients would tend toward low readiness. RIASEC and CIP theory provide several ideas for assessing client readiness and barriers related to career decision making; these ideas are discussed in the next section.

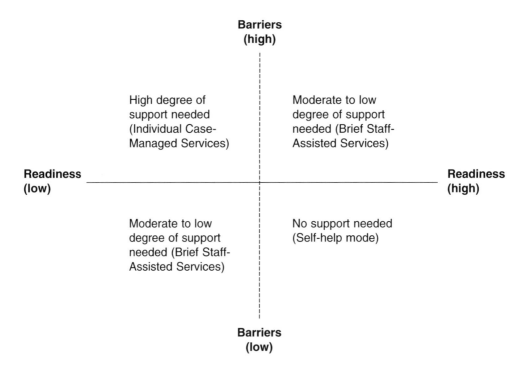

Figure 27. A model for determining the level of staff services needed for effective career assistance. From *Maximizing staff resources in meeting customer needs in one-stop centers* (Technical Report No. 22), by J. Sampson and R. Reardon. Copyright © 1996 by Florida State University, Center for the Study of Technology in Counseling and Career Development, Tallahassee, FL. Reproduced by permission.

Client screening options might include many activities, ranging from a client's brief answers to several questions to a battery of screening tests and questionnaires. One advantage to using a Holland-based approach or one based on CIP theory is that these theories provide some guides for screening to determine which clients might be most appropriate for a particular program of career services. A brief screening using Holland's theory might use client responses to counselor questions directed at determining levels of the eight indicators discussed in chapters 7 and 9. The format for this brief screening activity might include having the client examine the hexagon figure (see Figure 9) and self-identify a three-letter code after reading these brief descriptions. These indicators include congruence between aspirations and RIASEC code; the probable high-point code letter; coherence of aspirations; probable vocational identity level; and the level of consistency, differentiation, and commonness of the probable code. Other indicators might include the client's expressed level of anxiety about career decision making, the amount of negative thinking evident regarding career decision making, and the client's identification of barriers to career decision making.

Career counselors might want to rely on the results of tests and inventories in making screening judgments about the nature of an appropriate programmatic intervention. These instruments might also be used if a full range of services were available (e.g., self-help, brief staff-assisted, individual case-managed) and if many clients had to be screened in a short period of time. Screening instruments and the variables measured are described below:

1. *Self-Directed Search (Form R):* Congruence of aspirations and summary codes; RIASEC high-point code; list of aspirations and summary code; coherence of aspirations; and code consistency, differentiation, commonness (Holland, Powell, & Fritzsche, 1994).

2. *My Vocational Situation:* Vocational identity, need for information, barriers to career decision making (Holland, Daiger, & Power, 1980).

3. *Career Attitudes and Strategies Inventory:* Job Satisfaction, Work Involvement, Skill Development, Dominant Style, Career Worries, Interpersonal Abuse, Family Commitment, Risk-taking Style, and Geographical Barriers (Holland & Gottfredson, 1994).

4. *Career Thoughts Inventory:* Negative career thoughts based on CIP theory, including Decision Making Confusion, Commitment Anxiety, and External Conflict (Sampson, Peterson, Lenz, Reardon, & Saunders, 1996b).

5. *Career Decision Scale:* Career Certainty and Indecision (Osipow et al., 1976).

6. *Career Beliefs Inventory:* Beliefs that prevent clients from achieving career goals; 25 scales in five categories (Krumboltz, 1988).

7. *Career Decision Profile:* Decidedness, Comfort, Self-Clarity, Knowledge about Occupations and Training, Decisiveness, Career Choice Importance (Jones, 1988).

8. *Career Factors Inventory:* Career Choice Anxiety, Generalized Indecisiveness, Need for Career Information, and Need of Self-Knowledge (Chartrand, Robbins, & Morrill, 1997).

9. *Career Maturity Inventory* (revised): Career maturity attitude and competence (Crites & Savickas, 1995).

10. *Occupational Alternatives Question (OAQ)*: Level of career decidedness (Zener & Schnuelle, 1972; Slaney 1978, 1980).

Now that we have briefly discussed screening for client readiness to use the SDS or other Holland-based materials, we are ready to examine a basic 7-step model which is applicable to almost any career guidance program.

A Basic 7-Step Model for Career Service Delivery

A basic model for career service delivery was described by Peterson, Sampson, and Reardon (1991) and modified by Sampson and Reardon (1997). This model is based on the idea that career services in almost any setting follow the 7 steps shown in Figure 26. This 7-step sequence occurs in brief staff-assisted and individual case-managed services, although the time taken in each step varies across these service modes. Although initial contact (Step 1) is included in self-help services, the remaining 6 steps are often included in comprehensive self-help resource materials. These 7 steps may be shown as a flowchart describing how the counselor, client, and resources/materials connect during the process of service delivery.

1. *Initial Contact:* This might involve a scheduled intake interview, a brief visit in a hallway, a classroom presentation, a telephone conversation, or signing a register when entering a career resource room; the time period could vary from a few moments to more than an hour.

2. *Screening:* This involves a preliminary assessment by a counselor of client readiness and barriers to career decision making. Instruments such as the MVS and CTI might be used, or a brief interview might be conducted; in the latter, the counselor would listen for cues indicating low readiness or high barriers (i.e., low vocational identity, many negative metacognitions, lack of coherence in aspirations or work history, lack of ability to specify interests in any RIASEC code area, indecisiveness in career decision making).

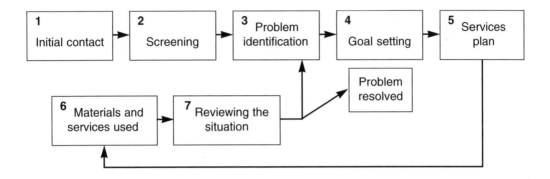

Figure 28. A model for career service delivery. From *Career development and services: A cognitive approach* (p. 231), by G. W. Peterson, J. P. Sampson, and R. C. Reardon. Copyright © 1991 by Brooks/Cole Publishing Company, Pacific Grove, CA 93950, a division of International Thomson Publishing, Inc. Reproduced by permission. All rights reserved.

3. *Problem Identification:* This involves the counselor and client agreeing about the nature of the gap between the current situation and a more desirable one (e.g., identify more options for future study or employment).

4. *Goal Setting:* This involves the counselor helping the client identify the outcome goals which, if completed, are likely to reduce the gap between the present and ideal situations (e.g., learn more about the pattern of my career interests, identify training programs most closely related to my strongest career interests, understand the relationship between my present job and my interests). Goal statements can be adapted from the National Career Development Guidelines Indicators (see Appendix K).

5. *Services Plan:* This involves the counselor and client collaborating to complete a plan that specifies a sequence for using Holland-based resources that will remedy the gap and meet the goals listed above. In some settings this might be called an Individual Education Plan or Individual Career Plan.

6. *Materials and Services Used:* This involves the client actually using the materials and resources identified in the plan; self-help and counselor assistance are used as indicated in the plan.

7. *Reviewing the Situation:* This involves the client and/or counselor reviewing the current situation to determine whether the gap has been removed. If the gap has been removed, career services

are discontinued until the next gap occurs; if the gap has not been removed, the services plan is revised as needed.

A developer can use this 7-step sequence to describe almost any career services program with respect to client involvement. In the following section, we will show how a developer might conceptualize a program proposal for a middle school.

Sample Program Scenarios

In the following sections, we will briefly sketch how a career services program could be conceptualized using the ideas described in this chapter. The first example provides a detailed description of how RIASEC and CIP theory might be applied in a program intervention using the CASVE process. This scenario is partly based on conversations with practitioners about successful programs. The other scenarios involving military and employment office applications provide less detail about the development process.

Scenario 1, Middle School Guidance: Project EXPLORE

Communication

The school advisory committee, which includes parents and school staff, has determined that middle school students are not prepared to select high school curriculum tracks in the eighth grade and that more emphasis on preparation for work should be incorporated into the school educational program. The committee wants to see career guidance incorporated into the educational program at the school and has directed that a pilot program be established. Consultation is obtained from the district office, and the school counselor is directed to develop a proposal for review.

Analysis

The counselor conducts an ERIC search for reports of middle school career guidance programs, creates a small ad hoc committee of teachers and parents, and begins to develop learner outcomes of a possible program. Using the National Career Development Guidelines, the following Competencies and Indicators are specified in the proposal:

V. Understanding the relationship between work and learning:
  - Describe the relationship of personal attitudes, beliefs, abilities, and skills to occupations.

VI. Skills to locate, understand, and use career information:
  - Identify a number of occupational groups for exploration.

VII. Skills to make decisions:
- Describe school courses related to personal, educational, and occupational interests.
- Identify advantages and disadvantages of various secondary and postsecondary programs for the attainment of career goals.

VIII. Understanding the process of career planning:
- Identify school courses that meet tentative career goals.
- Demonstrate knowledge of academic and vocational programs offered at the high school level.

After reviewing numerous program options, the ad hoc committee specified the following goals for Project EXPLORE:

1. Administer the SDS Career Explorer to 250 eighth-grade students during social studies classes in October as part of a unit on Exploring Careers.

2. Obtain computer-based SDS Career Explorer interpretive reports and make one copy available to each student and a parent.

3. Present a careers panel of parents representing RIASEC career fields for eighth-grade students.

4. Conduct orientation briefings by high school counselors on the RIASEC curriculum tracks at the high school level.

5. Assign a student research paper in which comparisons are made between two occupations or fields of study listed in the SDS Career Explorer interpretive report.

Synthesis

The counselor and ad hoc committee develop a written proposal for Project EXPLORE including a description of the program goals, activities, timelines, staff roles, costs, and evaluation, which is submitted to the school administration and the school advisory committee. Comments, suggestions, and concerns are noted, and the proposal is revised. The program evaluation includes a questionnaire and rating scale measuring the four sets of indicators listed in the Analysis section.

In developing the proposal, the committee decided to include the SDS Career Explorer paper components (i.e., Assessment Booklet, Careers Booklet, and Exploring Your Future with the SDS booklet), and to purchase the unlimited-use SDS Career Explorer software system to print the interpretive reports. The committee decided against the SDS Career Explorer Professional

Report Service because there were advantages to using the paper materials in classes, the paper Assessment Booklet could be used in writing the students' Individual Learning Plan, and an SDS code for expressed interests could be obtained from the Assessment Booklet. The committee noted that Professional Report Service advantages included less staff, less time, and less computer expenses for producing the student reports. The committee also recommended purchasing extra copies of the *SDS Professional User's Guide* and the *SDS Technical Manual*, as well as copies of *Making Vocational Choices*, for reference use by interested parents or teachers. Finally, the committee proposed expanding library holdings with multiple copies of the *Dictionary of Holland Occupational Codes*, the Educational Opportunities Finder, the *Occupational Outlook Handbook*, and the *Guide for Occupational Exploration*. These materials would be used by students in writing their research reports. Finally, it was proposed that students be taught how to use the Internet to obtain information about occupations and fields of postsecondary study that had been identified in the SDS Career Explorer interpretive report.

Valuing

At this point, the counselor and the staff must decide whether Project EXPLORE is worth doing. Will it remove the gap identified by the school advisory committee in a cost-effective way? The SDS Career Explorer Interpretive Report will enable students and parents to conceptualize career behavior and careers in the six RIASEC areas; it will also specify occupations and fields of study about which students can obtain more information as a basis for educational and occupational planning. In addition, the paper copy of the SDS Career Explorer Assessment Booklet will enable the counselor to identify the occupational daydreams of students experiencing particular difficulty in educational planning and to use the diagnostic signs embedded in the SDS to provide specialized assistance to students in greater need. A decision is made to execute Project EXPLORE.

Execution

Promotional and information materials for Project EXPLORE are prepared, testing materials are ordered, and arrangements are made to print the interpretive reports on computers at the school, staff are trained, and all arrangements have been made to operate the program. Program evaluation materials have been prepared, and a log has been prepared for collecting feedback and comments about the program. News stories about the program for the school paper and other publications have been scheduled. Stakeholders are kept informed of decisions about the program.

Communication

After Project EXPLORE has been completed, the school counselor and the ad hoc committee review all the reports and anecdotal comments of the participants, including those from parents, students, teachers, and administrators. A complete report is prepared with recommendations about continuing, changing, or eliminating the program for the following year. The basic question to be answered is whether the SDS Career Explorer, as incorporated into Project EXPLORE, increased student readiness for high school curriculum planning and preparation for work. Answers to this may be obtained from measures of the extent to which the four sets of indicators related to the national guidelines were achieved.

Scenario 2, Military Transition Program

This case involves a career transition program at a large military base that is designed to help persons who are separating from the military and seeking alternative career options. Persons receiving assistance can be at any rank in the military. Military spouses also have the option of getting help through this program. The program has been successfully operating for more than 5 years. Assistance is provided primarily through two different classes, one focusing on persons who will leave the military within a year, and the other focusing on individuals who are getting out in 2 to 5 years. The classes have proved quite popular, with the first class attracting 40 to 60 individuals per month and the other, 20 per month. For the military personnel who participate, time spent in this program is considered official duty time. All class participants complete the SDS Form R paper and pencil version. In the 3-day class format, participants complete the SDS as a homework assignment, and it is reviewed in class. In the half-day class format, participants complete the SDS in class and it is discussed during that same time period. Beyond the class activities, participants can also receive individual attention from program staff if they need it.

Program participants can follow up on their SDS results and other classwork by using materials in the career resource center which has more than 300 books and five computers for client use, including one with Internet access. The resource center is staffed by individuals who are participating in the Veterans Administration work-study program. These staff are on the GI Bill while attending school. They must be enrolled a minimum of $3/4$ time and can work up to 25 hours per week at minimum wage. These resource center staff are screened and trained by regular program staff and are viewed as an excellent cost-effective resource for extending the services of the resource center. Program coordinators have found it helpful to use the *Dictionary of Holland Occupational Codes* (DHOC) in conjunction with a computer-based *Dictionary of Occupational Titles* (DOT) program. These resources help individuals who are trying to identify options that will use the skills and experiences they acquired while in the military. The ultimate goal is to have all participants identify three occupational alternatives they wish to pursue and then develop a plan for pursuing additional education related to those alternatives or a job search strategy. Program participants also receive information and instruction from state Department of Labor personnel related to resume writing, interviewing, and labor market conditions.

Scenario 3, Employment Office Program

This example involves an organizational career development program that was developed for university employees. The program is open to all employees and averages 1,500 contacts per year. The components of the program include self-assessment activities, individual counseling, internal job market information (e.g., job postings, career path planning), organizational assessment, and developmental programs (e.g., job rotation, task enrichment, career exploration). The program manager chose Holland-based materials, including SDS Forms CP and E, and the Vocational Preference Inventory, for the self-assessment component of the program because of their "user friendliness, the fact that they provide immediate feedback and can be completed in a relatively brief period of time, and because they reduce participants' anxiety that they are being tested" (M. J. Healy, personal communication, June 19, 1997). Although most of the assistance is provided on a one-to-one basis, employees also participate in "lunch and learn" sessions where they receive information on career planning basics and receive a copy of the SDS. This activity is followed up by individual assistance as requested by the employees. The program is advertised through the employee newspaper. Another successful strategy for promoting the program and encouraging employee participation has been to set up tables in the cafeteria and share information while employees are on their lunch break. The program is currently staffed by one professional and one support staff person.

Holland's Ideas for Improved Career Programs

In the third edition of *Making Vocational Choices*, Holland (1997) has shared many ideas about strategies for improving career services programs. Reviewing the outcomes of studies, he writes that "the effects of different forms of career assistance are that almost any intervention helps, that group interventions may be as helpful as individual interventions, and that the search for special interventions for people with special problems has been less productive" (p. 203). He notes that standard interventions (e.g., counselors, inventories, courses, workshops, workbooks) have many common characteristics that contribute to their effectiveness. He further notes that interventions are helpful "because the average person has little career knowledge, has at least a moderate degree of career identity, and needs to rationalize his or her decisions or situation" (Holland, 1997, p. 204). We find the latter point especially useful, because in a chaotic, uncertain world, career services may be most helpful in providing clients with a solid rationale for doing what they want or need to do anyway.

In urging the development of balanced, broad-based career programs, Holland (1997) advocates providing comprehensive occupational information in an accessible form, individual and group sessions, an interest inventory (and perhaps a personality inventory or aptitude tests for some people), and some structured and unstructured exercises, including a report in which the client attempts to integrate all the treatment information and justify his or her vocational planning and current situation. We believe that components of such a balanced program can be obtained from the SDS and other Holland-based materials, when combined together with the work of skilled counselors and other helping persons.

Conclusion

This chapter has described the use of the CASVE cycle as a guide in program development. When followed, this 5-step sequence helps a program developer think through and make decisions about the issues that arise in solving individual career problems at the organizational level. The chapter also examined techniques and procedures for screening the level of client readiness for the use of the SDS and other Holland-based interventions, and briefly described a 7-step service delivery sequence that can be applied to all career interventions. A sample program scenario describing a middle school career guidance program application was described from a CASVE perspective, followed by brief descriptions of Holland-based programs in military and university employment office settings. Finally, readers were directed to the National Career Development Guidelines (Appendix K) for lists of competencies and indicators related to Holland-based materials. It is clear that Holland-based materials and resources are highly relevant to the development of programs that will help career services professionals and their clients become more competent career problem solvers and decision makers for many years to come.

12

Evaluation and Future Trends

In chapter 1, we began this book with a look at John L. Holland himself, the originator, manager, and evaluator of the RIASEC typological career theory that bears his name. In this chapter, we will move full circle from where we began. This chapter will help us obtain some external perspectives on the Self-Directed Search as well as on RIASEC theory. It will review what various experts and critics have said about both of these topics, and it will also present what Holland himself has said about the SDS and the theory after more than 40 years of work. The purpose of this chapter is to present a perspective on what the theory and related instruments have accomplished thus far and the directions that future work might follow. Hopefully, these ideas will help us become more confident and competent users of Holland's work in our career counseling and guidance activities.

We think there are two principle reasons. First, some practitioners question whether Holland's contributions are truly important in the field. They wonder about the status or stature of the theory and the related practical devices in relation to other career theories or instruments. Some scoffed at the SDS when it was first introduced. "If there is one word that characterizes and summarizes the construction and development of the SDS it is 'simplistic'" (Crites, 1978, p. 1611). Second, some leaders in career psychology, particularly those who have a more developmental or process orientation, do not now think Holland's work will be important in the future. There is a view that Holland's contributions, sometimes cast as an outmoded, outdated trait-factor approach, will not be important or useful in the future. Krumboltz (1996), for example, argues that deciding about an occupation in contemporary times may be not only impossible, but unwise. In speaking about person-environment congruence, Krumboltz says that "trying to place an evolving person into the changing work environment is like trying to hit a butterfly with a boomerang" (p. 263). The purpose of this chapter is to address these two issues and reaffirm the importance of Holland's theory and practical devices.

Holland's work has been controversial from the beginning. Perhaps it simply comes with being an Artistic type in any field. In an interview with Weinrach (1980), Holland noted that he had offended some by suggesting that their work in career theory and practice was imperfect, and they responded in kind. He noted that some of the criticism of RIASEC theory had come from those adhering to the developmentally oriented theories, who viewed these as more valuable than the structural theories. Perhaps a quote from that interview can be used to demonstrate the tone for the critical views from both sides: "I remain unimpressed by most of the 'career development' research. The attempts to document stages, problems, and solutions form a weak collection of work" (Weinrach, 1980, p. 412). More recently, Vondracek (1992) criticized Holland's use of the vocational identity construct as lacking the rich developmental, life-cycle formulation set forth by Erik Erickson. Holland (1997) responded:

> In the same way that scissors beat paper, evidence beats speculation—no matter who says it or how plausible it may seem. I developed a simple scale to capture the guts of the Erickson speculations, for I could not wait for my developmental colleagues to develop a brief, practical scale. (p. 150)

Those on the developmental side have often been unimpressed with Holland's work. John Crites (1978), a student of Donald Super's, was an early reviewer of the SDS in Buros' *Mental Measurement Yearbook*. Crites questioned the ethical basis for using the SDS by noting the following, "Practically, there is sufficient evidence to question seriously the ethics of indiscriminately making the SDS available to the public" (p. 1611). In listing his criticisms of the SDS, Crites concluded, "Until sophisticated attention is given to these overly simplified theoretical, psychometric, and practical issues, the caveat to users of the Self-Directed Search is that it might better be thought of as the Mis-Directed Search" (p. 1612). As we noted earlier, Holland's work has not been without controversy. We hope that the following sections of this chapter will help readers develop a personal view about the merits of Holland's theory and instruments.

What Others Say About RIASEC Theory

In taking a current sounding of what is being written about Holland's contributions to career theory and practice, we examined several of the most important textbooks in the field to see what these authors have written in their most recent editions. These texts are revised every 4 to 5 years, and the authors are respected, intellectual leaders in the career field. Several of these books are in their fifth or sixth edition, which means that they have become respected, continuous sources of information in the field. They are important influences in shaping how we view career theory and practice.

Herr and Cramer

Edwin Herr and Stanley Cramer (1996), writing in the fifth edition of their massive work, *Career Guidance and Counseling Through the Lifespan: Systematic Approaches*, offered the following summary on Holland's contributions:

> In sum, then, Holland's theory continues to stimulate other lines of inquiry, raise new questions, and find new applications. Although much research remains to be done on the hypotheses generated by the theory, it continues to be major conceptual structure for considering choice, persistence, and performance in educational and occupational settings." (p. 228)

They don't label his work as the best or most important.

In addition to their overall evaluation of Holland, Herr and Cramer (1996) summarized the important changes in the theory reported in an earlier work by Weinrach and Srebalus (1990, pp. 47-48, as cited in Herr & Cramer, 1996, p. 228):

1. The theory has expanded its constructs, becoming more comprehensive and explicit.

2. Throughout its evolution, new concepts (e.g., identity) have been added to prop up others. The theory's limitations are more explicit.

3. The theory remains in the tradition of differential psychology.

4. It has moved away from all-or-none distinctions among environmental and personality types and towards statements of degree and patterning.

5. All major constructs have operational definitions, and these enable careful empirical verification of the theory.

6. A two-dimensional scientific model (the hexagon) has been added.

7. Empirical evidence, pro and con, has been generated in more than 450 studies across populations of diverse characteristics.

8. Application of the theory to career planning and counseling has been encouraged through the development and refinement of practitioner and self-help tools.

9. Procedures have been developed to teach the theory and evaluate mastery of it.

10. Although continually open to revision based on empirical evidence, Holland's theory has successfully resisted modifications intended to satisfy prescriptive cultural and political pressures.

Isaacson and Brown

Another leading textbook in the field by Lee Isaacson and Duane Brown (1997), *Career Information, Career Counseling, and Career Development*, now in its sixth edition, offers the following observation regarding the status of Holland's theory: "Holland's theory of vocational choice and adjustment stands as the most influential of the extant theories" (p. 24). There's little doubt about where Isaacson and Brown stand regarding Holland's work. They go on to list some of the indicators of the impact of Holland's work on research and practice in the career field.

Zunker

Vernon Zunker (1994), in the fourth edition of *Career Counseling: Applied Concepts of Life Planning*, wrote the following:

> Holland's theory places emphasis on the accuracy of self-knowledge and career information necessary for career decision making. It has had a tremendous impact on interest-assessment and career-counseling procedures; a number of interest inventories present results using the Holland classification format. Its implications for counseling are apparent; a major counseling objective would be to develop strategies to enhance knowledge of self, occupational requirements, and differing occupational environments. (p. 49)

Zunker, although generally positive, appears to see limits in Holland's work with respect to counseling interventions.

All three of these basic texts in the career field acknowledge Holland's strong, persistent, long-standing contributions and their impact on service and research, but only Isaacson and Brown (1997) place it at the top of the current theories. But how do the authors of the basic textbooks on career theory itself evaluate Holland's work?

Osipow and Fitzgerald

In the fourth edition of *Theories of Career Development*, Osipow and Fitzgerald (1996) offered a mixed review of Holland's theory:

> The proposal [the theory] is comprehensive, covering not only vocational choices but life-style in the broadest sense. Tests of the theory indicate its validity in broad outline. Certain aspects are open to rigorous test, while others must of necessity be tested indirectly, or worse, crudely. The theory does not describe the development of personality types but does indicate the process of normal choice and misdirected choice from the point of an established

personal orientation and beyond. Unfortunately, few suggestions are made for the treatment of problems in career choice and for identifying relevant vocational counseling goals. The theory does logically and parsimoniously account for a good deal of vocational behavior, but falls down somewhat in respect to explanation of why people develop into various types. (p. 105)

They concluded, "The number of unanswered and answered questions that remain with respect to Holland's theory, however, suggests that the theory will exert an influence on research in career choice for some time and begin to have a growing impact on counseling itself" (p. 105).

Osipow and Fitzgerald (1996) cited no references authored by Holland later than 1990, so they have not included much of the work that we have referenced in this book. Also, some of the themes regarding the theory's impact on the career counseling process noted in their evaluation are similar to Zunker's observations.

Brown and Brooks

Perhaps the most widely read career theories book is edited by Duane Brown and Linda Brooks (1996), *Career Choice and Development*, now in its third edition. The chapter in this book on "Holland's Theory" was written by Arnie Spokane (1996), and was cited earlier in chapters 1, 2, and 3. In a concluding chapter in this book, "Status of Career Development Theories," Brown (1996) noted that Holland's theory is well constructed in most regards and that in stimulating research it "has no peer" (p. 518). Further, he noted that "because of the instruments Holland has produced to measure his constructs, his ideas are without question more influential than the ideas of any of the other theorists in the practice area" (p. 518).

Sharf

A second edition of *Applying Career Development Theory to Counseling* by Richard Sharf (1997a) offers a summary of Holland's work. Sharf notes that RIASEC theory has been widely accepted by counselors and psychologists because it is conceptually easy to use; the constructs of the theory are clearly defined and have generated much research applicable to all people, including women and persons of color; the occupational classification system is easy to use; and other inventories besides the SDS and VPI use the theory. Sharf concludes, "Because of its wide acceptance by counselors and the abundance of supportive research, Holland's theory is likely to be used widely in the future" (p. 111).

This review of some of the leading basic textbooks in the career field indicates that Holland's work has been, is now, and will continue to be very important. Indeed, this work is possibly unsurpassed in its impact on career research and practice. Again, why is this important to us? One anecdote comes to mind: A colleague recently had a conversation with a state-level developer of computer-assisted career guidance systems, who indicated that he would not incorporate Holland-based ideas or materials into that state system because they were too simplistic and outdated. Such a policy decision seems at odds with what the experts say and will ultimately shortchange the citizens of that state seeking high-quality career services.

Theory Convergence

Before examining Holland's own views of RIASEC theory and the SDS, we should pause a moment and examine the "theory convergence" movement as it has emerged in the past several years. This movement in career psychology has sought to promote a more unified, common theory base in the field. Osipow (1990), a psychologist at Ohio State University, has been particularly outspoken in noting that career theories have more in common than in differences, and Donald Super (1992) also strongly supported the idea of theory convergence. These efforts culminated in a theory convergence project which led to a conference and ultimately a book, *Convergence in Career Development Theories: Implications for Science and Practice* (Savickas & Lent, 1994). This book includes presentations by the leading career theorists and discussions by leaders in career psychology.

What are the implications of this movement for RIASEC theory? Savickas and Lent (1994) have been quick to point out that the movement is not intended to create some kind of homogenized theory, some blend of career theory that ignores past contributions of such persons as Holland. But, they say, the unique contributions of each theory can be viewed as complementary to one another, as providing special insights into common career problems. Others, such as Holland, have taken a different view.

Holland addressed the conference on theory convergence in April 1992. The title of his talk was "Separate but Unequal is Better" (Holland, 1994). Holland listed several barriers to theory integration, the first of which was the fact that theories have different goals: "Mine is aimed primarily at practitioners and their clients, so I have tried to develop a statement that is relatively simple to comprehend and apply" (p. 46). He continued:

> Theories have different audiences and goals. Some are oriented to
> practitioners; others are oriented to psychologists, sociologists, or

other groups. It's hard to do both, for practitioners want help and psychologists want perfection or scientific respectability. Vocational theories are also oriented to different human problems— field or kind of work, occupational level, satisfaction, involvement, vocational adjustment, and so on. To summarize, integration requires agreement about goals, but different goals are weighted differently by different people. (p. 46)

He concluded, "In short, it appears more productive to renovate old theories or strategies than to stitch together an integrated theory" (p. 50). Holland also suggested renovations for his own theory, and we will review these ideas in the following section of this chapter.

A second conference on convergence was held in 1994. This time the topic was the convergence of career theory and practice, or the degree to which career theory and practice might better inform one another. Papers presented at the conference led to the publication of the *Handbook of Career Counseling Theory and Practice* (Savickas & Walsh, 1996). The first chapter of the book featured a chapter by Holland (1996c), in which he shared observations about the relationship between career theory and practice. He noted that practice is hampered by inadequate counselor training, an addiction to one-to-one counseling intervention, a lack of familiarity with test manuals and other product documentation, a lack of scientific training, insensitivity to client aspirations, and environmental problems (e.g., large caseloads).

However, Holland (1996c) also mentioned several positive contributions of theory to practice. For example, he attributed the dominance of person-environment fit theories, such as the RIASEC typology, to the fact that they address two fundamental client questions: What kind of work will bring happiness? and Can I perform it well? He further noted that developmental and learning theories focus more on questions of interest to practitioners than their clients (e.g., What is my level of vocational maturity? What is my career life stage?). Holland also noted that RIASEC theory has demonstrated its usefulness to divergent groups in society and in considerable research about the practical effects of such tools as the SDS.

What Holland Says About RIASEC Theory

As noted earlier, Holland (1994) critiqued his own theory in the paper delivered at the 1992 theory convergence conference. Holland observed that one of the strengths of a typology like RIASEC theory is its ability to organize information and to help explain stability in personality and vocational behavior. In contrast, a weakness of typologies involves their explanation of the processes involved in change and development (i.e., learning, early childhood socialization). Holland also noted "...I should do a better job of linking the typology to vocational interventions" (p. 50). In this regard, it should be noted that the most recent edition of *Making Vocational Choices* (Holland, 1997) includes quite a bit of new material on career interventions and providing career assistance, which he describes as the most spontaneous writing in the book.

In the *SDS Technical Manual*, Holland, Fritzsche, and Powell (1994) offered additional critical comments about the typology. They cited the following strengths of RIASEC Theory:

- The typology is easily understood by most persons.
- The theory is easily applied to practical problems (i.e., assessment of interests, classifications of options, intervention strategies).
- The theory is useful (i.e., has clear definitions, an internally consistent structure, a broad scope, and accounts for personal development and change).
- There is broad research support (i.e., men and women, large samples, children through elderly persons have been studied).

They also found weaknesses:

- Hypotheses about career environments need more research support.
- Hypotheses about Person–Environment interactions have received some support but require more testing.
- Formulations about personal development and change have been supported but require more comprehensive examination.
- Classification of occupations may differ slightly according to the device used.
- Many important effects on career behavior are outside the typology (i.e., distribution of social power in a specific environment; impact of social class, great wealth or poverty, intelligence, and special aptitudes on career behavior).

In a pointed response to a generally positive critique of the theory offered by Duane Brown (1987), Holland (1987) made several comments about his theory that we think are especially relevant for practitioners. First, he noted that many evaluations of RIASEC theory offer two suggestions: (a) be more explicit about how types develop, and (b) women need a separate theory. Regarding the first suggestion, Holland reported that each revision of the theory has provided more information about how types develop, with more recent statements connecting learning theory to the development of types. "Different types are the outcomes of different learning histories" (Holland, 1987, p. 26). Holland disagrees that women need a separate theory because the "evidence from the application of the theory to men and women of different ages is that theoretical predictions work about as well for women as they do for men" (p. 26). Holland has generally sought to verify broad, general themes about career behavior that have the widest possible practical application.

In an address to the 1995 annual convention of the American Psychological Association (Holland, 1996a), Holland noted some of the high points in his past work and offered observations about the future of the theory:

1. The application of the RIASEC classification system to work histories "represents its most explicit success." It shows that the average career has substantial continuity across specific jobs (p. 397).

2. "The application of the typology to vocational aspirations or intentions of people of different ages also demonstrates the continuity or cohesiveness of an individual's intentions" (p. 400). Like the studies of work histories, they show that aspirations cohere over time.

3. Along with aspirations, interests are relatively stable over long periods of time and become more stable with age. People tend to act on their dominant interests and seek occupations in which they can express their interests.

4. A review of research findings indicates that "congruency of interests is conducive to stability and satisfaction in both interpersonal and person-job relations" (p. 401). However, the efficiency of this hypothesis is low, and improved research and/or a revision of the typology may be in order.

5. Theory revisions since 1987 have sought to make it more explanatory by incorporating information about a person's beliefs about career stability or change (e.g., the nine scales of the Career Attitudes and Strategies Inventory; Holland & Gottfredson, 1994).

6. Persons with high vocational identity, an explicit and relatively stable picture of their goals, interests, skills, and suitable occupations, are more likely to accept or find work that is congruent with their RIASEC type. Identity has increasingly become a key aspect of the theory.

7. Unfinished theory business includes an improved understanding of the nature of the hexagonal model (Rounds & Tracey, 1996) as it applies in other countries or cultural traditions outside the U.S.; the application of the RIASEC model in a changing

socio-economic world with transient, unpredictable work opportunities (Rifkin, 1995); and the need for renewed research into
the application of the typology to aspirations and work histories.

These seven items represent both a mountaintop view of the theory and a
leader's call for greater efforts to scale new heights. Many of the issues raised by
practitioners in our SDS workshops and by clients discussing their SDS results,
are related to these seven items. In some cases, we as counselors can make defin-
itive statements and provide evidence that we know something about vocational
behavior that might be helpful, but in other instances we know less.

In addition to Holland's personal evaluation, Fred Borgen, of Iowa State
University, summarized 20 years of Holland's work as seen through the *Journal
of Vocational Behavior*, with the following thoughts: "By any standard, the erup-
tion of Holland's influence is unmistakable in the last two decades of vocational psychology. Research on his theory is voluminous and unabating. His theoretical insights are now at the center of any comprehensive review... The
widespread use of his inventories is huge..." (Borgen, 1991, pp. 275-276). Later
Borgen notes, "Perhaps Holland himself provides the best explanation of why
the hexagon has traveled so far" (p. 276). The concluding paragraph of the
Holland, Magoon, and Spokane (1981) review asserted the following:

> Finally, the road to continued progress in this area may be a road
> that is paved more with perseverance, reading, and thinking rather
> than worrying about methodological perspectives. The tools, theo-
> ries, and substantive advances in this field owe very little to method
> and very much to a relatively small number of good ideas vigor-
> ously followed for long periods of time. (p. 300)

In the next section, we will move from our review of the theory to a summary of reviews of the SDS instrument. We will look first at what others have
said recently about the SDS and then at what Holland himself has had to say. We
will focus on the most recent reviews and statements about the SDS because
older reviews typically address problems that have since been corrected.

What Others Say About the SDS

Since the SDS was published in 1970, it has been reviewed many times in
professional journals, Buros' *Mental Measurements Yearbooks*, *Test Critiques*, and
elsewhere. In response to reviewer and customer comments, Holland has made
changes in the SDS in each new edition (Holland, Fritzsche, & Powell, 1994).
For example, Holland's colleague Gary Gottfredson and daughter Joan
Holland wrote a paper (never published) upon the release of the 1977 edition
of the SDS, in which they reported 139 changes made in the SDS to make it

more easily self-administered and quicker to complete. Ironically, they submitted this article to eight journals that had published articles or reviews on the SDS, but no editor was willing to publish it (Holland, 1977, personal communication). Perhaps the old line about "bad news is good news" also applies to professional matters involving career counseling.

We could find no reviews of the 1994 edition of the SDS published in the literature. Therefore, we reverted to several reviews of the 1985 edition that have been published most recently. These published reviews include Bodden (1987), Daniels (1989), and Manuelle-Adkins (1989). The most recent published review of the SDS was written by Harry Daniels (1994) in *A Counselor's Guide to Career Assessment Instruments*. He notes that Holland's purpose in creating the SDS was to provide a counseling tool that could serve many adolescents and adults seeking career counseling, a structural framework for organizing personal and occupational information to aid career decision making, and a psychometrically sound instrument for researchers to use in investigating the validity of RIASEC theory. Daniels concluded that Holland had achieved those purposes.

Despite many positive features reviewed in the SDS, Daniels (1994) had reservations about the use of raw scores to determine three-letter codes and about the inconsistent use of the typology within the SDS itself (i.e., actual numbers are used in the Self-Estimates section, whereas items are used in the other sections). Although Daniels noted that the SDS may not work for every client, that some clients will need follow-up by a counselor, and that the SDS, like other interest tests, has limited predictive validity, "the SDS remains an excellent vocational counseling tool that can be used with most adolescents and adults" (p. 211).

The use of raw scores in calculating the SDS summary score has sparked controversy from time to time. Some critics (Prediger, 1981) have suggested that sex-bias and age-bias could be corrected with the use of normed scores rather than raw scores in the SDS. (The SDS computer-based interpretive report presents both raw scores and percentiles related to gender and age.) Holland, however, argues that (according to his definition) a sex-fair inventory "uses one form for both sexes, does not modify scores because of a person's sex, and, most important, influences men and women positively and equally according to experimental tests" (Holland, Powell, & Fritzsche, 1994, p. 53). He cites evidence to support the latter claim (Holland, Fritzsche, & Powell, 1994). Lee Cronbach, whose *Essentials of Psychological Testing* (1984) has informed many counselors over the years about tests, weighed in on this issue in favor of raw scores and in support of Holland's approach with the SDS: "In my opinion, general norms should play little part in interpreting interests; if a person likes the work, it makes no difference whether 50% or 90% of other persons would also like it" (Cronbach, 1984, p. 421).

Borgen (1991) and Spokane (1990) picked up on a slightly different theme in their reviews of the SDS. Borgen, noting that career counseling has increasingly moved toward viewing clients as active rather than passive agents in shaping their careers, says:

> It is startling to reread Holland...and see how in today's hot emphases he was ahead of the curve on cognition, agency, and empowerment... . The subsequent success of his SDS was presaged by his beliefs about giving tools to clients to shape their career lives. (p. 281)

He further noted that the very name Self-Directed Search seems synonymous with personal agency.

Spokane (1990) viewed the SDS as a self-guided treatment that moved the focus of career intervention to the client's process rather than the counseling process, or more specifically, the work of the counselor. He viewed the SDS as unique among interest inventories in three ways: It is completely self-administering, self-scoring, and self-interpreting; its scales are based on Holland's theory and are not exclusively empirical in nature; and it is supported by a large body of research on its psychometric characteristics *and* its diagnostic indicators.

What Holland Says About the SDS

In reviewing the 1994 edition of the SDS (Holland, Powell, & Fritzsche, 1994), Holland observed that it closely resembled the 1985 edition, although more than 100 changes were made. He also noted that the 1994 edition is slightly more reliable than the 1985 edition and generally superior in most respects. In creating the most recent edition, Holland sought to increase the validity and reliability by trying out new or revised items, deleting weak or outdated items, and omitting items with extreme endorsement rates among either males or females. However, he noted that there have been nine item analyses of the four forms of the SDS and that "it has become increasingly difficult to create a better inventory" (Holland, Fritzsche, & Powell, 1994, p. 17). Detailed information about the reliability and validity of all editions of the SDS as well as the equivalence across all four editions of the SDS is given in the *SDS Technical Manual* (Holland, Fritzsche, & Powell, 1994).

Holland makes several other points in evaluating the SDS. First, he notes that the SDS, like the Strong-Campbell Interest Inventory (Campbell, 1977), does not provide more efficient predictions than a person's expressed choice when coded by RIASEC category. Indeed, the predictions of aspirations always exceed those of inventories, but when the inventory and aspiration share the same first-letter code, the predictive efficiency is 64% to 85% for intervals of

1-3 years (Holland, Fritzsche, & Powell, 1994, p. 30). Second, Holland observed that the usefulness and validity of the SDS as a comprehensive career assessment appears to flow from vocational interests, personality, values, competencies, and avocational interests (Holland, Fritzsche, & Powell, 1994). Third, the SDS affects test takers in several positive ways, whereas no negative effects have been documented in more than 20 studies. Moreover, the positive effects do not depend on age, race, gender, or intelligence (Holland, Fritzsche, & Powell, 1994, p. 58).

Of the many studies conducted over the years, we find one by Pallas, Dahmann, Gucer, and Holland (1983) particularly interesting. The researchers set out to assess the effects of the SDS and other psychological tests. A diverse sample (N = 334) was drawn from 13 sources (e.g., high schools, colleges, women's centers, working adults, retirees). One group in the sample included people (N = 84) who purchased the SDS for $.80 at a booth at the Baltimore City Fair staffed by psychologists. Evaluation measures included the Vocational Identity scale of the MVS, an eight-item Evaluation scale, a six-item Action scale to measure what a person had done since completing the SDS, a five-item Cool scale measuring how a person contends with ordinary life events, and a measure of the extent to which participants completed all SDS materials.

On average, participants evaluated the SDS positively, and these evaluations did not differ by race, sex, or educational level. Positive test-taking experiences were reported by 60%, 23% reported neither positive nor negative reactions, and 12% reported negative reactions (mostly as a result of poor test administration). Participants with greater vocational identity were more likely to rate the SDS positively, as were those scoring higher on the Cool scale. Although most test-takers only partially completed the SDS experience, the persons completing more of the experience had more positive evaluations of the SDS and were more likely to take positive action. In conclusion, the authors noted that test-takers had slightly positive evaluations of the SDS across various demographic characteristics, and that it is important to use effective test administration practices to maximize the positive outcomes of using such instruments as the SDS.

Spokane and Holland (1995) summarized the present and future of the SDS:

> The SDS is an inventory with desirable psychometric characteristics that incorporates a person's history of vocational daydreams, which can be used to increase predictive validity and to form an impression of a client's goals and background, and encourages the immediate preliminary exploration of more than 1,000 occupations. Because it is self-scored and can be interpreted by many, perhaps most, clients, it encourages active participation in the resolution of career problems and questions. (p. 388)

In addition, the effects of the SDS on the test-taker are now documented by 22 experimental studies. The interpretation of SDS scales is also supported by a substantial literature examining the RIASEC typology. Most recently, the relationship between the "Big Five" personality factors and the RIASEC types continues to both clarify the interpretation of the types and contribute to our understanding of the nature of, and overlap between, interests and personality. (p. 388)

They concluded by noting that there is much to be learned about interest inventories, such as the SDS. For example, which sections of the SDS promote exploration, and how does the SDS aid in career decision making? It is ironic that we know so much about the SDS relative to other career interventions and inventories, but there remains a great deal yet to be learned and understood.

Conclusion

This chapter has highlighted the impact of Holland's theory and the SDS on the career counseling profession and the field of career psychology. This chapter reviewed what textbook writers and leading scholars have said about Holland's work because these persons shape many of our ideas about what is important in the field. We also examined what Holland himself has had to say about the theory and the SDS. Readers can take heart that RIASEC theory seems to still be on an ascending slope of relevance and energy in the field of career research. Holland, nearing his eighth decade, continues to direct the work associated with the theory that bears his name. In the most recent edition of *Making Vocational Choices*, Holland (1997) wrote:

> The theory, the classification, and the related assessment devices (i.e., VPI, SDS, MVS, DHOC, PCI, CASI) offer a variety of explanatory possibilities for coping with common diagnostic problems in career practice. The typological formulations can be used to interpret interest inventories, to clarify the divergent occupational choices of people in conflict, to interpret work histories, to estimate the outcomes of proposed person-environment combinations, to explain the origins of interests, and to explain the reasons for adaptive and maladaptive career development. And of equal importance, the theory suggests remedial actions or treatments for facilitating more adaptive vocational behavior. (p. 194)

This book has sought to move the state of the art in career services a little bit forward in these areas.

Epilog

In writing this book and in reflecting on our years of working with Holland's RIASEC theory and the SDS, we have heard many stories from practitioners in the field about their work in applying Holland's ideas. Some of these stories are funny, some show incredible creativity, some show success, some show failure. Some are inspiring—one particular story, which provides an appropriate epilog for a book on using the SDS. The names and identifying information in this story have been changed, but the facts are accurate as I (Reardon) recall them.

"Ted's" Story

This story was told to me several years ago by a former doctoral student in our counseling program who had completed an internship in a state forensic hospital. He had stayed on after the internship and taken a job working in a ward occupied by female inmates who had been judged criminally insane. One particular inmate—we'll call her Mary—had become particularly difficult to manage. She had a reputation for being the most difficult, dangerous patient in the hospital. She had been in the hospital prison for about 30 years. She had murdered someone and had been sentenced to this forensic unit. Ted told me that she had several thick folders containing the results of many psychological and medical tests conducted over the years, but that the staff had pretty much given up on working with her. She was very withdrawn, seldom spoke, and had again started self-mutilation. She had attempted suicide several times and was taking several medications designed to help her control her self-destructive behavior. She was often placed in restraints.

In trying to help Mary overcome the self-mutilation, Ted had been given the green light by the supervising staff to try anything. It seemed to be a hopeless situation. Over a period of weeks, Ted met with Mary in the ward where she was under very close supervision and confinement. He tried to talk with her about her interests and to learn about things that she might like to do. It was very difficult—Mary had really never thought about herself in such ways. Moreover, no one had ever really asked. As Mary and Ted began to establish a fragile counseling relationship, Ted got the idea of having Mary take the SDS. He thought it might help him learn more about what she liked and was interested in doing. It was also very simple and straightforward; there was nothing mysterious about it. Initially, Mary didn't want to do it because she had already taken so many different tests.

Ted checked with his supervisor about administering the SDS. The supervisor had heard of the Strong, but didn't know about the SDS. After being briefed, the supervisor said, "Go ahead. Nothing else has ever worked with Mary." So, Ted obtained a copy of the SDS and showed it to Mary. She was surprised that she could keep the booklet herself and work on it when she felt like it. Ted was not prepared for how difficult it was for her to complete the items. It took her almost a week to complete the SDS, and several times she wanted to quit or was overwhelmed by the task. Some days she could only complete a few items before taking a cigarette break. She had just not thought about herself in terms of the SDS items. The fact that someone else was interested in her interests was also unprecedented in all the past years.

After completing the SDS and scoring it, Mary broke down completely in tears. Why? Because she could not remember that anyone had ever before shown her the results of the tests she had taken or explained these results to her. Here were Ted and Mary, spending time talking about her interests, the things she had done, could do, and liked to do. Moreover, it was possible to look at her interests and identify things in the hospital that she might be able to do. As I recall, Mary had Conventional and Realistic interests, and Ted arranged for her to begin to make choices that would enable her to spend time in the ward and on the grounds doing things that interested her.

As all of this was happening with the SDS, Mary's self-mutilation behavior had dramatically stopped. Other hospital staff were puzzled and asked what was happening because Mary for the first time in many years had stopped abusing herself and acting so crazy. Other psychological tests were administered, and the psychiatrists did various medical workups on Mary. Unbelievably, Mary was getting better. She was no longer looking and acting insane. She was slowly moved from the maximum security areas in the facility into other areas. Mary was given some work privileges involving tending the gardens and plants at the entrance to the hospital. She handled these tasks very well; the grounds never looked better. Eventually, there were medical and judicial hearings, and Mary was judged competent to be released to a halfway house, where she obtained a job in the local community.

If you're like me, you find this story difficult to believe. However, it was told to me as truth about 10 years ago, and I believe it to be so. The counselor involved was of unimpeachable character and is still working as a prison psychologist in the southeastern part of the country. Interestingly, the SDS was added to the battery of tests used at the hospital after this incident.

A Call to Network and Share

We suspect there are many other stories like this one involving the SDS. It is a loss to the career counseling profession and to all of us helping persons that these case reports seldom find their way into our professional literature. We invite readers with inspiring and illuminating reports of SDS use, either with individual cases or group programs, to share them with us by phone, fax, or e-mail. We would seek to enrich the next edition of this book with such reports.

We hope Ted's story helps you redouble your efforts in helping people to better discover their interests and to explore their career options more fully. The SDS awaits your creative application as a helping person.

To share your stories and cases contact us at:

Robert C. Reardon
rreardon@admin.fsu.edu
(850) 644-9777
(850) 644-3273 (FAX)

or

Janet G. Lenz
jlenz@admin.fsu.edu
(850) 644-9547
(850) 644-3273 (FAX)

References

American Psychological Association. (1995). John L. Holland: Award for distinguished professional contributions. *American Psychologist, 50,* 236-247.

Arbona, C. (1989). Hispanic employment and the Holland typology of work. *The Career Development Quarterly, 37,* 257-268.

Austin, J. (1993). Gary D. Gottfredson's and John L. Holland's Position Classification Inventory (Form HS). *Measurement & Evaluation in Counseling & Development, 26,* 206-206.

Bandura, A. (1977). Self-efficacy: Toward a unifying theory of behavioral change. *Psychology Review, 84,* 191-215.

Barker, S., White, P., Reardon, R., & Johnson, P. (1980). An evaluation of the effectiveness of an adaptation of the Self-Directed Search for use of the blind. *Rehabilitation Counseling Bulletin, 23,* 177-182.

Bauernfeind, R. H. (1992). Self-Directed Search—Form CP—Career Planning. *Newsnotes, 27*(2), 5-7.

Betz, N., Borgen, F., & Harmon, L. (1996). *Manual for the Skills Confidence Inventory.* Palo Alto, CA: Consulting Psychologists Press.

Bodden, J. (1987). Review of the Self-Directed Search. In D. Keyser & R. Sweetland (Eds.), *Test critiques* (Vol. 5, pp. 419-424). Kansas City, MO: Test Corporation of America.

Bolles, R. (1996). *What color is your parachute?* San Francisco, CA: Ten Speed Press.

Borgen, F. (1991). Megatrends and milestones in vocational behavior: A 20-year counseling psychology retrospective. *Journal of Vocational Behavior, 39,* 263-290.

Brown, D. (1987). The status of Holland's theory of vocational choice. *Career Development Quarterly, 36,* 13-23.

Brown, D. (1996). Status of career development theories. In D. Brown & L. Brooks (Eds.), *Career choice and development* (3rd ed., pp. 513-526). San Francisco: Jossey-Bass.

Brown, D., & Brooks, L. (Eds.). (1996). *Career choice and development* (3rd ed.). San Francisco: Jossey-Bass.

Brown, M. B. (1996). Review of the Career Attitudes and Strategies Inventory: An inventory for understanding adult careers. In J. Impara & J. Conoley (Eds.), *Supplement to the twelfth mental measurements yearbook* (pp. 60-61). Lincoln, NE: Buros Institute of Mental Measurements of the University of Nebraska, Lincoln.

Bureau of Labor Statistics. (1996). *Occupational outlook handbook.* Washington, DC: U.S. Government Printing Office.

Campbell, D. P. (1971). *Handbook for the Strong Vocational Interest Blank.* Stanford, CA: Stanford University Press.

Campbell, D. P. (1977). *Manual for the Strong-Campbell Interest Inventory T325 (Merged form).* Stanford, CA: Stanford University Press.

Campbell, D. P. (1995). The Campbell Interest & Skill Survey (CISS): A product of ninety years of psychometric evolution. *Journal of Career Assessment, 3,* 391-410.

Career Design Associates. (1988). *Discovering career options: Introduction to the Self-Directed Search*. Dallas, TX: Author.

Chartrand, J., Robbins, S., & Morrill, W. (1997). *Career Factors Inventory*. Palo Alto, CA: Consulting Psychologists Press.

Chung, Y. B., & Harmon, L. W. (1994). The career interests and aspirations of gay men: How sex-role orientation is related. *Journal of Vocational Behavior, 45*, 223-239.

Ciechalski, J. (1996). Review of the Self-Directed Search, Form E–1990 Revision. In J. Impara & J. Conoley (Eds.), *Supplement to the twelfth mental measurements yearbook* (pp. 313-314). Lincoln, NE: Buros Institute of Mental Measurements of the University of Nebraska, Lincoln.

Cole, N., Whitney, D., & Holland, J. (1971). A spatial configuration of occupations. *Journal of Vocational Behavior, 1*, 1-9.

Costa, P. T., Jr., & McCrae, R. R. (1992). *NEO PI-R professional manual*. Odessa, FL: Psychological Assessment Resources.

Crenshaw, A. B. (1995, January 2-8). So much for the myth of a mobile work force. *Washington Post National Weekly Edition*.

Crites, J. (1978). The Self-Directed Search. In O. K. Buros (Ed.), *Eighth mental measurements yearbook* (pp. 109-122). Highland Park, NJ: Gryphon Press.

Crites, J., & Savickas, M. (1995). *The Career Maturity Inventory–Revised*. Boulder CO: John O. Crites. (Available from ISM Information Systems Management, Inc., Careerware, Ottawa, Ontario).

Cronbach, L. J. (1984). *Essentials of psychological testing* (4th ed.). New York: Harper & Row.

Cummings, R., & Maddux, C. (1987). Self-administration and scoring errors of learning disabled and non-learning disabled students on two forms of the Self-Directed Search. *Journal of Counseling Psychology, 34*, 83-85.

Daniels, H. (1989). Review of the Self-Directed Search: 1985 Revision. In J. Conoley & J. Kramer (Eds.), *Tenth mental measurements yearbook*. Lincoln, NE: Buros Institute of Mental Measurements of the University of Nebraska, Lincoln.

Daniels, H. (1994). Self-Directed Search (SDS). In J. Kapes, M. Mastie, & E. Whitfield (Eds.), *A counselor's guide to career assessment instruments* (3rd ed., pp. 206-212). Alexandria, VA: National Career Development Association.

Daniels, M. H. (1985). Vocational Exploration and Insight Kit. In J. V. Mitchell, Jr. (Ed.), *Ninth mental measurements yearbook* (pp. 1675-1676). Lincoln, NE: University of Nebraska Press.

Daniels, M. H. (1994). Review of the Self-Directed Search. In J. T. Kapes, M. M. Mastie, & E. A. Whitfield, (Eds.), *A counselor's guide to career assessment instruments* (3rd ed., pp. 206-212). Alexandria, VA: National Career Development Association.

Day, S., Rounds, J., Tracey, T., & Swaney, K. (1996, August). *The structure of vocational interests for diverse groups in the United States*. Paper presented at the annual meeting of the American Psychological Association, Toronto, Canada.

DeFruyt, F., & Mervielde, I. (1997). The Five-Factor model of personality and Holland's RIASEC interest types. *Personality & Individual Differences, 23*, 87-103.

DeVito, A. J. (1985). Review of Myers-Briggs Type Indicator. In J. Mitchell, Jr. (Ed.), *Ninth mental measurements yearbook* (pp. 1030-1032). Lincoln: University of Nebraska Press.

Diamond, E. (1996). Review of the Self-Directed Search, Form E—1990 Revision. In J. Impara & J. Conoley (Eds.), *Supplement to the twelfth mental measurements yearbook* (pp. 314-316). Lincoln, NE: Buros Institute of Mental Measurements of the University of Nebraska, Lincoln.

Dillon, M., & Weissman, S. (1987). Relationship between personality types on the Strong-Campbell and Myers-Briggs instruments. *Measurement & Evaluation in Counseling & Development, 20,* 68-79.

Dolliver, R. (1969). Strong Vocational Interest Blank versus expressed vocational interests: A review. *Psychological Bulletin, 72,* 95-107.

Downes, M., & Kroeck, K. (1996). Discrepancies between existing jobs and individual interests: An empirical application of Holland's model. *Journal of Vocational Behavior, 48,* 107-117.

Drummond, R. J. (1986). Vocational Preference Inventory. In D. J. Keyser & R. C. Sweetland (Eds.), *Test critiques* (Vol. 2, pp. 545-548). Kansas City, MO: Test Corporation of America.

Feller, R., & Walz, G. (1996). *Career transitions in turbulent times.* Greensboro, NC: ERIC Counseling and Student Services Clearinghouse.

Fouad, N., & Dancer, L. S. (1992). Cross-cultural structure of interests: Mexico and the United States. *Journal of Vocational Behavior, 40,* 129-143.

Funder, K., Taylor, K., & Kelso, G. (1986). Developmental trends in adolescents' expressed and inventoried career choices. In J. J. Lokan & K. F. Taylor (Eds.), *Holland in Australia: A vocational choice theory in research and practice* (pp. 123-135). Melbourne: Australian Council for Educational Research.

Gade, E., Fuqua, D., & Hurlburt, G. (1984). Use of the Self-Directed Search with Native American high school students. *Journal of Counseling Psychology, 31,* 585-589.

Gibson, E. (1995). Self-Directed Search Career Explorer. Australian Journal of Career Development, Spring, 37-38.

Glidden-Tracey, C., & Greenwood, A. K. (1997). A validation study of the Spanish Self-Directed Search using back-translation procedures. *Journal of Career Assessment, 5,* 105-113.

Gottfredson, G. D. (1977). Career stability and redirection in adulthood. *Journal of Applied Psychology, 62,* 436-445.

Gottfredson, G. D. (1980, September). *A review and evaluation of John Holland's contributions.* Paper presented at the annual meeting of the American Psychological Association, Montreal, Canada.

Gottfredson, G. D. (1982). An assessment of a mobility-based occupational classification for placement and counseling. *Journal of Vocational Behavior, 21,* 71-98.

Gottfredson, G. D. (1984, August). *An empirical classification of occupations based on job analysis data: Development and applications.* Paper presented at the annual meeting of the American Psychological Association, Toronto, Canada.

Gottfredson, G. D. (1985, August). *Holland's theory and person-environment interactions.* Paper presented at the annual meeting of the American Psychological Association, Los Angeles.

Gottfredson, G. D., & Decision Research Associates. (1984, August). *An empirical classification of occupations based on job analysis data: Development and applications.* Paper presented at the annual meeting of the American Psychological Association, Toronto, Canada.

Gottfredson, G. D., & Holland, J. L. (1989). *Dictionary of Holland occupational codes* (2nd ed.). Odessa, FL: Psychological Assessment Resources.

Gottfredson, G. D., & Holland, J. L. (1991). *Position Classification Inventory professional manual.* Odessa, FL: Psychological Assessment Resources.

Gottfredson, G. D., & Holland, J. L. (1996a). *Dictionary of Holland occupational codes* (3rd ed.). Odessa, FL: Psychological Assessment Resources.

Gottfredson, G. D., & Holland, J. L. (1996b). *Environmental Identity Scale.* Unpublished instrument.

Gottfredson, G. D., Holland, J. L., & Gottfredson, L. S. (1975). The relation of vocational aspirations and assessments to employment reality. *Journal of Vocational Behavior, 7,* 135-148.

Gottfredson, G. D., Holland, J. L., & Ogawa, D. (1982). *Dictionary of Holland occupational codes.* Palo Alto, CA: Consulting Psychologists Press.

Gottfredson, L. (1979). Aspiration–job match: Age trends in a large, nationally representative sample of young white men. *Journal of Counseling Psychology, 26,* 319-328.

Harmon, L., & Borgen, F. (1995). Advances in career assessment and the 1994 Strong Interest Inventory. *Journal of Career Assessment, 3,* 374-372.

Harmon, L. W., Hansen, J. C., Borgen, F. H., & Hammer, A. L. (1994). *Strong Interest Inventory applications and technical guide.* Stanford, CA: Stanford University Press.

Herr, E. L., & Cramer, S. H. (1996). *Career guidance and counseling through the life span: Systematic Approaches* (5th ed.). New York: HarperCollins.

Hogan, T. L. (1997). Using Holland's theory in staff development. *Journal of College Student Development, 38,* 301-303.

Holland, J. L. (1973). *Making vocational choices: A theory of careers.* Englewood Cliffs, NJ: Prentice-Hall.

Holland, J. L. (1974). Vocational guidance for everyone. *Educational Researcher, 3,* 9-15.

Holland, J. L. (1985a). *Making vocational choices: A theory of vocational personalities and work environments.* Odessa, FL: Psychological Assessment Resources.

Holland, J. L. (1985b). *Manual for the Vocational Preference Inventory.* Odessa, FL: Psychological Assessment Resources.

Holland, J. L. (1987). Current status of Holland's theory of careers: Another perspective. *Career Development Quarterly, 36,* 24-30.

Holland, J. L. (1990). *Self-Directed Search Form CP: Career planning.* Odessa, FL: Psychological Assessment Resources.

Holland, J. L. (1992). *Vocational Exploration and Insight Kit.* Odessa, FL: Psychological Assessment Resources.

Holland, J. L. (1994). Separate but unequal is better. In M. Savickas & R. Lent (Eds.), *Convergence in career development theories: Implications for science and practice* (pp. 45-51). Palo Alto, CA: CPP Books.

Holland, J. L. (1996a). Exploring careers with a typology: What we have learned and some new directions. *American Psychologist, 51,* 397-406.

Holland, J. L. (1996b). *Self-Directed Search Form E: A guide to educational and vocational planning.* Odessa, FL: Psychological Assessment Resources.

Holland, J. L. (1996c). Integrating career theory and practice. In M. Savickas & W. B. Walsh (Eds.), *Handbook of career counseling theory and practice* (pp. 1-12). Palo Alto, CA: CPP Books.

Holland, J. L. (1997). *Making vocational choices: A theory of vocational personalities and work environments* (3rd ed.). Odessa, FL: Psychological Assessment Resources.

Holland, J. L., Daiger, D. C., & Power, P. G. (1980). *My Vocational Situation: Description of an experimental diagnostic form for the selection of vocational assistance.* Palo Alto, CA: Consulting Psychologists Press.

Holland, J. L., Fritzsche, B., & Powell, A. (1994). *Self-Directed Search technical manual.* Odessa, FL: Psychological Assessment Resources.

Holland, J. L., Gottfredson, D., & Power, P. (1980). Some diagnostic scales for research in decision-making and personality: Identity, information, and barriers. *Journal of Personality and Social Psychology, 39,* 1191-1200.

Holland, J. L., & Gottfredson, G. D. (1992). Studies of the hexagonal model: An evaluation (or, perils of stalking the perfect hexagon). *Journal of Vocational Behavior, 40,* 158-170.

Holland, J. L., & Gottfredson, G. D. (1994). *Career Attitudes and Strategies Inventory: An inventory for understanding adult careers.* Odessa, FL: Psychological Assessment Resources.

Holland, J. L., Gottfredson, G. D., & Baker, H. G. (1990). Validity of vocational aspirations and interest inventories: Extended, replicated, and reinterpreted. *Journal of Counseling Psychology, 37,* 337-342.

Holland, J. L., & Holland, J. E. (1977a). Distributions of personalities within occupations and fields of study. *Vocational Guidance Quarterly, 25,* 226-231.

Holland, J. L., & Holland, J. E. (1977b). Vocational indecision: More evidence and speculation. *Journal of Counseling Psychology, 24,* 404-414.

Holland, J. L., Hollifield, J., Nafziger, D., & Helms, S. (1972). *A guide to the self-directed career program: A practical and inexpensive vocational guidance system* (Report No. 126). Baltimore: Center for Social Organization of Schools, Johns Hopkins University.

Holland, J. L., Johnston, J., & Asama, N. (1993). The Vocational Identity Scale: A diagnostic and treatment tool. *Journal of Career Assessment, 1,* 1-12.

Holland, J. L., Magoon, T., & Spokane, A. (1981). Counseling psychology: Career interventions, research and theory. *Annual Review of Psychology, 32,* 279-305.

Holland, J. L., & Powell, A. (1994). *Self-Directed Search Career Explorer.* Odessa, FL: Psychological Assessment Resources.

Holland, J. L., Powell, A., & Fritzsche, B. (1994). *Self-Directed Search professional users guide*. Odessa, FL: Psychological Assessment Resources.

Hollifield, J. (1971). An extension of Holland's theory to its unnatural conclusion. *Personnel & Guidance Journal, 50,* 209-212.

Holmberg, K., Rosen, D., & Holland, J. L. (1990). *The Leisure Activities Finder*. Odessa, FL: Psychological Assessment Resources.

Humes, C. W. (1992). Career planning implications for learning disabled high school students using the MBTI and the SDS-E. *School Counselor, 39,* 362-368.

Hyland, A., & Muchinsky, P. (1991). Assessment of the structural validity of Holland's model with job analysis (PAQ) information. *Journal of Applied Psychology, 76*(1), 75-80.

Impara, J., & Conoley, J. (Eds.). (1996). *Supplement to the twelfth mental measurements yearbook*. Lincoln, NE: Buros Institute of Mental Measurements of the University of Nebraska, Lincoln.

Isaacson, L. E., & Brown, D. (1997). *Career information, career counseling, and career development* (6th ed.). Boston: Allyn & Bacon.

Jackson, D. H. (1985). *Jackson Vocational Interest Survey*. Port Huron, MI: Research Psychologists Press.

Jacoby, B., Rue, P., & Allen, K. (1984). UMaps: A person-environment approach to helping students make critical choices. *Personnel & Guidance Journal, 62,* 426-428.

Jin, S. R. (1986). Holland typology: An empirical study of its factorial structure. *Bulletin of Educational Psychology, 19,* 219-253.

Jones, L. (1988). *The Career Decision Profile*. (Available from Lawrence K. Jones, North Carolina State University, College of Education and Psychology, Department of Counselor Education, Box 7801, Raleigh, NC 27695).

Jung, C. (1933). *Psychological types*. New York: Harcourt-Brace-Jovanovich.

Keirsey, D., & Bates, M. (1978). *Please understand me: Character and temperament types*. Del Mar, CA: Prometheus Nemesis Books.

Kinnier, R. T. (1996). Review of the Career Attitudes and Strategies Inventory: An inventory for understanding adult careers. In J. Impara & J. Conoley (Eds.), *Supplement to the twelfth mental measurements yearbook* (pp. 61-64). Lincoln, NE: Buros Institute of Mental Measurements of the University of Nebraska, Lincoln.

Kivlighan, D. M., & Shapiro, R. M. (1987). Holland type as a predictor of benefit from self-help career counseling. *Journal of Counseling Psychology, 34,* 326-329.

Kobylarz, L. (Ed.). (1996). *National career development guidelines: K–adult handbook*. Stillwater, OK: NOICC Training Support Center.

Krumboltz, J. (1988). *The Career Beliefs Inventory*. Palo Alto, CA: Consulting Psychologists Press.

Krumboltz, J. D. (1996). A learning theory of career counseling. In M. L. Savickas & W. B. Walsh (Eds.), *Handbook of career counseling theory and practice* (pp. 55-80). Palo Alto, CA: Davies-Black.

Kuder, G. R., & Diamond, E. E. (1979). *General manual for the Kuder DD Occupational Interest Survey*. Chicago: Science Research Associates.

Kummerow, J. M. (1991). *New directions in career planning and the workplace: Practical strategies for counselors*. Palo Alto, CA: Davies-Black.

Lackey, A. (1975). An annotated bibliography for Holland's theory, the Self-Directed Search, and the Vocational Preference Inventory (1972-1975). *JSAS Catalog of Selected Documents in Psychology, 5*, 352. (Ms. No. 1149)

Leierer, S. (1990). *A casual model of supervisor's evaluation using employee satisfaction, work ethic and Holland type*. Unpublished manuscript.

Lenz, J., Reardon, R., & Sampson, J. P., Jr. (1993). Holland's theory and the effective use of computer-assisted career guidance systems. *Journal of Career Development, 19*, 245-253.

Lokan, J. J., & Taylor, K. F. (1986). *Holland in Australia: A vocational choice theory in research and practice*. Melbourne: Australian Council for Education and Research.

Loughead, T., & Linehan, P. (1996). The basics of using the Self-Directed Search in business and industry. In M. Shahnasarian (Ed.), *The Self-Directed Search in business and industry: A resource guide* (pp. 1-26). Odessa, FL: Psychological Assessment Resources.

Lunneborg, P. (1985). Review of My Vocational Situation. In J. Mitchell (Ed.), *Ninth mental measurements yearbook* (pp. 1026-1027). Lincoln, NE: Buros Institute of Mental Measurements of the University of Nebraska, Lincoln.

Macdaid, G., McCaulley, M., & Kainz, R. (1987). *Myers-Briggs Type Indicator atlas of type tables*. Gainesville, FL: Center for Applications of Psychological Type.

Maddux, C. D., & Cummings, R. E. (1986). Alternate form reliability of the Self-Directed Search—Form E. *Career Development Quarterly, 35*, 136-140.

Mahalik, J. R. (1996). Client vocational interests as predictors of client reactions to counselor intentions. *Journal of Counseling and Development, 74*, 416-421.

Manuelle-Adkins, C. (1989). Review of the Self-Directed Search: 1985 Revision. In J. Conoley & J. Kramer (Eds.), *Tenth mental measurements yearbook*. Lincoln, NE: Buros Institute of Mental Measurements of the University of Nebraska, Lincoln.

McCaulley, M. (1990). The Myers-Briggs Type Indicator: A measure for individuals and groups. *Measurement & Evaluation in Counseling & Development, 22*, 181-195.

McCaulley, M., & Martin, C. (1995). Career assessment and the Myers-Briggs Type Indicator. *Journal of Career Assessment, 3*, 219-239.

McCormick, E. J. (1974). *Job analysis: Methods and applications*. New York: AMACOM, American Management Association.

McCrae, R., & Costa, P. (1989). Reinterpreting the Myers-Briggs Type Indicator from the perspective of the five-factor model of personality. *Journal of Personality, 57*, 17-40.

McKee, L. M., & Levinson, E. M. (1990). A review of the computerized version of the Self-Directed Search. *Career Development Quarterly, 38*, 325-333.

McLaughlin, D. H., & Tiedeman, D. V. (1974). Eleven year career stability and change as reflected in Project Talent data through the Flanagan, Holland, and Roe occupational classification systems. *Journal of Vocational Behavior, 5*, 177-196.

Miller, M. (1991). Accuracy of the Leisure Activities Finder: Expanding Holland's typology. *Journal of Vocational Behavior, 39*, 362-368.

Moore, T. (1987, March 30). Personality tests are back. *Fortune*, 76-81.

Murray, H. (1938). *Explorations in personality*. New York: Oxford.

Myers, I. B., & McCaulley, M. H. (1992). *Manual: A guide to the development and use of the Myers-Briggs Type Indicator*. Palo Alto, CA: Consulting Psychologists Press.

Osipow, S. (1990). Convergence in theories of career choice and development. *Journal of Vocational Behavior, 36*, 122-131.

Osipow, S., Carney, C., Winer, J., Yanico, B., & Koschir, M. (1976). *Career Decision Scale* (3rd ed.). Odessa, FL: Psychological Assessment Resources.

Osipow, S. H., & Fitzgerald, L. F. (1996). *Theories of career development* (4th ed.) Boston: Allyn & Bacon.

Pallas, A. M., Dahmann, J. S., Gucer, P. W. , & Holland, J. L. (1983). Test-taker evaluations of the Self-Directed Search and other psychological tests. *Psychology Documents, 13*, 11 (Ms. No. 2550).

Peterson, G. W., Sampson, J. P., Jr., & Reardon, R. C. (1991). *Career development and services: A cognitive approach*. Pacific Grove, CA: Brooks/Cole.

Peterson, G. W., Sampson, J. P., Jr., Reardon, R. C., & Lenz, J. G. (1996). Becoming career problem solvers and decision makers: A cognitive information processing approach. In D. Brown & L. Brooks (Eds.), *Career choice and development* (3rd. ed., pp. 423-475). San Francisco, CA: Jossey-Bass.

Peterson, G. W., Sampson, J. P., Jr., Reardon, R. C., & Lenz, J. G. (1997). *Readiness for career problem solving and decision making: Definition and components from a cognitive information processing perspective*. Unpublished manuscript, Center for the Study of Technology in Counseling and Career Development, Florida State University, Tallahassee.

Pittenger, D J. (1993). Measuring the MBTI...and coming up short. *Journal of Career Planning and Employment, 54*(1), 48-52.

Powell, A., & Holland, J. L. (1996). *Self-Directed Search (SDS) Form E (4th ed.): Supplement to the SDS professional user's guide*. Odessa, FL: Psychological Assessment Resources.

Prediger, D. (1981). A note on Self-Directed Search validity for females. *Vocational Guidance Quarterly, 30*, 117-129.

Prediger, D., & Vansickle, T. (1992). Locating occupations on Holland's hexagon: Beyond RIASEC. *Journal of Vocational Behavior, 40*, 111-128.

Reardon, R. C. (1987). Development of the computer version of the Self-Directed Search. *Measurement & Evaluation in Counseling & Development, 20*, 62-67.

Reardon, R. C. (1996). A program and cost analysis of self-directed career advising services in a university career center. *Journal of Counseling & Development, 74*, 280-285.

Reardon, R. C., Domkowski, D., & Jackson, E. (1980). Career center evaluation methods: A case study. *The Vocational Guidance Quarterly, 29*, 150-158.

Reardon, R. C., & Kahnweiler, B. (1980). A comparison of paper-pencil and tactile board forms of the Self-Directed Search. *Journal of Counseling Psychology, 27*, 328-331.

Reardon, R. C., Lenz, J., & Strausberger, S. (1996). Integrating theory, practice, and research with the Self-Directed Search: Computer version (Form R). *Measurement & Evaluation in Counseling & Development, 28*, 211-218.

Reardon, R. C., & Loughead, T. (1988). A comparison of paper-and-pencil and computer versions of the Self-Directed Search. *Journal of Counseling and Development, 67*, 249-252.

Reardon, R. C., & Minor, C. (1975). Revitalizing the career information service. *The Personnel & Guidance Journal, 54*, 169-171.

Reardon, R. C., & Ona, N. (1996). Self-Directed Search Form R computer version user's guide. [Windows Version 4]. Odessa, FL: Psychological Assessment Resources.

Reardon, R. C., & PAR Staff (1996). Self-Directed Search Form R computer version (Windows Version 4) [Computer software]. Odessa, FL: Psychological Assessment Resources.

Redmond, R. E. (1973). Increasing vocational information behaviors of high school students. *Dissertation Abstracts International, 34*(046), 2311A-2312A. (University Microfilms No. 73-17)

Reich, R. B. (1993). *The work of nations: Preparing ourselves for 21st century capitalism.* New York: Knopf.

Rifkin, J. (1995). *The end of work.* New York: Putnam.

Rose, R. G. (1996). Using the RIASEC scales in selection and development in business. In M. Shahnasarian (Ed.), *Using the SDS in business and industry* (pp. 59-80). Odessa, FL: Psychological Assessment Resources.

Rose, R. G., & Holland, J. L. (1985). *Vocational Preference Inventory: Computer version* [Computer software]. Odessa, FL: Psychological Assessment Resources.

Rosen, D., Holmberg, K., & Holland, J. L. (1994). *The Educational Opportunities Finder.* Odessa, FL: Psychological Assessment Resources.

Rosenberg, H. G., & Smith, S. S. (1985). Six strategies for career counseling. *Journal of College Placement, Spring*, 42-46.

Rounds, J., & Tracey, T. (1996). Cross-cultural structural equivalence of RIASEC models and measures. *Journal of Counseling Psychology, 43*, 310-329.

Sampson, J., & Reardon, R. (1997). *Maximizing staff resources in meeting customer needs in one-stop centers* (Technical Report No. 22). Tallahassee: Florida State University.

Sampson, J. P., Jr., Peterson, G. W., Lenz, J. G., & Reardon, R. C. (1992). A cognitive approach to career services: Translating concepts into practice. *The Career Development Quarterly, 41*, 67-74.

Sampson, J. P., Jr., Peterson, G. W., Lenz, J. G., Reardon, R. C., & Saunders, D. E. (1996a). *Career Thoughts Inventory.* Odessa, FL: Psychological Assessment Resources.

Sampson, J. P., Jr., Peterson, G. W., Lenz, J. G., Reardon, R. C., & Saunders, D. E. (1996b). *Career Thoughts Inventory: Professional manual.* Odessa, FL: Psychological Assessment Resources.

Sampson, J. P., Jr., Peterson, G. W., Lenz, J. G., Reardon, R. C., & Saunders, D. E. (1996c). *Improving your career thoughts: A workbook for the Career Thoughts Inventory.* Odessa, FL: Psychological Assessment Resources.

Sampson, J. P., Jr., Peterson, G. W., Lenz, J. G., Reardon, R. C., & Saunders, D. E. (1996d). Negative thinking and career choice. In R. Feller & G. Walz (Eds.), *Optimizing life transitions in turbulent times: Exploring work, learning and careers* (pp. 323-330). Greensboro: University of North Carolina at Greensboro. (ERIC Clearinghouse on Counseling and Student Services)

Saunders, D. (1996). *The contribution of depression and dysfunctional career thinking to career indecision.* Unpublished doctoral dissertation, Florida State University, Tallahassee.

Saunders, D. E., Sampson, J. P., Jr., Peterson, G. W., Lenz, J. G., & Reardon, R. C. (1993, November). *An investigation of the relationship between dysfunctional career thinking and career decidedness and vocational identity.* Paper presented at the Division 17 southeast regional conference, Psychology for an Era of Change, Gainesville, FL.

Savickas, M., & Lent, R. (1993). *Convergence in theories of career development* [Videotape]. (Available from National Career Development Association, 5999 Stevenson Ave., Alexandria, VA 22304-3300)

Savickas, M., & Lent, R. (Eds.). (1994). *Convergence in career development theories: Implications for science and practice.* Palo Alto, CA: CPP Books.

Savickas, M., & Walsh, B. (Eds.). (1996). *Handbook of career counseling theory and practice.* Palo Alto, CA: Davis-Black.

Shahnasarian, M. (1996a). Applications of the Self-Directed Search with various human resource functions. In M. Shahnasarian (Ed.), *The Self-Directed Search in business and industry: A resource guide* (pp. 47-57). Odessa, FL: Psychological Assessment Resources.

Shahnasarian, M. (Ed.). (1996b). *The Self-Directed Search in business and industry: A resource guide.* Odessa, FL: Psychological Assessment Resources.

Sharf, R. (1997a). *Applying career development theory to counseling* (2nd ed.). Pacific Grove, CA: Brooks/Cole.

Sharf, R. (1997b, January). *Using career development theory to understand technological change.* Paper presented at the meeting of the National Career Development Association, Daytona Beach, FL.

Shepard, J. W. (1989). Review of the Vocational Preference Inventory. In J. C. Conoley & J. J. Kramer (Eds.), *Tenth mental measurements yearbook* (p. 882). Lincoln, NE: Buros Institute of Mental Measurements of the University of Nebraska, Lincoln.

Slaney, R. B. (1978). Expressed and inventoried vocational interests: A comparison of instruments. *Journal of Counseling Psychology, 25,* 520-529.

Slaney, R. B. (1980). Expressed vocational choice and vocational indecision. *Journal of Counseling Psychology, 27,* 122-129.

Slaney, R. B. (1983). Influence of career indecision on treatments exploring the vocational interests of college women. *Journal of Counseling Psychology, 30,* 55-63.

Slaney, R. B., & Lewis, E. T. (1986). Effects of career exploration on career undecided reentry women: An intervention and follow-up study. *Journal of Vocational Behavior, 28,* 97-109.

Slaney, R. B., Stafford, M. J., & Russell, J. E. A. (1981). Career indecision in adult women: A comparative and descriptive study. *Journal of Vocational Behavior, 10,* 156-166.

Spokane, A. (1990). Self-guided interest inventories as career interventions: The Self-Directed Search. In C. Watkins & V. Campbell (Eds.), *Testing in counseling practice* (pp. 28-317). Hillsdale, NJ: Erlbaum.

Spokane, A. (1996). Holland's theory. In D. Brown & L. Brooks (Eds.), *Career choice and development* (3rd ed., pp. 33-74). San Francisco: Jossey-Bass.

Spokane, A., & Holland, J. L. (1995). The Self-Directed Search: A family of self-guided career interventions. *Journal of Career Assessment, 3,* 373-390.

Spokane, A., & Shultheis, S. (1996). There is nothing so practical as a good theory. In M. Shahnasarian (Ed.), *The Self-Directed Search in business and industry: A resource guide* (pp. 27-46). Odessa, FL: Psychological Assessment Resources.

Super, D. (1992). Toward a comprehensive theory of career development. In D. Montross & C. Shinkman (Eds.), *Career development: Theory and practice* (pp. 35-64). Springfield, IL: Charles C. Thomas.

Swanson, J. (1992). The structure of vocational interests for African-American college students. *Journal of Vocational Behavior, 40,* 144-157.

Takai, R., & Holland, J. (1979). Comparison of the Vocational Card Sort, the SDS, and the Vocational Exploration and Insight Kit. *Vocational Guidance Quarterly, 27,* 312-318.

Talbot, D. B., & Birk, J. M. (1979). Does the Vocational Exploration and Insight Kit equal the sum of its parts?: A comparison study. *Journal of Counseling Psychology, 26,* 359-362.

Taylor, N. B. (1986). Vocational identity and brief career counseling. In J. J. Lokan & K. F. Taylor (Eds.), *Holland in Australia: A vocational choice theory in research and practice* (pp. 196-203). Melbourne: Australian Council for Educational Research.

Taymans, J. M. (1991). The use of the Self-Directed Search and the Self-Directed Search Form E with people with learning disabilities. *Learning Disabilities Research and Practice, 6,* 54-58.

Thompson, B., & Ackerman, C. M. (1994). Review of the Myers-Briggs Type Indicator. In J. Kapes, M. Mastie, & E. Whitfield (Eds.), *A counselor's guide to career assessment instruments* (3rd ed., pp. 283-287). Alexandria, VA: National Career Development Association.

Tinsley, H. E. A. (Ed.). (1985). My Vocational Situation. In D. J. Keyser & R. C. Sweetland (Eds.), *Test critiques* (Vol. 2, pp. 509-516). Kansas City, MO: Test Corporation of America.

Tinsley, H. E. A. (1992). Special issue on Holland's theory. *Journal of Vocational Behavior, 40,* 109-267.

Tittle, C. K. (1985). Vocational Exploration and Insight Kit. In J. V. Mitchell, Jr. (Ed.), *Ninth mental measurements yearbook* (p. 1676). Lincoln, NE: University of Nebraska Press.

Tokar, D., & Swanson, J. (1995). Evaluation of the correspondence between Holland's vocational personality typology and the five-factor model of personality. *Journal of Vocational Behavior, 46,* 89-108.

Tracey, T., & Rounds, J. (1995). The arbitrary nature of Holland's RIASEC types: A concentric-circles structure. *Journal of Counseling Psychology, 42,* 431-439.

Urich, M. (1990). Self-Directed Search: Computer version [Software review]. *Measurement & Evaluation in Counseling & Development, 23,* 92-94.

U. S. Department of Labor. (1977). *Dictionary of occupational titles* (4th ed.). Washington, DC: U. S. Government Printing Office.

U. S. Department of Labor. (1979). *Guide for occupational exploration.* Washington, DC: U. S. Government Printing Office.

Vacc, N. A. (1989). Review of the Vocational Preference Inventory. In J. C. Conoley & J. J. Kramer (Eds.), *Tenth mental measurements yearbook* (pp. 882-883). Lincoln, NE: Buros Institute of Mental Measurements of the University of Nebraska, Lincoln.

Vondracek, F. (1992). The construct of identity and its use in career theory and research. *Career Development Quarterly, 41,* 130-144.

Walsh, B., & Betz, N. (1995). *Tests and assessment* (3rd ed.). Englewood Cliffs, NJ: Prentice Hall.

Watkins, C., Bradford, B., Lew, D., & Himmell, C. (1986). Major contributors and contributions to the vocational behavior literature. *Journal of Vocational Behavior, 28,* 42-47.

Weinrach, S. (1980). Have hexagon will travel: Interview with John Holland. *Personnel & Guidance Journal, 58,* 406-414.

Weinrach, S. (1996). The psychological and vocational interest patterns of Donald Super and John Holland. *Journal of Counseling & Development, 75,* 5-16.

Weinrach, S., & Srebalus, D. (1990). Holland's theory of careers. In D. Brown & L. Brooks (Eds.), *Career choice and development* (2nd ed., pp. 37-67). San Francisco: Jossey-Bass.

Westbrook, B. (1985). Review of My Vocational Situation. In J. Mitchell (Ed.), *Ninth mental measurements yearbook* (pp. 1027-1029). Lincoln, NE: Buros Institute of Mental Measurements of the University of Nebraska, Lincoln.

Westbrook, B., & Norton, J. (1994). Review of the Strong Interest Inventory. In J. Kapes, M. Mastie, & E. Whitfield (Eds.), *A counselor's guide to career assessment instruments* (3rd ed., pp. 215-218). Alexandria, VA: National Career Development Association.

Wheelahan, H. (1995). Self-Directed Search—Form CP (Career Planning). *Australian Journal of Career Development, Spring,* 38.

Whyte, J., & Rayman, J. (1985, August). *Macrostructural implications of Holland's theory.* Paper presented at the annual meeting of the American Psychological Association, Los Angeles.

Winer, J., Wilson, D., & Pierce, R. (1983). Using the Self-Directed Search—Form E with high school remedial reading students. *Vocational Guidance Quarterly, 32,* 130-135.

Yu, J., & Alvi, S. A. (1996). A study of Holland's typology in China. *Journal of Career Assessment, 4,* 245-252.

Zener, T. B., & Schnuelle, L. (1972). *An evaluation of the Self-Directed Search* (Report No. 124). Baltimore: Johns Hopkins University, Center for Social Organization of Schools. (ERIC Document Reproduction Service No. ED 061 458)

Zener, T. B., & Schnuelle, L. (1976). Effects of the Self-Directed Search on high school students. *Journal of Counseling Psychology, 23,* 353-359.

Zunker, V. G. (1994). *Career counseling: Applied concepts of life planning.* Pacific Grove, CA: Brooks/Cole.

Appendix A

Glossary

Analysis. A phase of career decision making (CASVE cycle) marked by career thoughts associated with identifying the causes and relationships among components of a career problem; a period of reflection to fully grasp all aspects of the problem.

Calculus. The relationships within and between types or environments ordered according to a hexagonal model in which the distances between types or environments are inversely proportional to the theoretical relationships between them.

Career. The combination of a person's multiple life roles, including worker, student, parent, child, spouse/partner, citizen, retiree. Occupation is an important part of one's life and career, as well as educational field of study, leisure pursuits, and family roles.

Career problem. A gap between an existing state of career indecision and a more desired state of decidedness; may be multifaceted in nature involving feelings, beliefs, behavior, family, community, leisure, and spiritual dimensions.

Career thought. Outcomes of one's thinking about behaviors, beliefs, feelings, plans, and/or strategies related to career problem solving and decision making.

Career Thoughts Inventory (CTI). A 48-item inventory of career thoughts that is a single global indicator of negative thinking in career problem solving and decision making. As scores on the CTI increase, the extent of negative career thinking increases as well. The CTI total score is negatively correlated with the Identity scale of My Vocational Situation (MVS).

CASVE cycle (pronounced Ca SA' Veh). A career decision-making model using a logical, rational approach to decision making that also recognizes the role that feelings play in this process. The simplest way to think about the CASVE cycle is as the means by which clients recognize and solve a career problem— they need to resolve the "gap" between where they are now and where they'd like to be. The CASVE cycle includes the five phases of Communication, Analysis, Synthesis, Valuing, and Execution.

Code. One to three RIASEC letters that indicate which Holland types a person, occupation, field of study, or leisure area most resembles.

Coherence of aspirations. Degree to which codes of a person's set of vocational aspirations or occupational daydreams belong in the same Holland category. Scores of high, average, or low are determined from analysis of the first three occupational aspirations listed in the Daydreams section of the SDS: High = first letter of first occupation same as first letter of second and third occupations; Average = first letter of first occupation same as first letter of second or third occupation; Low = first letter of first occupation does not appear as first letter of either second or third occupation. Coherence is related to consistency; high coherence may indicate future persistence in occupations with the same first letter code as that of the first aspiration.

Commitment Anxiety. A CTI scale that reflects an inability to make a commitment to a specific career choice, accompanied by generalized anxiety about the outcome of the decision making process, with anxiety perpetuating the indecision.

Commonness. The frequency with which a given code is observed; there is an extremely uneven frequency of various persons across the RIASEC types. Some code combinations (e.g., AC, CA) are rare. SDS summary codes that occur with a frequency of greater than 4.5% are High; those that occur with frequencies of .11–4.49% are Average; and those that occur with a frequency of less than .11% are Low. Common codes are associated with stability of choice.

Communication. A phase of career decision making (see CASVE cycle) marked by career thoughts related to becoming fully "in touch" with all aspects of a career problem, or the gap between the present and an ideal career situation. Cues about a gap may come from external sources (e.g., a parent's remark) or internal sources (e.g., negative emotions, avoidance behavior). Awareness of a gap leads to seeking a solution to the career problem.

Congruence. The degree of match between **two** codes (e.g., a person and an occupation). A Realistic person in a Realistic occupation is very congruent, whereas a Realistic person in a Social occupation is incongruent. Degrees of congruence are defined according to the hexagonal model in which Realistic, Investigative, Artistic, Social, Enterprising, and Conventional types (in that order) are at the six points of the hexagon. High levels of congruence are indicative of a person who will maintain the code of his or her first aspiration in the future.

Consistency. The degree of consistency in an SDS code is determined by the distance between the first two code letters on the hexagon: High = first two letters are adjacent on the hexagon (e.g., RI); Average = first two letters are alternate on the hexagon (e.g., RA); Low = first two letters are opposite on the hexagon (e.g., RS). High consistency is positively correlated with more stability in work history and the direction of career preferences or work histories.

Decision Making Confusion. A CTI scale that reflects an inability to initiate or sustain the career decision making process as a result of disabling emotions and/or a lack of understanding about the decision making process itself.

Decision-Making Skills Domain. Includes the five elements of the CASVE cycle, comprised of Communication, Analysis, Synthesis, Valuing, and Execution.

Differentiation. The level of definition or distinctness of a personality profile. A person who resembles one type and no other type is highly differentiated, whereas a person who resembles all six types to an equal degree is undifferentiated. Differentiation is usually computed by subtracting the lowest score in the profile from the highest; sometimes a more technical Iachan index is used. High differentiation is positively related to the person's exhibition of characteristics attributed to the types, especially the highest and lowest profile scores. In this way, persons with differentiated profiles are more predictable with respect to their interests.

Execution. A phase in career decision making (see CASVE cycle) marked by career thoughts that involve the planning and implementation of steps to resolve a career problem; may involve a tryout or reality testing of a first choice solution to a gap.

Executive processing. Career thoughts associated with monitoring, controlling, regulating, and evaluating lower-order information processing, including an awareness of one's self as a career problem solver via self-talk, with the complementary attitudes about one's ability to solve career problems.

External Conflict. A CTI scale that reflects an inability to balance the importance of one's own self-perceptions with the importance of input from significant others, resulting in a reluctance to assume responsibility for decision making.

Hexagon. A six-sided figure showing the order and similarity of the RIASEC types according to Holland's theory; can also be used to show the degree of agreement between a person's type and alternative occupational environments; persons can use a Personal Career Theory to think about careers in terms of personal typologies and matching jobs (e.g., "Where is she on the hexagon?").

Iachan congruence index. An index of congruence between persons and environments proposed by Ronaldo Iachan. This method of calculating congruence uses a three-letter code for an occupation (or other environment) and a three-letter code for a person to produce a number ranging from 0 to 28.

Iachan differentiation index. An index of differentiation of a personality or environmental profile proposed by Ronaldo Iachan. This way of describing differentiation uses the first, second, and fourth highest scores in a profile.

Identity (Vocational). The clarity and stability of a person's goals, interests, and talents. The Identity scale of My Vocational Situation is used to measure identity. High identity leads to relatively untroubled decision making and confidence in one's ability to make good decisions in the face of some inevitable environmental ambiguities.

Occupational level. The prestige, status, education required, usual remuneration, or substantive complexity of an occupation.

Occupational knowledge. Career thoughts related to the acquisition, storage and retrieval of information about individual occupations, fields of study, training programs, and the structure of the world of work.

Permutation. Alternative orderings of letters in a code: RIE, IRE, IER, etc.

Personal Career Theory (PCT). Personal views about careers and work that most people have which may include ideas about a typology of work personalities and environments, as well as a variety of career thoughts about educational and career decision making, job hunting, and life roles. A weak PCT may lead to career problems. PCTs may be related to the RIASEC hexagon and the CIP pyramid.

Personality pattern. The profile of resemblances of a person to the six personality types.

Profile. A pattern indicating degree of resemblance to the six ideal models or types.

Pyramid. Based on Cognitive Information Processing (CIP) theory, a figure showing three domains: Knowledge (self- and occupational) is at the base, decision-making skills are in the middle (CASVE cycle), and executive processing is at the top. Career thoughts operate at all three levels to inform, guide, and control career decision making. A person's career situation can be understood in terms of the quality and content of his/her unique pyramid (e.g., "Where is she in the CASVE cycle?").

Rule of 8. RIASEC summary scale differences of fewer than 8 on the SDS Form R should be regarded as trivial because they are within the limits of the standard error of measurement of the inventory.

Rule of Asymmetrical Distributions of Types and Subtypes. The distributions of persons across the six types are extremely uneven.

Rule of Full Exploration. Persons completing various forms of the SDS are encouraged to use all permutations and combinations of their three-letter summary code to generate lists of occupations and fields of study for further exploration and consideration; the computerized version of the SDS Form R automatically searches and reports all code combinations in the interpretive report.

Rule of Intraoccupational Variability. Research indicates that occupations and fields of study include a variety of types and subtypes. Many occupations tolerate a variety of types. Individuals employed in the same occupation have a variety of Holland codes. Different positions within the same occupation often have a variety of codes as well. Put another way, codes describe people in an occupation on average, but it is a mistake to assume that all persons or positions in an occupation will have the same SDS or PCI profiles.

Self-knowledge. Career thoughts related to the acquisition, storage, or recall of information about one's personal characteristics (e.g., interests, skills, and values).

Subtype. A two- or three-letter code. For example, saying that a person is identified with the RI subtype means that the person resembles the R type most, followed by the I type.

Synthesis. A phase of career decision making (see CASVE cycle) marked by career thoughts related to the formulation of a plausible set of alternatives for resolving a career problem; synthesis elaboration involves brainstorming a wide variety of possible solutions, and synthesis crystallization involves narrowing the potential solutions to the best three to five options.

Tied codes. A term describing an equal or nearly equal degree of resemblance to two or more types or environmental models.

Type. Holland's theory makes use of six personality types and six environmental models in explaining behavior in environments. No person is a true type, but indicating the types a person resembles helps to describe the person.

Valuing. A phase of career decision making (see CASVE cycle) marked by career thoughts related to the prioritizing of possible solutions in terms of what is best for the individual, significant others, and society; a tentative best choice emerges from this phase of decision making.

Vocational aspiration. A person's desired occupational or career aim. Similar terms include vocational expectation, (expected career role at a point in future time), occupational aspiration, occupational daydream, and occupational expectation. Classified aspirations or expectations can be used to estimate a person's Holland code. Aspirations are assessed by expressed interest measurement techniques.

Vocational history. The history of a person's positions, occupations, or vocational aspirations can be classified to estimate his or her Holland code.

Appendix B

A Handout Describing the Self-Directed Search Form R: Computer Version

The Self-Directed Search Form R: Computer Version (SDS-R:CV) for Windows® is an on-screen instrument designed to help you organize information about your interests and abilities. The program takes 45-60 minutes to complete. After you complete the inventory, a personalized 10- to 12-page interpretive report will be printed. This report may contain any or all of the following:

- a description of the Holland code types, including information about the RIASEC theory and the hexagonal model

- a list of occupations for possible further study based on all combinations of your three-letter summary code, including *Dictionary of Occupational Titles* reference numbers and estimated level of education and training time for each occupation

- a list of possible leisure activities, based on the first two letters of your Summary Code

- suggestions for continued educational and career planning

The SDS-R:CV also produces a 2- to 3-page Professional Summary for counselor reference.

Experience suggests that you will find it helpful to meet with a career advisor or counselor after completing the SDS-R:CV to discuss the printout and implications for career planning. You may be asked to complete an evaluation form after using the program.

The SDS-R:CV is published by Psychological Assessment Resources, Inc., P.O. Box 998, Odessa, FL 33556, 1-800-331-8378.

Appendix C

Undergraduate Academic Program Guide: Sample Page

ENGLISH EDUCATION
College of Education

Major Code: 220202   Holland Code: ASE

The *Undergraduate Academic Program Guide* is only a general resource guide. Students are urged to consult with representatives from the academic department for the most current information, additional details, and planning.

Program Office   Resource Personnel
209 Corothers Building   Dr. L. Baines, Dr. P. Carroll
644-6553   Dr. J. Simmons

Description of Major
The English Education major is a teacher preparation program designed to prepare personnel to teach English in secondary school settings (grades 6-12). The program includes required coursework in literature, linguistics, composition and rhetoric, and speech, as well as coursework in teaching methodology. Some flexibility is afforded the individual student in selecting both required and elective coursework in order to capitalize on personal interests and career inclinations.

Common Prerequisites
Fall, 1996, freshmen and transfers from schools and other than Florida public supported colleges must meet common prerequisites in order to be admitted to some majors in the State University System. Students enrolled prior to Fall, 1996, shall come under the catalog year in effect at the time of entry, or have the option of coming under the new catalog. Listed below are prerequisites as published by the Articulation Coordinating Committee for this major. However, the publication does not always distinguish between prerequisites required for admission to the program, prerequisites required as preparation for the major but not required for admission to the program, or suggested courses. Contact resource personnel immediately for this information.

  See General Degree Prerequisites and Pre-education Core below.

General Admission Requirements
This program is a Limited Access Teacher Education program and admits a limited number of students each year in the fall and spring semester. Students seeking admission to this teacher education program must meet the following requirements:

1) meet the general criteria for transfer into a FSU degree-granting program (see *Bulletin*),
2) complete Liberal Studies requirements or an A.A. degree with a grade of "C–" or higher in each freshman English and each basic mathematics course,
3) achieve a minimum score of 20 on the ACT or 950 combined on the SAT,
4) complete the Pre-education core listed below,
5) complete the General Degree Prerequisites listed below, and
6) achieve an overall 2.5 GPA

Florida State University is committed to increasing the proportion of teacher candidates who have historically been under-represented among Florida's public school teachers. Applicants representing such groups will be considered for exceptions to the general admissions criteria.

Program Planning and Continuation
Students should complete all Liberal Studies prior to entry into this program; gain admission to teacher education by the end of the first term in the program; and achieve a "C" or higher in each required course for the major.

Students must also gain admission to student teaching at the appropriate time. In order to be admitted to student teaching, students must satisfactorily complete all required coursework with an overall minimum GPA of 2.75 in English courses, an overall 2.75 in professional education courses and an overall GPA of 3.0 in English education courses. NOTE: Certification to teach in Florida requires a 2.5 GPA in the field of specialization.

Minimum Program Requirements – Summary   Notes:
Liberal Studies   36* sem. hrs.   60 hours must be earned at a senior institution;
Pre-education Core   9 sem. hrs.   the final 30 hours must be in residence at FSU;
General Degree Prerequisites   15 sem. hrs.   40 hours must be 3000/4000 level.
Major Coursework   59 sem. hrs.
Electives   1 sem. hrs.
Min. Hrs. Required   120 sem. hrs.

Please see following page for continuation of summary.

Minimum Program Requirements – Summary (Continued)

*NOTE: Students are encouraged to select survey courses in English, American, or world history and literature in partial satisfaction of the Liberal Studies requirements.

Program Requirements – Detail

General Degree Prerequisites: 15 semester hours. Courses satisfying the general program requirements are those taken beyond the Liberal Studies requirement.

- (3)   Fundamentals of speech course
- (3)   Literature course
- (9)   Elective courses in English composition/language study

Pre-education Code: 9 semester hours

EDF 1005	(3)	Introduction to Education
EDG 2701	(3)	Teaching Diverse Populations
EME 2040	(3)	Introduction to Educational Technology

Major Coursework: 59 semester hours   **(Subject to change)**

Teaching Field Coursework in <u>English</u>: 24 semester hours

- (3) hours in general American literature
- (3) hours in minority American literature
- (3) hours in British literature
- (3) hours in Shakespeare
- (3) hours in ENC 3310, Article and Essay Workshop or approved alternate
- (3) hours in language study chosen from either LIN 3010 or LAE 4332
- (3) hours in literature that reflects multicultural emphases (see adviser)
- (3) hours in literature, composition, or language study of the students choice (or EDM 3001, Intro. to the Middle School)

Teaching Field Coursework in <u>English Education</u>: 17 semester hours

LAE 3331	(3)	Teaching Literature and Drama in High Schools
LAE 3333	(3)	Teaching Writing and Language in High Schools
LAE 4323	(3)	Teaching English in Middle Schools
LAE xxxx	(3)	Technology for Teachers of English
LAE 4360	(3)	Classroom Management & Planning Instructor in Middle/High School English
LAE 4941	(2)	Methods & Observation/Participation in Middle/Secondary English

Professional Education Coursework: 6 semester hours

EDF 4604	(3)	Schooling in American Society
EDF 4214	(3)	Classroom Applications of Educational Psychology

Student Teaching: 12 semester hours. Note: All required coursework must be completed prior to student teaching.

LAE 4942	(12)	Student Teaching in Secondary School English

Employment Information

Representative Job Titles Related to this Major:

Teacher of English: Middle School, Junior High, Senior High, Adult Education, Principal or Superintendent of Schools

School Librarian	Sales Representative, books
Audiovisual Specialist	Teacher of English as a foreign language
Youth Organization Worker	Television Educational Specialist
Tutor	Editor/Editorial Assistant
Reporter	Writer, Technical Publications

Representative Employers:

Government Agencies:	Overseas schools for military
Department of Education	School Boards
Department of State: Indian reservations,	Immigrant Service Agencies
Peace Corps	Publishing Companies
Bookstores	
Television	

Reprinted with permission of the Undergraduate Academic Advising Center, Florida State University, Tallahassee, FL.

Appendix D

Florida State University Undergraduate Programs Arranged by Holland/RIASEC Categories

Realistic

Classical Archaeology
Chemical Engineering
Civil Engineering
Electrical Engineering
Environmental Engineering
  (See Civil Engineering)

Exercise Physiology
Geography
Geology
Mechanical Engineering

Investigative

Actuarial Mathematics
Anthropology
Communication Disorders
  (Audiology/Speech Path)
Biochemistry
Biological Science
Chemical Engineering
Systems
Chemical Science
Chemistry
Civil Engineering
Classical Archaeology
Computer Science
Criminology/Criminal Justice
Dietetics
Economics
Electrical Engineering
Environmental Chemistry
  (see Chemistry)
Environmental Studies
Exercise Physiology

Food & Nutrition Science
Geography
Geology
International Affairs
Industrial Engineering
Information Studies
Management and Information

Mathematics
Mechanical Engineering
Meteorology
Nutrition and Fitness
Physics
Physics, Interdisciplinary
Program in Medical Sciences
  (PIMS)*
Psychology
Sociology
Social Science, Interdisciplinary
  Program
Textiles

Artistic

Acting
Apparel Design & Technology
Art Education
Art History
Art, Studio
Classical Civilization
Classics/Religion – Joint Major
Dance

Design Technology
English
English Education
French
German
Greek
Greek & Latin
Housing

Artistic (cont.)

Humanities
Interior Design
Italian
Latin
Motion Picture, TV & Recording Arts
Multinational/Multicultural Education
Music
Music Composition
Music Education

Music History & Literature
Music Performance
Music Theater (Music)
Music Theater (Theater)
Music Theory
Philosophy
Russian (Slavic)
Spanish
Theater

Social

American Studies
Art Education
Art History
Asian Studies
Communication Disorders
  (Audiology/Speech Path)
Criminology
Dietetics
Early Childhood Education
Elementary Education
English Education
Food & Nutrition Science
Family & Nutrition Science
Family & Child Sciences
Family & Consumer Science
Education
Health Education
History
Home Economics
Home Economics Education
Housing
Human Resource Management
Humanities
International Affairs
Latin American & Caribbean
  Studies

Mathematics Education
Multicultural/Multilingual
  Education (Foreign
  Language Education)
Music Education
Music History and Theory
Music Therapy
Nursing
Nutrition & Fitness
Philosophy
Physical Education
Political Science
Pre-Art Therapy
Pre-Physical Therapy
Psychology
Real Estate
Recreation and Leisure Services
  Administration
Rehabilitation Services
Religion
Russian and Eastern European
  Studies
Science Education
Social Science,
  Interdisciplinary Program
Social Sciences Education

Social (cont.)

Social Work

Special Education
  (see specific majors)

Teacher Certification for
  Non-Education majors*

Women's Studies

Enterprising

Advertising, Communication for
  Business, Public Relations

Art History

Communication for Business

Communication Studies

Entrepreneurship and Small
  Business Management

Finance

Food and Nutrition Science

General Communication

History

Hospital Administration

Human Resource Management

Industrial Engineering

Management

Marketing

Mass Communication

Merchandising

Multinational Business
  Operations

Music Therapy

Nutrition & Fitness

Operations Management

Political Science

Pre-Art Therapy

Real Estate

Risk Management & Insurance

Recreation and Leisure Services
  Administration

Sports Management

Conventional

Accounting

*Program Option: Refer to the Florida State University Bulletin or Undergraduate
Academic Program Guide for more information.

Classification of FSU undergraduate programs derived from the *Dictionary of Holland
Occupational Codes* (Gottfredson & Holland, 1996a) and *The Educational Opportunities
Finder* (Rosen, Holmberg, & Holland, 1994).

Appendix E

Counselor Training Questions/Activities

1. Name the six types.

   a.   d.

   b.   e.

   c.   f.

2. Draw and label the hexagon.

3. How many times is a person's resemblance to a type estimated?

4. What kind of SDS scales have been substituted for aptitude tests and/or self-efficacy scales?

5. The Occupations scale of the SDS Form R comes from what inventory?

6. The SDS is a simulation of the career counseling experience because all of the following activities take place:
   performing a personal _____, arriving at a
   _____ formulation, searching an _____ file.

7. Name three reasons that a person might have a flat or undifferentiated profile.

   a._____

   b._____

   c._____

8. Which version(s) of the SDS do not include the Daydreams section?

9. People whose summary codes do not correspond to codes in The Occupations Finder usually have rare codes.

   T   or   F   (circle one)

10. What publication provides Holland summary codes for all the occupations in the *Dictionary of Occupational Titles?*

11. Which version of the SDS is designed for individuals with poor reading skills?

12. What diagnostic screening tool is embedded in the Form R computer version?

13. Which version of the SDS is designed to be used with middle school students?

14. Adult work histories tend to be random.

   T   or   F   (circle one)

15. The "Rule of 8" means that differences less than 8 between any two summary codes should be regarded as trivial.

   T   or   F   (circle one)

16. The "Rule of Intraoccupational Variability" means that an occupation usually tolerates only a single type.

   T   or   F   (circle one)

17. The "Rule of Asymmetrical Distribution of Types and Subtypes" means that all SDS codes are about equally common.

    T   or   F   (circle one)

18. The predictive efficiency of a person's occupational daydreams increases the more the daydreams share the same first-letter code.

    T   or   F   (circle one)

19. Why do users search for all permutations of their Summary codes? (circle one)

    a. To increase the range of possible alternatives.

    b. To lessen informational errors due to a small score or profile differences.

    c. Both of the above.

20. What instrument would you use to generate a 3-letter Holland code for a particular job within an organization?

21. The weaknesses in the SDS include the following: (circle one)

    a. It appears too simple to some professionals.

    b. Directions fail to stimulate everyone to explore all permutations of their code.

    c. Scoring is not perfectly reliable.

    d. Occupational codes are not precise.

    e. Competency tests need more validation.

    f. It fails to help everyone and upsets a few people.

    g. All of the above.

22. If a person has a low score on the Vocational Identity scale (MVS), he or she is likely to have a high total score on the Career Thoughts Inventory (CTI).

    T   or   F   (circle one)

23. A client's Personal Career Theory (PCT) can be explored with respect to the RIASEC typology hexagon and the pyramid of information processing domains.

    T   or   F   (circle one)

24. The CASVE cycle can be used to increase understanding of individual career decision making, as well as to guide the development of a career program proposal.

    T   or   F   (circle one)

25. Coherence of aspirations, like consistency, can be used as a measure of career stability and direction.

    T   or   F   (circle one)

Answer Key for Counselor Training Questions

1. Name the six types.
   a. Realistic
   b. Investigative
   c. Artistic
   d. Social
   e. Enterprising
   f. Conventional

2. See Figure 1, page 16

3. 5 times

4. Competency, self-estimates of abilities

5. Vocational Preference Inventory (VPI)

6. assessment; diagnostic; occupational

7. a. personal confusion and conflict
   b. immaturity and lack of experience
   c. multiple talents and interests

8. SDS Form CP

9. T

10. Dictionary of Holland Occupational Codes (DHOC)

11. SDS Form E

12. My Vocational Situation

13. SDS Career Explorer

14. F

15. T

16. F

17. F

18. T

19. c.

20. Position Classification Inventory (PCI)

21. g.

22. T

23. T

24. T

25. T

Note. Adapted from the *SDS Professional User's Guide*, 1994, by J. L. Holland, A. B. Powell, and B. A. Fritzsche (p. 94), Odessa, FL: Psychological Assessment Resources.

Appendix F

Career Information Follow-Up Exercise

This exercise is designed to help you narrow down a list of occupations you may have received as a result of completing one or more assessment activities. After completing this exercise you will have an organized plan for using information resources. It is important to complete Steps 1, 2, and 3 of this exercise **before** you begin a more detailed use of information resources. Complete Step 4 of this exercise as you use the various information resources.

Step 1: Initial Review of Occupations

As you review the list of occupations that were generated during your assessment activities, list in the first column of Career Information Exercise A each occupation *in which you have no interest*. It is best to eliminate an occupation from consideration only on the basis of accurate and realistic job knowledge. If you think your decision might be based on a stereotype or a second-hand impression, list that occupation in the column labeled Uncertain. A staff member can help you determine whether stereotypes are influencing your decision.

In the column labeled Uncertain, list all the occupations that might be interesting to you but are **unfamiliar**. For example, Industrial Designer might be an interesting occupation, but you lack enough information about typical work activities and the education required to decide whether you want to seriously consider this occupation. Also in this column, list all the occupations about which you are uncertain—in other words, occupations in which you have some interest, but which you view as having some important negative characteristics as well.

In the column labeled Follow Up, list occupations in which you have a **definite interest** and wish to explore.

Step 2: Narrowing Your List

The next step in the process involves obtaining enough basic information about the occupations you listed in the Uncertain column so that you can decide whether to reject an occupation. Basic information about an occupation can be obtained by reviewing the following information in the most recent edition of the *Occupational Outlook Handbook* (Bureau of Labor Statistics, 1996):

- Nature of the work
- Training, other qualifications, and advancement
- Earnings

You may want to seek information related to other factors that are especially important to your career decision making, such as working conditions, employment settings, job prospects, and related occupations. If occupations on your list are not found in the *Occupational Outlook Handbook*, consult the *Dictionary of*

Occupational Titles (U.S. Department of Labor, 1977) to obtain a brief description to use in evaluating an occupation.

After completing this step, move all the occupations from the Uncertain category to either the No Interest or the Follow Up column.

Step 3: Deciding What Information You Need

Use the Checklist of Questions to guide your search for more detailed information in Step 4. Place a check beside each category of information that is important to you in learning about your follow up occupations. Obtaining similar types of information about each different occupation in your Follow Up column will make it easier for you to compare the occupations on your list.

Step 4: Obtaining Detailed Information About Occupations

The fourth step involves obtaining detailed information about occupations in the follow up category. Career resource centers and libraries have a variety of materials that may help you to research occupations more thoroughly. These include computer systems, print, microfiche, and audiovisual materials. Sources of career information that may be helpful in your research include the following:

- Occupational books, monographs, CDs, video tapes, and guides
- Literature from various employers
- Descriptions of academic/training programs
- Professional association and trade union publications/descriptive literature
- Personal interviews with individuals in various occupations
- Computer-assisted career guidance systems
- Work experience (volunteer, part-time, summer, and cooperative work)
- Academic courses related to various occupations
- State Employment Service information (computer-based/microfiche occupational information systems)
- Internet sites

The accuracy and quality of occupational information can vary. It is important to be a critical reader/listener. The time lag between collecting information and publishing the results may make the salary and employment outlook information out of date, and information from personal interviews, employers, and organizations may be biased in favor of a particular occupation. Most information, however, is accurate and objective. A staff member can assist you in locating, evaluating, and using these resources.

Make copies of specific information that is of interest to you for future reference in your career decision making.

Career Information Exercise A

Occupations Generated Through Assessment Activities

No Interest	Uncertain	Follow Up

Note. You may also wish to include on this sheet additional occupations you are considering that did not appear on any of your other lists. Some initial resources for evaluating occupations are listed earlier in this exercise. A staff member can help you locate additional resources for obtaining information.

Career Information Exercise B

Checklist of Questions

Career information resources can help you decide which occupations are worth further consideration and which occupations can be eliminated. Place a check next to each category of information that you would like to determine about your Follow Up occupations. Remember to check those questions concerning values, interests, and skills that are important to you.

Description

_____ 1. Description of occupation?
_____ 2. Typical work activities?
_____ 3. Sample job titles?
_____ 4. Work settings(s)? Indoors/outside?
_____ 5. Physical demands?

Education and Training

_____ 6. Educational requirements?
_____ 7. Suggested courses?
_____ 8. Specialized occupational training?
_____ 9. Personal qualities?
_____ 10. Specific skills required?
_____ 11. Experience required?

Earnings

_____ 12. Beginning earnings?
_____ 13. Average earnings?
_____ 14. Top earnings potential?
_____ 15. How/why earnings vary?

Personal Requirements

_____ 16. Contribution to others?
_____ 17. Interests?
_____ 18. Leadership?
_____ 19. Leisure?
_____ 20. Independence?
_____ 21. Prestige?
_____ 22. Variety?

Employment Opportunities

_____ 23. Employment prospects?
_____ 24. Typical employers?
_____ 25. Security?
_____ 26. Advancement?

Additional Information

_____ 27. Sources of additional information?

From "Career Information Exercise," by J. P. Sampson, Jr., and J. G. Lenz, 1990. Copyright © 1990 by the Center for the Study of Technology in Counseling and Career Development at Florida State University. Adapted with permission.

Appendix G

Career Exploration Activity Worksheet

Name:_____ Date:_____

Grade in School: _____ Age: _____

Please list all the occupations you are currently considering in the blank spaces below, and list the Holland code for each:

Holland Code

_____ ____ ____ ____

_____ ____ ____ ____

_____ ____ ____ ____

_____ ____ ____ ____

_____ ____ ____ ____

List below the occupation that is your first choice. If undecided, write "undecided."

_____

List below the titles of occupations for which you obtained computer printouts:

_____

_____

_____

Three-letter Holland Code from "RIASEC Game."

_____ _____ _____

Holland "RIASEC Game" Summary Code occupations.

_____   _____

_____   _____

_____   _____

Appendix H

Individual Learning Plan

Goal(s) (1) _____

(2) _____

(3) _____

(4) _____

Goal	Priority	Activity	Purpose/Outcome

_____   _____   __/__/__

Employee   Staff Member   Date

A similar figure can be found in *Career development and services: A cognitive approach* (p. 239), by G. W. Peterson, J. P. Sampson, Jr., and R. C. Reardon. Copyright © 1991 by Brooks/Cole Publishing Company, Pacific Grove, CA 93950, a division of International Thomson Publishing, Inc. Reproduced by permission. All rights reserved.

Appendix I

SDS Case Study Analysis Worksheet

Indicators	Case #1	Case #2	Case #3
Summary Code			
Aspirations Summary Code			
Code of first aspiration			
Congruence			
Coherence			
My Vocational Situation Vocational Identity Occupational Information Barriers			
Consistency			
Differentiation			
Commonness			
Additional Assessment Information			
Additional Notes			
Possible Interventions			

Note. Permission to copy this form for educational purposes is hereby granted by Psychological Assessment Resources, Inc.

Appendix J

SDS Case Study Analysis Results

SDS Case Study Analysis Worksheet

Indicators	Martha	Kisha	Ariel
Summary Code	SAE	SCE	AIS
Aspirations Summary Code	SEI	ESA	AES
Code of first aspiration	SAI	ESR	AIR
Congruence	Average	Average	Average
Coherence	High	Average	Low

My Vocational Situation
 	
  Vocational Identity
  Occupational Information
  Barriers
	N/A
	
		0
		0
		1
			
			3
			0
			2

Consistency	High	Average	High
Differentiation	Average	High	Average
Commonness	High	High	Average
Additional Assessment Information	See PCI and CASI profiles	CTI Total: 61 (57th %ile) DMC: 13 (53rd %ile) CA: 26 (99th %ile) EC: 1 (14th %ile)	N/A
Additional Notes	Some anger and depression. Ageism issues.	Lots of positives to draw on. Needs help deciding between closely related alternatives. May need particular help in the Valuing phase.	Diversity of aspirations Desire to please father. Conflict between A and need for more secure future. Blocked from first choice. Lack of E competencies.
Possible Interventions	Help with networking. Job leads in consulting & religious settings. Update resume. Counseling to manage emotional issues associated with job change. Reinforce strong points/positive indicators.	Try out choices/volunteer. Use CTI Workbook to change negative thinking. Informational interviews. Use decision-making exercise to compare and contrast options, and identify first choice.	Understanding hexagon may help Ariel clarify the nature of his PCT. Full exploration of code is important; needs to identify alternatives to first choice. Discuss how Es and Is differ in terms of values, skills, interests.

SDS Case Study Analysis Worksheet

Indicators	Linda	Susana	Frank
Summary Code	SAI	ECS	EAS
Aspirations Summary Code	EAS	SRE	SEI
Code of first aspiration	AES	SEA	SEI
Congruence	Average	Average	Average
Coherence	Low	Low	Average
My Vocational Situation Vocational Identity Occupational Information Barriers	3 0 2	N/A	N/A
Consistency	High	High	Average
Differentiation	Average	Low	Average
Commonness	Average	Average	Low
Additional Assessment Information	CTI Total 59 (84th %ile) DMC: 17 (90th %ile) CA: 17 (92nd %ile) EC: 6 (92nd %ile) 7 obstacles on CASI Elevated scores on Career Worries, Interpersonal Abuse. PCI code for current occupation: SRC	N/A	CTI Total 51 (76th %ile) DMC: 15 (84th %ile) CA: 13 (76th %ile) EC: 3 (50th %ile)
Additional Notes	Single parent	Victim of domestic violence. History of substance abuse. Highly motivated.	Suffering from stress of running small business. Health problems associated with stress. Pressure to support family.
Possible Interventions	Build trusting counseling relationship; provide lots of support/encouragement. Cognitive reframing. Exploration of alternative careers in health professions.	Support efforts to complete GED; use occupational information to show relationship between education, employment options, and income. Help with employability skills, completing applications, preparing resume, practice interviewing. Ongoing counseling to deal with self-esteem issues.	Check to make sure he is attending to health issues. Have him use E competencies for networking/informational interviews. Encourage occupational research to better understand differences in aspirations. Use values card sort to help prioritize what's most important. Look at lifestyle issues—how can he use hobbies to pursue A interests or volunteer work for S interests?

Appendix K

Selected National Career Development Guidelines Related to Holland-Based Materials

In examining where the SDS fits within the larger scheme of things, it seemed important to us to focus on how the SDS intervention program relates to the *National Career Development Guidelines* (Kobylarz, 1996). For those not familiar with these guidelines, the following is a brief review.

The guidelines represent a nationwide effort to foster career development at all levels. Persons knowledgeable about career guidance and strategies for preparing persons for work, including members of eight professional associations (e.g., American School Counselor Association, National Career Development Association, Council of Chief State School Officers) developed statements of desired competencies for students and adults relative to educational and career decision making. The idea was to use these guidelines to design and implement comprehensive programs of career guidance and counseling. Ideally, any product or service in the career area would increase the competencies of users of the program to solve career problems and make career decisions.

The numbered competencies and related indicators included in the guidelines describe the outcomes that can be expected for individuals who have participated in career development programs and are the basis for program content. Three areas of competencies are self-knowledge, educational and occupational exploration, and career planning for elementary, middle/junior high school and high school students, and adults. [Note: We have not included elementary-level competencies in our own analysis because the SDS would not be used at this age.] *Competencies* are viewed as broad goals, whereas *indicators* describe specific knowledge, skills, and abilities related to a person's career development.

The following section illustrates our judgment of how Holland-based materials match the competency statements for middle/junior high, high school, and adult competencies found in the guidelines. The bulleted items below each competency statement specify the indicators that career counselors or program developers might examine to determine whether a program intervention is meeting the stated guideline or to assess the impact of the intervention on a specific client or user of the program. The items in parentheses following each indicator provide examples of specific Holland materials that would enable a client to demonstrate the desired knowledge, skill, or attitude.

Middle/Junior High School

<u>Self-Knowledge</u>

Competency I: Knowledge of the influence of a positive self-concept.

- Describe personal likes and dislikes (e.g., SDS Career Explorer Self-Assessment Booklet [AB], Exploring Your Future [EYF], SDS Career Explorer: Interpretive Report [IR]).

- Describe individual skills required to fulfill different life roles (e.g., SDS Career Explorer Careers Booklet [CB], SDS Career Explorer: IR, AB, EYF; *Dictionary of Holland Occupational Codes* [DHOC]).

Competency II: Skills to interact positively with others.

- Demonstrate respect for the feelings and beliefs of others (e.g., SDS Career Explorer: IR, EYF).

- Demonstrate an appreciation for the similarities and differences among people (e.g., SDS Career Explorer: IR, EYF; DHOC; The Educational Opportunities Finder [EOF]).

Educational and Occupational Exploration

Competency IV: Knowledge of the benefits of educational achievement to career opportunities.

- Describe the importance of academic and occupational skills in the work world (e.g., SDS Career Explorer: IR, EYF; DHOC).

- Identify how the skills taught in school subjects—academic and contextual— are used in various occupations (e.g., SDS Career Explorer: IR, EYF; DHOC; EOF).

- Describe how skills are related to the selection of high school courses of study (e.g., SDS Career Explorer: IR, EYF; EOF).

- Describe how aptitudes and abilities relate to broad occupational groups (e.g., SDS Career Explorer: IR, EYF; DHOC; The Occupations Finder [OF])

Competency V: Understanding the relationship between work and learning.

- Describe the relationship of personal attitudes, beliefs, abilities and skills to occupations (e.g., SDS Career Explorer: IR, EYF; OF; DHOC).

Competency VI: Skills to locate, understand, and use career information.

- Identify various ways that occupations can be classified (e.g., SDS Career Explorer: IR, EYF; DHOC).

- Identify a number of occupational groups for exploration (e.g., SDS Career Explorer: IR, EYF; DHOC; OF).

- Identify sources to obtain information about occupational groups including self-employment (e.g., SDS Career Explorer: IR, EYF; DHOC).

- Identify skills that are transferable from one occupation to another (e.g., SDS Career Explorer: IR, EYF; DHOC).

Career Planning

Competency IX: Skills to make decisions.

- Describe personal beliefs and attitudes (e.g., SDS Career Explorer: IR, EYF).

- Identify possible outcomes of decisions (e.g., SDS Career Explorer: IR, EYF).
- Describe school courses related to personal, educational, and occupational interests (e.g., SDS Career Explorer: IR, EYF; DHOC; EOF).
- Identify the requirements for secondary and postsecondary programs (e.g., SDS Career Explorer: IR, EYF; EOF).

Competency X: Knowledge of the interrelationship of life roles.

- Identify personal leisure choices in relations to lifestyle and the attainment of future goals (e.g., SDS Career Explorer: IR, EYF; The Leisure Activities Finder [LAF]; DHOC).
- Describe the interrelationships among family, work, and leisure decisions (e.g., SDS Career Explorer: IR, EYF; DHOC; LAF).

Competency XII: Understanding the process of career planning.

- Identify school courses that meet tentative career goals (e.g., SDS Career Explorer: IR, EYF; EOF; DHOC).
- Demonstrate knowledge of academic and school-to-work transition opportunities offered at the high school level (e.g., SDS Career Explorer: IR, EYF; EOF; DHOC).
- Describe skills needed in a variety of occupations, including self-employment (e.g., SDS Career Explorer: IR, EYF; DHOC).

High School

Self-Knowledge

Competency I: Understanding the influence of a positive self-concept.

- Identify and appreciate personal interests, abilities, and skills (e.g., SDS Form R You and Your Career [YYC]; My Vocational Situation [MVS]).
- Demonstrate an understanding of how individual characteristics relate to achieving personal, social, educational, and career goals (e.g., SDS Form R: IR, OF, YYC; MVS).
- Demonstrate an understanding of environmental influences on one's behaviors (e.g., SDS Form R: IR, YYC; MVS).

Educational and Occupational Exploration

Competency IV: Understanding the relationship between educational achievement and career planning.

- Describe the relationship of academic and vocational skills to personal interests (e.g., SDS Form R: IR, YYC; EOF).
- Describe how skills developed in academic and vocational programs relate to career goals (e.g., SDS Form R: IR; EOF; DHOC).

- Describe how education relates to the selection of college majors, further training, and/or entry into the job market (e.g., SDS Form R OF; EOF; DHOC).

Competency VI: Skills to locate, evaluate, and interpret career information.

- Describe the educational requirements of various occupations (e.g., SDS Form R OF; DHOC).
- Demonstrate knowledge of various classifications systems that categorize occupations and industries (e.g., SDS Form R OF; DHOC).

Career Planning

Competency IX: Skills to make decisions.

- Demonstrate responsibility for making tentative educational and occupational choices (e.g., SDS Form R: IR; MVS; Vocational Exploration and Insight Kit [VEIK]).
- Identify alternatives in given decision making situations (e.g., SDS Form R: IR, OF; EOF).
- Describe skills and aptitudes needed to qualify for desired postsecondary education/training (e.g., SDS Form R: IR; EOF).

Competency X: Understanding the interrelationship of life roles.

- Describe ways in which work, family, and leisure roles are interrelated (e.g., SDS Form R: IR, OF, YYC; LAF).
- Demonstrate ways that occupational skills and knowledge can be acquired through leisure (e.g., SDS Form R: IR; DHOC; LAF).

Competency XII: Skills in career planning.

- Demonstrate knowledge of postsecondary occupational and academic programs (e.g., EOF; DHOC).
- Describe school and community resources to explore educational and occupational choices (e.g., SDS Form R: IR, YYC; DHOC; VEIK).

Adult

Self-Knowledge

Competency I: Skills to maintain a positive self-concept.

- Identify skills, abilities, interests, experiences, values, and personality traits and their influence on career decisions (e.g., SDS Form R: IR, YYC; Career Attitudes and Strategies Inventory [CASI]).
- Identify achievements related to work, learning, and leisure and their influence on self-perception (e.g., SDS Form R: IR, YYC, EOF, LAF).
- Demonstrate a realistic understanding of self (e.g., SDS Form R; MVS; CASI; Position Classification Inventory [PCI]).

Competency II: Skills to maintain effective behaviors.

- Identify symptoms of stress (e.g., SDS Form R; MVS; CASI; PCI).

Competency III: Understanding developmental changes and transitions.

- Describe how personal motivations and aspirations may change over time (e.g., SDS Form R: IR, YYC).
- Identify external events (e.g., job loss, job transfer) that require life changes (e.g., CASI; MVS).

Educational and Occupational Exploration

Competency IV: Skills to enter and participate in education and training.

- Describe short- and long-range plans to achieve career goals through appropriate educational and training paths (e.g., SDS Form R: IR; DHOC; EOF).
- Identify information that describes educational opportunities, such as job training programs, employer-sponsored training, and graduate and professional study (e.g., DHOC; EOF).

Competency V: Skills to participate in work and lifelong learning.

- Describe how educational achievements and life experiences relate to occupational opportunities (e.g., SDS Form R: IR; LAF; EOF; CASI).

Competency VI: Skills to locate, evaluate, and interpret information.

- Identify and use current career information resources (e.g., computerized career information systems, print and media materials, and mentors) (e.g., SDS Form R: IR; DHOC).
- Identify the diverse job opportunities available to an individual with a given set of occupational skills (e.g., SDS Form R: IR; DHOC).
- Identify opportunities available through self-employment (e.g., DHOC).

Competency VII: Skills to prepare to seek, obtain, maintain, and change jobs.

- Demonstrate skills and abilities essential to prepare for and participate in a successful job interview (e.g., SDS Form R OF; DHOC; CASI; PCI).
- Demonstrate effective work attitudes and behaviors (e.g., CASI; PCI).
- Identify skills that are transferable from one job to another (e.g., CASI; PCI).

Career Planning

Competency IX: Skills to make decisions.

- Describe personal criteria for making decisions about education, training, and career goals. (SDS Form R: IR; CASI).
- Describe the effects of education, work, and family decisions on individual career decisions (e.g., DHOC; PCI; CASI).

- Identify personal and environmental conditions that affect decision making (e.g., PCI; CASI; MVS).

Competency X: Understanding the impact of work on individual and family life.

- Describe how family and leisure functions affect occupational roles and decisions (e.g., CASI; MVS; LAF; SDS).
- Describe how work, family, and leisure activities interrelate (e.g., SDS Form R: IR; LAF; DHOC; CASI).

Competency XII. Skills to make career transitions.

- Identify transition activities (e.g., reassessment of current position and occupational changes) as a normal aspect of career development (e.g., SDS Form R YYC; PCI; CASI; MVS; DHOC).
- Describe skills and knowledge needed for pre-retirement planning (e.g., SDS Form R: IR, YYC; LAF; PCI; CASI).

The preceding analyses illustrates the application of Holland-based materials to the National Career Development Guidelines.

Appendix L

Selected Additional Resources

Many practitioners have an interest in creating a career resource center built on Holland's theory and assessment instruments. In addition to Holland's instruments and the numerous publications that have grown out of those instruments, such as the DHOC, there are other resource materials that use the Holland typology. Selected examples are described below.

Note: The inclusion of materials in this list does not imply any endorsement by the authors. Readers wanting more information on a particular resource should contact the publisher listed for the specific resource.

Career Planning Guides

If you're teaching a career planning class or group, several texts describe Holland's theory and give examples of how it can be used in career planning.

Decision Time (1994), by Michael Shahnasarian. Psychological Assessment Resources, Inc., P.O. Box 998, Odessa, FL: 33556, 1-800-331-8378.

> This book covers all aspects of the career choice process, from assessment to exploration to decision-making to lifelong career management. It includes exercises to help individuals develop their unique career plan. Of particular interest is a card sort that is designed to help users determine their Holland type and locate occupations from a list of 1,300 alternatives.

Taking Charge of Your Career Direction: Career Planning Guide, Book 1 (3rd ed., 1996), by Robert D. Lock. Brooks/Cole Publishing, 511 Forest Lodge Rd., Pacific Grove, CA 93950-5089; 1-800-354-9706.

> A section in chapter 3 of this book provides an overview of the basic concepts in Holland's theory and describes the RIASEC personality types and environments. Users are given suggestions for generating occupational alternatives using Holland codes; one activity involves using a "Personality Pattern Word List" to assess one's Holland type. The book includes a table showing a link between Holland categories and the interest categories used in several other career assessment instruments.

How to Succeed Without a Career Path (1995), by Howard Rosenberg. Impact Publications, 9104-N Manassas Drive, Manassas, VA 22111-5211.

> This book disputes the notion that everyone has to have a career track. The book explores a wide range of issues related to one's total lifestyle, including career decision making and personal development. Rosenberg uses Holland's typology to discuss the role of relationships and communications as keys to career success. He provides suggestions on how persons can improve relationships with others by better

understanding Holland typology, including how to use type to achieve more positive interactions with supervisors.

Take Charge of Your Own Career (1994), by Donna Moore with Susan VanderWey. Previously published by Psychological Assessment Resources, now available from the first author at P.O. Box 10723 Bainbridge Island, WA, 98110.

This publication is designed to help white-collar federal employees in planning their career paths. In addition to including a section where two-letter Holland codes are related to federal employment, the book includes 26 exercises that can be helpful to individuals in planning and making career moves. One note of caution: The version of the SDS included in the text is an adaptation of the 1990 edition. Persons working in federal agencies who are considering using this as a resource could have participants complete the 1994 version of the SDS and still use the book's various exercises as appropriate for their setting and population.

The 1997 What Color is Your Parachute? (1996), by Richard Bolles. Ten Speed Press, P.O. Box 7123, Berkeley, CA 94707; 1-800-841-BOOK.

This best-selling self-help career book endorses Holland's RIASEC system and related materials. It includes directions for the "Party Exercise," a 1-minute technique for quickly estimating a person's Holland code.

Career Information

Careers for Creative and Unconventional Types (1995), by Jill Eikenberry. Ten Speed Press, P.O. Box 7123, Berkeley, CA 94707; 1-800-841-BOOK.

Many users of the SDS have often noted the difficulties encountered in working with A types and helping them locate suitable occupational alternatives. The 130 occupations with a first code letter of A in The Occupations Finder can seem small in comparison to some of the other types. We find ourselves working in a government (CES-oriented) town on a campus that is to some extent dominated by A types because of the presence of nationally acclaimed music, film, and theater schools. This book is a useful supplement to other publications listing occupations by Holland types because it expands the possibilities for A types. It includes activities to help readers think about themselves in Holland terms, provides some real world examples of how individuals have used their A, as well as descriptions of occupational alternatives that allow for expression of an individual's A characteristics.

Real People, Real Jobs (1995), by David H. Montross, Zandy B. Leibowitz, & Christopher J. Shinkman. Davies-Black Publishing, 3808 East Bayshore Rd., P. O. Box 10096, Palo Alto, CA 94303.

> These authors use Holland's theory as a taking off point for sharing interviews with "real people" in "real jobs." The chapters go through each of the six types providing examples of how people have success-fully matched their interests with satisfying positions that match their "type." Each chapter includes a series of questions that might help readers determine whether their views of themselves are consistent with that particular type, as well as resources and organizations related to that type. The book concludes with some information, activities, and exercises designed to help readers take the next step in their career development.

Computer-Assisted Career Guidance Systems

In working with some of your clients, you also may wish to use computer-assisted career guidance systems (CACGS). Holland's typology and the SDS are incorporated in several ways. Some systems allow for the input of RIASEC scores to search for occupational alternatives; others allow users to simply use one or more of the types to generate options; and other systems actually produce a Holland code associated with a specific assessment activity. Some examples of these are provided below. This list is not intended to be comprehensive, but rather highlights the variety of approaches used by CACGS to incorporate Holland codes.

CHOICES, Careerware: ISM Systems Corp., 2220 Walkley Road, Ottawa, Ontario K1G 5L2, Canada; 1-800-267-1544; http://www.careerware.com

> This software uses Holland types as one of the criteria available to clients in searching for occupations. Users can enter up to two one-letter Holland codes, and the program provides a list of occupational options, detailed information on each occupation, and where to get training to enter the field. All the printouts for specific occupations include the occupation's Holland code.

DISCOVER, ACT, Inc. ACT Technology Center, Executive Plaza 11350 McCormick Road, Suite 200, Hunt Valley, MD 21031-1107; 1-800-645-1992; http://www.act.org

> In the assessment module of both DISCOVER for Colleges and Adults (DCA) and DISCOVER for High Schools (DHS), entitled "Looking at You," users have the option of entering the results from their Self-Directed Search. In addition, users completing the paper version of

ACT's Inventory of Work Related Abilities (which is one of the assessment activities included in DISCOVER) will obtain a Holland code associated with their ability ratings. These ability ratings can then be used to search for occupations in the DISCOVER module, "Looking at Occupations."

Guidance Information System (GIS); Versions 17 and II; Riverside Publishing Company, 425 Spring Lake Drive, Itasca, IL 60143; 1-800-767-8420; http://www.hmco.com/riverside

The career decision making approach included in GIS is based on John Holland's theory; in the Exploring Your Interests and Abilities section, users can enter their scores from the SDS.

MICROSkills, Richmond, CA: The California Career Information System, P.O. Box 647, Richmond, CA 94808-9900; 415-884-0818

Users can complete a paper and pencil inventory to identify their skills based on past accomplishments or work history and then enter the results into the computer, or they may complete this process on-line. Users classify their skills in three categories: very satisfying, moderately satisfying, and somewhat satisfying. The printout provides a link between users' skills and the six Holland types.

For additional information on systems that allow you to search for occupational alternatives by Holland codes, see the report, *A differential feature–cost analysis of seventeen computer-assisted career guidance systems (1996)*, published by the Center for the Study of Technology in Counseling and Career Development, Florida State University, Tallahassee, FL (http://www.aus.fsu.edu/techcntr/).

For a further discussion of the connection between computer-based systems and the SDS Form R, see also Deborah Bloch's chapter in *The Self-Directed Search in Business & Industry* (Shahnasarian, 1996b).

Career Assessments

Strong Interest Inventory; Consulting Psychologists Press, 3803 East Bayshore Road, P.O. Box 10096, Palo Alto, CA 94303; 1-800-624-1765

See the description of the Strong in chapter 4. The RIASEC typology is included in the General Occupational Themes, and the occupations presented in users' results include Holland codes.

Armed Services Vocational Aptitude Battery (ASVAB); published by the U.S. Department of Defense; DOD Center Monterey Bay, 400 Gigling Road, Seaside, CA 93955-6771; 408-583-2400

The recently revised ASVAB includes an Interest Finder assessment that is linked to the Holland typology; the Exploring Careers Workbook includes activities and information organized by RIASEC letters. The *Counselor's Manual* provides learning activities that help users understand the RIASEC classification system (e.g., a RIASEC quiz that asks students to match tools used in different occupations with the appropriate Holland code).

The book, *A Counselor's Guide to Career Assessment Instruments* (3rd ed.), by Kapes, Mastie, and Whitfield (1994), published by the National Career Development Association, 5999 Stevenson Avenue, Alexandria, VA 22304 (1-800-347-6647) describes a number of instruments and card sorts that have incorporated Holland codes into their materials. Some of these may no longer be in print, so it is best to contact the publishers listed in the back of the guide for the most current information.

Subject Index

Author Index